Case 17 How Should I Grade Danielle?	X	
Case 18 Rewarding Respectful Behavior	X	
Chapter 6 Religion		
Case 19 Isn't the Christmas Tree a Christian Symbol?	X	X
Case 20 My Persuasive Essay Is "Why We Should Follow Jesus"	X	X
Case 21 Planning for Religious Diversity: Special Needs of Muslim Students		
Case 22 Faith-Based Teasing, Student Curiosity, and the Question of Infusing Religion into the Curriculum	X	X
Chapter 7 Special Needs		
Case 23 We Only Meant It as a Joke	X	
Case 24 Structuring for Success in a Mainstreamed Classroom	X	
Case 25 Inaccessibility of Web Sites to Students Who Are Blind		
Case 26 Modifications for Special Students: Autism Spectrum Disorder	X	
Chapter 8 Sexual Orientation		
Case 27 Not in My Group—He's Gay!	X	
Case 28 Homosexuality and Religion: "In Islam, Homosexuality Is a Sin and a Crime"	X	X
Case 29 "Lesbian!": Dealing with the Interaction of Sexuality, Special Needs, and Culture		
Case 30 A Paperwork Problem: A Transgendered Student Teaches about Gender Identity	X	
Chapter 9 Language		
Case 31 You'll Need Both Black Vernacular and Standard English	X	X
Case 32 They Speak English and Spanish Well, but a Learning Disability Creates Problems in Reading and Writing	X	
Case 33 A Bilingual Teacher's Aide Assesses His New School	X	X
Case 34 Computers and Culturally Diverse Learners	X	
Chapter 10 Ageism		
Case 35 Age as a Factor in Bullying and "Cyberbullying"	X	
Case 36 The Wages We Will Get as Adults Will Pay for the Elderly? What's Up with That?	X	X
Case 37 You're Teaching Our Kids to Disrespect the Elderly?	X	X
Case 38 Age-Related Cultural Needs of Children and Youth	X	

A Casebook for Exploring Diversity

FOURTH EDITION

George L. Redman
Hamline University

Angela R. Redman
New Millennium Academy, Minneapolis

Boston Columbus Indianapolis New York San Francisco Upper Saddle River Amsterdam
Cape Town Dubai London Madrid Milan Munich Paris Montreal Toronto Delhi
Mexico City Sao Paulo Sydney Hong Kong Seoul Singapore Taipei Tokyo

Editor in Chief: Paul A. Smith
Senior Editor: Kelly Villella Canton
Editorial Assistant: Annalea Manalili
Cover Administrator: Jayne Conte
Production Manager: Holly Shufeldt
Cover Photo: Getty Images
Vice President, Director of Marketing: Quinn Perkson
Senior Marketing Manager: Darcy Betts Prybella

Photo Credits: Bob Daemmrich Photography, pp. 13, 73, 105; Digital Vision/Getty Images, p. 1; Frank Siteman, p. 31; Jupiter Unlimited, p. 139; Shutterstock, pp. 49, 89, 121, 157.

Library of Congress Cataloging-in-Publication Data

Redman, George
A casebook for exploring diversity / George L. Redman, Angela R. Redman.—4th ed.
p. cm.
Includes bibliographical references and index.
ISBN-13: 978-0-13-706128-0
ISBN-10: 0-13-706128-5
1. Multicultural education—United States. 2. Cultural pluralism—United States. 3. Case method. 4. Teachers—Training of—United States. I. Redman, Angela R. II. Title.
LC1099.3.R43 2003
370.1170973—dc22

2010001288

13

Allyn & Bacon
is an imprint of

www.pearsonhighered.com

ISBN 10: 0-13-706128-5
ISBN 13: 978-0-13-706128-0

About the Authors

George Redman taught in the public schools for 7 years, including 4 years in the Los Angeles area and 3 in an urban school in Minneapolis. He has also served as professor for over 30 years in the undergraduate teacher education program at Hamline University in St. Paul, Minnesota. He has taught in the Hamline Continuing Education for Teachers Program for more than 15 years and has conducted numerous in-service professional development workshops and courses for teachers throughout the region.

Dr. Redman's primary undergraduate responsibility has been for three courses: Education and Cultural Diversity, a core course in the program; Teaching in the Secondary School, a general methods course; and Student Teaching. He has also taught courses entitled Interpersonal and Intercultural Relations: Bridges and Barriers to Community, City as Classroom, Values Education, Theory to Practice K–8, Families, Schools, and Communities, and Self and Other. He served as chair of the department for more than 10 years. For over 30 years, he has supervised student teachers in urban schools in the Minneapolis/St. Paul metropolitan area.

Professor Redman is a recipient of the Association of Teacher Educators (ATE) national award for outstanding research, and he has published numerous articles in professional journals. His other books include *Teaching in Today's Classrooms: Cases from Elementary School, Teaching in Today's Classrooms: Cases from Middle and Secondary School, Building Self-Esteem in Students: A Skill and Strategy Workbook for Teachers,* and *Building Self-Esteem in Children: A Skill and Strategy Workbook for Parents.* He is co-author of *Self-Esteem for Tots to Teens.*

Angela Redman has over 10 years of experience in K–8 classrooms. She is currently working in an administrative capacity as an academic coordinator, supervising and mentoring new and seasoned teachers. Her teaching experience spans from multiaged classrooms K–8 to working as the Director of Exceptional Student Services. In urban settings in Minneapolis, Minnesota, as well as in suburban settings around the Phoenix area, she has worked directly with cross-categorical special education students, and has taught reading to English language learners. She holds an advanced degree in curriculum and instruction as well as in special education.

Contents

Note: Every effort has been made to provide accurate and current Internet information in this book. However, the Internet and information posted on it are constantly changing, so it is inevitable that some of the Internet addresses in this textbook will be altered or even dropped entirely by the time of publication.

PREFACE

Book Overview

The fourth edition of *A Casebook for Exploring Diversity* contains 38 case examples of realistic classroom events, situations, and issues for analysis and inquiry, focusing on the topics of gender, ethnicity, race, socioeconomic status, religion, special needs, sexual orientation, language, and ageism. The stories in this collection represent real classroom situations, presented to be relevant to teachers and prospective teachers in grades pre-K to 12 and across the full range of subject matter areas.

This casebook is a text supplement for use in courses on multicultural/inclusive/urban education, as well as in foundations, methods courses, and student teaching seminars, in which course or program goals reflect concern for diversity. It is also a useful resource in professional development programs designed to stimulate reflection and action in schools in an increasingly diverse society.

It is assumed that your primary course text will introduce, provide the theoretical and/or research base for, and show relationships among basic terms and concepts such as:

prejudice	classism	multicultural curriculum	power
stereotype	self-esteem	racism	cultur
white privilege	sexism	oppression	ethnicity

To assist in identifying definitions for key terms commonly used in discussions of diversity issues, a glossary of selected terms is provided in the Appendix of this text.

As a text supplement, this casebook provides (1) illustrations or examples of real classroom events, (2) problems for analysis and inquiry, and (3) frames for developing storied knowledge of teaching. The cases herein can for some students create a need to know about important concepts and for others extend thinking about such concepts. The questions at the end of each case encourage the reader to think about diversity issues as well as teaching methods, student learning, child or adolescent needs, and moral aspects of teaching within a diverse setting.

The case analysis approach in this text is consistent with the trend toward constructivism in teacher education, in which teachers are invited to become active inquirers in their work, and in so doing, to engage in reflection, interaction, speculative thinking, contextual influence, and personal meaning making. The orientation toward multicultural education represented in this text is that of social reconstructivism. Within the classroom setting, we believe in treating the whole child as having unique, individualized, prior experience and current needs, interests, and abilities.

Organization of this Text

Chapter 1 provides an introduction to the text, with a brief discussion of definitions, research, and benefits of case methodology, a description of the nature and scope of the cases in this text, and a process for analyzing and discussing the cases and for pursuing follow up activities. Chapters 2 through 10 consist of cases depicting key issues within major areas of cultural diversity in education. Each case:

- Begins with a brief overview of an authentic classroom or school incident
- Provides a concise story illustrating at least one diversity issue (some cases also provide the opportunity for analysis of other learning or teaching issues)
- Offers "Questions for Reflection" and "Activities for Extending Thinking" to stimulate immediate and long-term thinking about critical diversity issues

At the end of each chapter, students are invited to construct a case of their own. Finally, a bibliography and a listing of selected Internet sites that relate to the diversity area of that section are provided.

At the back of the book, **Resource A** includes guidelines for creating additional context for a given case, a table illustrating proportions of ethnic groups represented in the U.S. population, and projections of the number of students who would comprise a "typical" classroom based on those projections. **Resource B** offers a model illustrating four levels of integration of multicultural curriculum (Banks, 2005). **Resource C** provides a form to use in designing your own cases. **Resource D** provides a bibliography of multicultural children's literature. **Resource E** offers rubrics for self, peer, and instructor assessment of student responses to cases.

New to This Edition

- New cases have been added in the following areas: gender, religion, and sexual orientation that deal with faith-based teaching and religion in the curriculum (Case 22), autism spectrum syndrome (Case 26), and transgendered sexual orientation (Case 30).
- New subtopics embedded into new and current cases, such as confidentiality regarding student information, pressures for sexual involvement, anxiety and depression, social networking sites such as Facebook and MySpace, and identity of persons of mixed race.
- Retention and updates of best cases: Based on analysis of ratings of over 200 students in an urban-based pre-service teacher education program, cases rated most highly in terms of quality and perceived benefit have been retained, and those not as highly rated have been deleted or revised.
- A number of "Questions for Reflection" and "Activities for Extending Thinking" that relate the cases to clinical experiences, curriculum development, and local, state, and national standards have been added.

- Over 30 key terms have been added to the glossary to assist students as they discuss issues embedded in the cases.
- Over 60 of the most recent print and Internet resources reflecting the current research and best practice in the profession have been added.

Benefits of this Casebook

This supplemental text is designed to offer the following advantages to preservice teacher preparation:

Provides Focused Cases

First, although the cases offer opportunities for analysis on more than one level and sufficient complexity to invite multiple interpretations, they are also more focused than cases in most other texts so that they can be used more flexibly (e.g., using one case in a 20-30 minute portion of a given class, or using more than one if class time permits).

Stimulates Thinking at Various Levels

Questions for Reflection invite students to reflect on prior knowledge, collect further data, consider alternative perspectives, share their thoughts with others, and formulate individual or group responses. Activities for Extending Thinking encourage students to think about cause-and-effect relationships; develop and use categories of knowledge, skills, and dispositions; and build and evaluate new paradigms and models. Students are invited to relate insights to the course text, field experiences, the lesson and unit planning process, and local, state, and national standards in teacher education. Some of the questions and activities encourage students to deepen and broaden their understanding of diversity issues by investigating resources beyond those listed in this casebook (e.g., local or regional advocacy agencies in their own geographical area).

Provides Resources for Connecting to the Knowledge Base

Extensive references and resources are offered as a bridge to the knowledge base. Selected readings and Internet resources related to each of the 9 diversity domains are provided at the end of each chapter. In addition, a list of relevant general sources is provided at the end of the book.

Provides Opportunities for Students to Become Actively Involved in Case Design

This book provides the opportunity for readers to help construct the context in which they will analyze a given case, as well as to design cases of their own. Individuals or small groups in a course or workshop can consider a given case within more than one context. Doing so serves to highlight the importance of contextual conditions that affect teaching and learning. Suggestions for adding context to any of the cases in this text are provided in Resource A.

To encourage active involvement in their own learning, students are invited to construct a case of their own at the end of each chapter.

(Writing) cases involves skills central to reflective practice. Choosing what to write, the particular focus or frame, developing a story, and learning what to accentuate are all components of reflection. (Richert, 1991).

Provides Cases Representing Interpersonal Competence and Multicultural Content

Each case herein falls under one or both of the classifications *interpersonal competence* or *multicultural content*. As a guide for both students and instructors, the matrix in the inside front of the book places each case into the categories of interpersonal competence (cases that focus on personal skills that demonstrate cultural sensitivity) and/or multicultural content (cases that illustrate the use of multicultural curriculum in a subject matter context).

Consistent with characteristics of cases suggested by Fauske (2000), the cases in this casebook:

- Are intentionally shorter in length than cases in other texts
- Allow an instructor to have students focus on one, or more than one, objective (issue)
- Encourage discussion of multiple perspectives including both divergent and convergent responses of students
- Allow student analysis, either as individuals or in small groups, followed by instructor guidance in the form of questions for reflection
- Allow flexibility for amount of instructor direction, that is, relating of case to students' prior experience, curriculum development, current clinical experience, professional standards, or an outcome determined by the instructor to be critical
- Provide resources for further exploration of issues related to the case

Acknowledgments

For their ongoing love and support, not only in the writing of this casebook, but in all aspects of my life, I thank my wife Shari, our son Ryan, and our daughter Angie. Each truly has been a blessing in my life.

In acknowledging others who contributed to the book, I begin by thanking Dr. Eugene Anderson, professor of education (retired), University of Minnesota. His mentorship in ways of thinking about education and teacher education has been invaluable. I have valued deeply his friendship, guidance, and support over the years. His suggestions regarding the organization and overall readability of this book have been most appreciated.

For her analysis of case-study format, validity, and integrity of concepts and her multicultural sensitivity, I thank Darcia Narvaez, Department of Curriculum and Instruction, University of Minnesota. Her work significantly strengthened the conceptual and theoretical aspects of the book.

I thank the many pre-K-to-12 teachers and undergraduate and graduate students in teacher education who reviewed the cases. Their assessment of the degree of clarity and realism of each of the cases helped greatly in confirming their potential for wider use. In particular, I thank Jon Halpern and Jeff Fink, veteran elementary teachers; Ann Mabbott, director of Second Language Teaching and Learning at Hamline University; Sam Hernandez, veteran secondary teacher; and Deborah L. Harris, parent, for their valuable reviews.

Kelly Villella Canton, Acquisitions Editor, Pearson Teacher Education, and Annalea Manalili, Editorial Assistant, Pearson Teacher Education, have done a superb job in establishing a comfortable working environment for creating and writing. I appreciate the guidance they have so generously provided.

Deborah Brown, of Hamline University, helped greatly in the preparation of the manuscript, and I thank Julie Johnson for her work on the bibliography of multicultural children's literature.

I am also grateful to the following reviewers:

> Greg Czysczon, James Madison University; Cary Gillenwater, University of North Carolina at Chapel Hill; Yoko Mogi-Hein, St. Norbert College; Reynaldo Reyes III, University of Texas at El Paso; Jayminn Sanford-DeShields, Temple University.

I thank Dr. Dwight C. Watson, for his encouragement and support on the development of cases related to race and ethnicity, especially the case designed to help with the deconstruction of the "N" word (Case 13), the context for the case on oppression and whiteness (Case 15), and on the development of the assessment rubrics in Resource E. As a colleague and close friend, he has generously shared his expertise in various areas within multicultural education, as well as in the areas of reading and literacy, and curriculum and instruction. His many contributions have indeed enriched this edition of this casebook.

Last, without the encouragement and support of my colleagues at Hamline University, completion of this casebook would not have been possible. I extend sincere thanks to each of the following: Colleen Bell, Jim Bonilla, Nancy Desmond, Steve Jongewaard, Letitia Basford, Sarah Hick, Lenore Kinne, Kim Koeppen, Jean Strait, Dwight Watson, and Joy Wimsatt, as well as to the college faculty as a whole.

George Redman

If we are lucky, we encounter people in our lives who change the way we see the world. They deepen our understanding of all people and open our hearts to new levels of compassion. These same people teach us how important it is to love, whole heartedly and unconditionally. I thank all who have inspired me. You have proven to be a gift to me and make the world a better place to be. Peace~much love~namaste.

Angela Redman

References

Banks, J. A. (2001). Approaches to multicultural curriculum reform. In J. A. Banks & C. A. M. Banks (Eds.), *Multicultural education: Issues and perspectives* (4th ed., pp. 225–246). New York: Wiley.

Darling-Hammond, L., & Bransford, J. (2005). *Preparing teachers for a changing world: What teachers should learn and be able to do.* San Francisco: Jossey-Bass.

Fauske, J. R. (2000). Linguistic and instructional precision in teaching with cases and problems. *Journal of Cases in Educational Leadership, 3*(2), feature essay.

Merseth, K. (1996). Cases and case methods in teacher education. In J. Sikula, T. J. Buttery, & E. Guyton (Eds.), *Handbook of research on teacher education* (2nd ed., pp. 722–744). New York: Macmillan.

Redman, G. L. (1999). *Teaching in today's classrooms: Cases from elementary school.* Upper Saddle River, NJ: Merrill/Prentice Hall.

Redman, G. L. (1999). *Teaching in today's classrooms: Cases from middle and secondary school.* Upper Saddle River, NJ: Merrill/Prentice Hall.

Richert, A. E. (1991) Case methods and teacher education: Using cases to teach teacher reflection. In B. R. Tabachnik & K. Zeichner (Eds.), *Issues and practices in inquiry-oriented teacher education* (pp. 130–150). London: Falmer.

Whittaker, C. A., & vanGarderen, D. (2007). *Enhancing teacher development using a metacognitive problem solving approach with case-based instruction.* Manuscript submitted for publication.

Chapter 1

Introduction

Cases: What Are They?

Cases have been defined as engaging narrative stories containing events that unfold over a period of time in a specified place (Shulman, 1992). Within teacher education, such stories describe *events that commonly occur in classrooms and schools*. They are stories of either real problems or hypothetical problems representing real ones and can be as short as a paragraph or as long as 50 pages. McNergney, Herbert, and Ford (1994, p. 340) asserted that "good cases have possibilities for multiple levels of analysis and they are sufficiently complex to allow multiple interpretations."

Cases and the Knowledge Base in Teacher Education

Case-based instruction is supported by the portion of the knowledge base that asserts teachers' knowledge (1) is situation-specific (contextual), (2) is informed and informing through interaction (interactive), and (3) involves uncertainty (is speculative; Clark & Lampert, 1986). Cases, then, provide situation-specific circumstances that can help students connect theory with practice in a supportive, interactive environment.

Schon (1987) observed that teachers acquire the bulk of their professional knowledge through continuous action and reflection on everyday problems. Case studies provide a common point of departure for reflecting on such problems and thus help teachers create meaning from complex teaching and learning situations.

A growing research base suggests varied benefits from reflecting on everyday problems. Through the analysis of authentic cases, teachers, businesspeople, lawyers, and others are said to develop the power to reason (Sprinthall & Theis-Sprinthall, 1983), enhance their cognitive complexity (Hunt & Sullivan, 1974; Oja & Sprinthall, 1978), perceive meaningfulness (Kennedy, 1991), alter their belief structure (Peterson, Carpenter, & Fennema, 1989), think like professionals (Kleinfeld, 1992; Morine-Dershimer, 1991), and develop other capacities through reflection. Cases focusing on moral dilemmas, interpersonal difficulties, and cultural differences have been used to promote deliberation and problem solving, in programs that prepare teachers for the complexities of teaching in diverse classrooms (Levin, 2002, Whitcomb, 2002).

Some scholars think of teacher reflection in terms of critical theory. McLaren (1989) viewed knowledge as determined by the surrounding culture, context, customs, and historical era. He observed that "critical pedagogy attempts to provide teachers with a better means of understanding the role that schools actually play within a race-, class-, and gender-divided society" (p. 163).

Darling-Hammond (2000, p. 170) posited that "good teachers must develop an awareness of their own perspectives and how these can be enlarged to avoid a 'communicentric bias' (Gordon, Miller, & Rollock, 1990), which limits their understanding of those whom they teach." Case analysis in which multiple perspectives are explored can help expand one's communicentric bias. (For a review of this literature, see Darling-Hammond & Snyder, 1998.)

Merseth (1995) reviewed developments regarding the nature of teacher knowledge, focusing in particular on the field of teacher cognition. She posited that:

> The apparent ability of cases and case-based instruction to present theoretical knowledge as well as to provide an opportunity to exercise judgment and to develop analytical skills matches well with the current views of teacher knowledge and what teachers need." (Merseth, 1995)

The Benefits of Case Studies

Cases provide an opportunity for both prospective and in-service teachers to anticipate real problems, to retrieve principles *from theories* of teaching and learning to resolve those problems, and to construct, discuss, and evaluate responses in a community of learners. More specifically, according to Merseth (1991), as cited in Cooper (1995), case methods

1. Help develop skills of critical analysis and problem solving, including skills of observing, making inferences, identifying relationships, and articulating organizing principles
2. Encourage reflective practice and deliberate action—they require students to discuss and choose from competing interpretations advanced by one another
3. Provide a context in which students can make decisions in complex situations when there is not an exact match between theory and practice
4. Involve students in their own learning—active responsibility takes the place of passive acceptance that might exist in a lecture situation
5. Encourage the development of a community of learners by/through lively and engaging discussion and collaborative teamwork

Merseth (1995) also offers a simple and useful conceptual framework for thinking about cases and case methods, a framework that identifies three purposes for analyzing cases: (1) "to exemplify a principle, theory or instructional technique" (Sykes & Bird, 1992, p. 480), (2) to "practice professional, skills such as interpreting situations, framing problems, generating various solutions to the problems posed and choosing among them" (Sykes & Bird, 1992, p. 482), and (3) to stimulate personal reflection (Richert, 1991; Zeichner & Liston, 1987).

Over the past several years, when asked how the analysis of cases personally benefitted them, preservice teacher education classes taught by this author have repeatedly recognized as benefits all three of the purposes outlined in the Merseth's conceptual framework. Many of the students surveyed indicated that as a result of case analyses, they felt better able to connect practice described in the cases to theories of which they were aware. Others reported feeling more adept at problem solving and decision making, and still others stated that they thought more reflectively or more deeply about the complexities of teaching. Indeed, many students reported that they benefitted personally in more than one of these ways.

The Cases in This Casebook

> I've never taught in a school, urban or suburban, in which staff members freely discussed issues of race and class with one another. Racial tensions are almost always a factor among faculty, but they're almost never addressed. Because our society is so segregated, most of us don't discuss race in integrated settings, and schools don't provide opportunities for teachers—or students—to develop the skills and knowledge needed to examine "hot" issues, like race, with civility. (Weiner, 1999)

The cases in this collection describe events that occur in elementary, middle, and high school classrooms in urban, suburban, and rural settings. They represent dilemmas common to all classrooms, regardless of subject matter and grade level.

Each case focuses on at least one issue involving race, socioeconomic status, language, ethnicity, gender, sexual orientation, religion, disability, or age. In addition, each contains at least one issue related to planning, classroom environment, instruction, or professional responsibilities. Thus, each case can be used to stimulate thinking about diversity and/or pedagogical issues, depending on the orientation of a given course or workshop, and on the needs and interests of participants. Some of the cases offer examples of good teaching, and some provide examples of teacher behaviors known to be ineffective. They all offer opportunities for connecting theory to practice, to practice skills of problem solving, decision making, and action planning, while at the same time, encouraging deeper, more reflective thinking.

Multicultural Education

A definition of the term *culture* is basic to the understanding of multicultural education. Although the term can be defined in various ways, the broad definition offered by Pusch (1979) best serves the purpose of this text:

> Culture is the sum total of ways of living, including values, beliefs, aesthetic standards, linguistic expression, patterns of thinking, behavioral norms, and styles of communication which a group of people has developed to assure its survival in a particular physical and human environment. (p. 3)

Multiculturalism, then, invites teachers to integrate into their teaching information about the many cultures in their schools, communities, and the world. It has as its central goal the development in all students of an understanding of, and appreciation for, the human potential of persons of all backgrounds.

Carl Grant (1994, p. 4) defined multicultural education as a "philosophical concept and an educational process." As a philosophical concept, it is based on the ideals of "freedom, justice, equality, equity, and human dignity that are contained in United States documents such as the Constitution and the Declaration of Independence" (Grant, 1994, p. 4). As an educational process, multicultural education informs all academic disciplines and other aspects of the curriculum. It prepares all students to work actively toward structural equality in the organizations and institutions of the United States. It helps students to develop positive self-concepts and to discover who they are, particularly in terms of their multiple group memberships. Multicultural education does this by providing knowledge about the history, culture, and contributions of the diverse groups that have shaped the history, politics, and culture of the United States. (Grant, 1994, p. 4)

The orientation of the authors of this text is consistent with that expressed by Grant and closely aligned with the "multicultural and social reconstructionist approach" of Sleeter and Grant (2006) and Genor (2005). Further, it should be emphasized that multicultural content and education for intercultural competence should be integrated into all content areas, rather than viewed as an "add-on" subject in itself.

Finally, Banks and Banks (2001, p. 20) identified dimensions of multicultural education that can guide school reform: (1) integration of cultural content, (2) the knowledge construction process, (3) prejudice reduction, (4) an equity pedagogy, and (5) an empowering school culture and social structure.

The more teachers examine, reflect on, and discuss these important dimensions, the more informed they will become and the more confident they will be when implementing them in classrooms and schools. The examination of authentic cases is one effective method for stimulating such reflection. Indeed,

> the case method . . . is uniquely suited to the analysis of the complex and emotionally charged issues of teaching in culturally unfamiliar contexts. (Kleinfield, 1990, in Merseth, 1995)

Creating Additional Context for the Cases

In Resource A, you will find an invitation to list community, school, and classroom factors that might make a case more rich, authentic, or personally relevant. You are invited to list factors such as characteristics of the school and community (e.g., proportion of socioeconomic, ethnic, and religious groups) and the nature of the individuals and the classroom in the case (e.g., personal characteristics, type of curriculum). You may also find the information in Resource A on national estimates of various ethnic groups, children in poverty, exceptionality, and sexual orientation helpful.

We recommend limiting the number of details that you add to a given case—perhaps to four or five—so that the key issues in the case are not lost. Take a few minutes to list in writing the contextual details you will add. To further encourage your active participation in learning, your instructor may invite you to design a case study of your own. Directions for doing so are provided in Resource C.

Preparing and Participating in Discussions of Cases

Participation in class discussions of case studies should take place in the spirit of cooperation. Whether discussion occurs in large or small groups, your learning will be maximized if everyone has an equal opportunity to share ideas about an issue in the case. Participants should use good listening skills, such as those described in Anderson, Redman, and Rogers (1991) and Redman (1992), including paraphrasing, empathizing, asking open questions, asking clarifying questions, and nonverbal attending. Destructive criticism, ridicule, interrupting, and other rejecting behaviors should be avoided.

The following steps are recommended for analyzing a case.

A. Understanding the Case

1. Read the case. Note key facts that might affect your understanding of the main issue(s). For example, what happened to the characters in the story (i.e., who did what to whom, what factors such as gender, race, class, age, etc. appear to have affected the events in the story?).

   List any questions that you might have about events in the story.

   If working in a group, encourage group members to ask their questions, and give others an opportunity to assist in responding to each others' questions.
2. Consider adding the cultural and educational context in which the case is set. Suggestions for doing so are offered in Resource A (see "Creating Additional Context for a Given Case"). You may decide to create a story context similar to a personal experience that you had when you were a P–12 student or a volunteer teacher's aid.

B. Analyzing the Case

1. For your small or large group, summarize key facts, pedagogical as well as cultural, that might have affected the development of the story. In addition, identify any conditions in the classroom in the case that might have fostered or allowed events to unfold. If the case is assigned for a future session, and if so advised by the instructor, examine outside resources (e.g., pertinent theories) that might be helpful.
2. Generate alternatives for addressing the key problem(s) in the case.
3. Identify criteria to be used in choosing "the best" alternative among those listed. Examples of quantitative criteria include cost, delivery time, and risk. Examples of qualitative criteria include student morale, safety, cultural sensitivity, and ease of implementation.
4. Evaluate the alternatives generated in point 2 above, using the criteria selected. You may want to assign a number or "weight" for each criteria so that the alternatives can be more objectively scored.
5. Outline briefly an action plan that specifies what, when, where, and how you would address the key issue in the case.

C. Following Up

1. Complete the questions at the end of the case and any Activities for Extending Thinking assigned by your instructor. Identify the central issue and a theory (developmental, multicultural, pedagogical, etc.) that would be helpful in addressing the key issue in more depth. Be prepared to share your responses with others.
2. Suggest ideas for activities that might extend thinking about the issue(s) in the case. For example, if you are aware of a resource or a Web site that could be

helpful to classmates to expand thinking about an issue, suggest it to your instructor and your classmates.

3. Finally, it is recommended that prior to the close of the discussion, participants share insights on *changes* in particular ideas and in the *patterns* of the responses as the discussion progresses. For example, participants may initially take the view of the student, but through discussion may come to support the teacher's perspective (or vice versa). Your instructor may ask you to record these changes in writing.

Alternative Analysis Process: Multidimensional Analysis of Cases

Although the central focus of the cases in this casebook is intended to be on issues of cultural sensitivity, it is possible examine most of the cases from additional perspectives (e.g., from a pedagogical perspective). In addition to focusing on cultural issues, students can explore almost any given case as it relates to curriculum, or instruction (such as differentiated instruction), or to a particular theory, such as multiple intelligences, developmental psychology, critical literacy, or any number of other areas of study pertinent to the instructor's goals and students' needs and interests.

Multidimensional analysis can be done by individuals, small groups, or even the entire class focusing on more than one dimension, such as those mentioned earlier, and then sharing the results of their study in class. For example, a small group of three students could assign one person the task of analyzing the case for cultural issues (e.g., stereotyping), a second group member the task of identifying stages of racial/ethnic identity represented in the story, and the third looking at ways to structure curriculum and/or instruction to address shortcomings of same identified in the case. Each group member could then share their findings in their own group or with group members from other groups who had the same task, or they could respond in a large-group discussion. Because some cases harbor more and varied issues than others, your instructor will weigh the benefits of this strategy with the costs (e.g., time) to determine whether the particular strategy should be used with a particular case.

Analysis of yet another dimension can be done on the basis of the two concepts delineated on the inside covers of this casebook: interpersonal competence and multicultural content. The task might be to identify the specific interpersonal skills and the specific multicultural content embedded in the case and to suggest the benefits and limitations, if any, of them. Using this strategy, some students—whether working individually or in small groups—can examine the case and report on their findings relative to these two dimensions. Again, instructors will want to make modifications based on their own interests and the needs, interests, and abilities of their students.

Conclusion

Be assured that the cases you are about to examine represent real problems related to the most critical components of teaching in today's elementary, middle, and high schools—components grounded in sound research and an extensive knowledge base. The purpose of this Casebook is to focus on diversity, equity, and social justice issues in teaching and learning, thereby raising awareness, elevating dialogue, and promoting action planning, all of which will increase your cultural competence and, hence, your overall effectiveness in the classroom. Be creative as you explore issues in the cases, relate the issues to field experiences or teaching experiences and/or to teacher education standards, design cases of your own, and utilize insights thus derived as you develop lesson and unit plans. This process helps good teachers learn and grow and become even better—it is the epitome of professional development.

Readings for Extending Thinking

Aaronsohn, E., Howell, M., & Carter, C. J. (1995). Preparing monocultural teachers for a multicultural world: Attitudes toward inner-city schools. *Equity & Excellence in Education, 28*(1). Upper Saddle River, NJ: Prentice Hall.

Anderson, E. M., Redman, G. L., & Rogers, C. (1991). *Self-esteem for tots to teens.* Wayzata, MN: Parenting and Teaching Publications. Available at Parenting and Teaching for Self-Esteem, 1480. Arden View Drive, Arden Hills, MN 55112.

Banks, J. A., & Banks, C. A. M. (2001). *Multicultural education: Issues and perspectives.* New York: Wiley.

Clark, C., & Lampert, M. (1986). The study of teacher thinking: Implications for teacher education. *Journal of Teacher Education, 37,* 27–31.

Cooper, J. M. (1995). *Teacher's problem solving: A casebook of award-winning cases.* Boston: Allyn & Bacon.

Darling-Hammond, L. (2000, May/June). How teacher education matters. *Journal of Teacher Education, 51*(3), 166–173.

Darling-Hammond, L., & Bransford, J. (Eds.). (2005). *Preparing teachers for a changing world.* San Francisco: Wiley.

Darling-Hammond, L., & Snyder, J. (1998). Authentic assessment of teaching in context. In *Contextual teaching and learning: Preparing teachers to enhance student success in the workplace and beyond.* Washington, DC: Office of Educational Research and Improvement.

Dworkin, A.G. (2005). The No Child Left Behind Act: Accountability, high-stakes testing, and roles for sociologists. *Sociology of Education, 78,* 170–174.

Epstein, J. L. (2005). Attainable goals? The spirit and letter of the No Child Left Behind Act on parental involvement. *Sociology of Education, 78,* 179–182.

Genor, M. (2005). A social reconstructionist framework for reflection: The "problematizing" of teaching. *Issues in Teacher Education, 14*(2), 45–62.

Gordon, E. W., Miller, F., & Rollock, D. (1990, April). Coping with communicentric bias in knowledge production in the social sciences. *Educational Researcher, 19,* 14–19.

Grant, C. A. (1994). Challenging the myths about multicultural education. *Multicultural Education, 2*(2), 4–9.

Hammerness, K., Darling-Hammond, L., and Shulman, L. (2002, April, 10-14). *Towards expert thinking: How case-writing contributes to the development of theory-based professional knowledge in student-teachers.* Paper presented at the annual meeting of the American Educational Research Association, Seattle, WA.

Hunt, D. E., & Sullivan, E. V. (1974). *Between psychology and education.* New York: Holt, Rinehart and Winston.

Kennedy, M. M. (1991). *An agenda for research on teacher learning* (Special Report). East Lansing, MI: National Center for Research on Teacher Learning.

Kleinfeld, J. (1990, Winter). The special virtues of the case method in preparing teachers for minority schools. *Teacher Education Quarterly, 17,* 43–51.

Kleinfeld, J. (1992). Learning to think like a teacher: The study of cases. In J. H. Schulman (Ed.), *Case methods in teacher education* (pp. 33–49). New York: Teachers College Press.

Ladson-Billings, G. (2001). *Crossing over to Canaan: The journey of new teachers in diverse classrooms.* San Francisco: Jossey-Bass.

Levin, B. B. (2002). *Case studies of teacher development: An in-depth look at how thinking about pedagogy develops over time.* Hillsdale, NJ: Erlbaum.

McLaren, P. (1989). *Life in schools: An introduction to critical pedagogy in the foundations of education*. White Plains, NY: Longman.

McNergney, R., Herbert, J., & Ford, R. (1993). *Anatomy of a team case competition*. Paper presented at the annual meeting of the American Educational Research Association, Atlanta, Georgia.

McNergney, R., Herbert, J., & Ford, R. (1994). Cooperation and competition in case-based teacher education. *Journal of Teacher Education, 45*(5), 339–345.

Merseth, K. K. (1991). *The case for cases in teacher education.* Washington, DC: American Association for Higher Education and the American Association of Colleges for Teacher Education.

Merseth, K. K. (1995). Cases and case methods in teacher education. In J. Sikula, T. J. Buttery, & E. Guyton (Eds.), *Handbook of research on teacher education* (2nd ed., pp. 722–744). New York: Macmillan.

Morine-Dershimer, G. (1991). Learning to think like a teacher. *Teaching and Teacher Education, 7*(2), 159–168.

Oja, S., & Sprinthall, N. A. (1978). Psychological and moral development for teachers. In N. A. Sprinthall & R. L. Mosher (Eds.), *Value development as the aim of education* (pp. 117–134). Schenectady, NY: Charter Press.

Peterson, P. L., Carpenter, T., & Fennema, E. (1989). Teachers' knowledge of students' knowledge in mathematics problem solving: Correlational and case analyses. *Journal of Educational Psychology, 81,* 558–569.

Pusch, M. D. (Ed.). (1979). *Multicultural education: A cross-cultural training approach.* Yarmouth, ME: Intercultural Press.

Redman, G. L. (1992). *Building self-esteem in students: A skill and strategy workbook for teachers*. Wayzata, MN: Parenting and Teaching for Self-Esteem. Available at Parenting and Teaching for Self-Esteem, 1480. Arden View Drive, Arden Hills, MN 55112.

Richert, A. E. (1991). Using teacher cases for reflection and enhanced understanding. In A. Lieberman & L. Miller (Eds.), *Staff development for education in the '90s* (pp. 113–132). New York: Teachers College Press.

Salend, S. J. (2008). *Creating inclusive classrooms: Effective and reflective practices* (6th ed.). Upper Saddle River, NJ: Merrill/Prentice Hall.

Schon, D. A. (1987). *Educating the reflective practitioner*. San Francisco: Jossey-Bass.

Shulman, L. (1992). Toward a pedagogy of cases. In J. H. Shulman (Ed.), *Case methods in teacher education* (p. x). New York: Teachers College Press.

Shulman, L. (1996). Tender feelings, hidden thoughts: Confronting bias, innocence and racism through case discussion. In A. Colbert, P. Desberg, & K. Trimble (Eds.), *The case for education: Contemporary approaches for using case methods* (pp. 137–158). Boston: Allyn & Bacon.

Sprinthall, N. A., & Theis-Sprinthall, L. (1983). *The teacher as an adult learner: A cognitive-developmental view*. National Society for the Study of Education Yearbook (Pt. 2), 13–35.

Stake, R. E. (1995). *The art of case study research*. Thousand Oaks: Sage Publications.

Sykes, G., & Bird, T. (1992). Teacher education and the case idea. In G. Grant (Ed.), *Review of Research in Education* (Vol. 18, pp. 457–521). Washington, DC: American Educational Research Association.

van Garderen, D., & Whittaker, C. R. (2006). Planning differentiated, multicultural instruction for secondary inclusive classrooms. *Teaching Exceptional Children, 38*(3), 12–21.

Weiner, L. (1999). *Urban teaching: The essentials*. New York: Teachers College Press.

Whitcomb, J. A. (2002). Composing dilemma cases: An opportunity to understand moral dimensions of teaching. *Teaching Education, 13*(2), 125–135.

Zeichner, K. M., & Liston, D. (1987). Teaching student teachers to reflect. *Harvard Educational Review, 57*(1), 23–48.

Internet Sites for Extending Thinking

http://www.adl.org/
Anti-Defamation League materials on fighting prejudice and racism.

http://ublib.buffalo.edu/libraries/projects/cases/case.html
University at Buffalo, collection of several hundred cases and teaching notes in the natural sciences.

http://www.edchange.org/multicultural
The multicultural pavilion offers lists, tools, fact sheets poems, songs, research reports, and dialogue opportunities for educators and activists dedicated to equity, diversity, social justice, and multicultural education.

http://hallway.org/
A repository of teaching cases and other curriculum materials for faculty who teach public policy and related subjects, including education, environment, human services, urban issues, and international affairs. (From the Evans School of Public Affairs, University of Washington.)

http://mingo.info-science.uiowa.edu/~stevens/critped/page1.htm
Provides an overview of critical pedagogy and brief description of prominent theorists including Freire and Giroux.

Chapter 2

Gender

Introduction

Many, perhaps most, teachers are aware of the various forms of gender bias, the ways in which it is perpetuated, and its impact on both boys and girls in schools. For some, however, gender equity is still elusive. In a recent conversation with several experienced and well-respected veteran teachers, awareness of issues related to racism seemed high. When asked about sexism, however, knowledge was limited, that is, they related only to the issue of sexual harassment and seemed unaware of other important gender-related issues, such as pressures for having sex, sexism in the media, the relation of brain chemistry and sex hormones to learning styles, exclusion of women in curriculum, date rape, teaching practices that favor one gender over the other, promotional inequities, and use of gender-neutral terms (e.g., "students" rather than "you guys"). Most were unaware of the fact that since the 1980s, boys have "consistently and increasingly underperformed" in school compared to girls (Coates, J., co-author of *Smart Boys, Bad Grades,* a report released by the Learning Resources Network in March 2002, quoted in Cook, 2006).

Educators who believe that gender bias lowers student self-confidence, contributes to academic failure, and even leads to emotional and physical violence in the nation's schools are likely to actively address such issues. It is critical that teachers explore thoughts and feelings about gender biases, raise awareness and understanding of key issues, and help other prospective and current teachers think about strategies for countering gender-based bias, both on a personal and an institutional (e.g., school and community) level.

The cases in Chapter 2 provide an opportunity to think more broadly and deeply about gender-based issues as they relate to curriculum, instruction, and student behavior management in classrooms and schools. Discussions of the cases in this section often invoke key terms and phrases such as the following.

critical thinking
discrimination
gender
gender equity
prejudice
reinforcement (of learning and/or behavior)
relevant curriculum
sexism
sexuality
social-emotional classroom climate
teacher flexibility and responsiveness
teacher–student interaction patterns
traditional social and role concepts
wait time

Definitions of key terms are located in the glossary of this text.

Case 1

Reinforcement of Student Work

Students perform assigned tasks in a class activity and receive encouragement and praise from their teacher for their efforts.

It was the last week of school before the spring break. For the past two weeks, Ms. Bell's class had worked hard on a series of lab experiments focused on factors affecting the growth rate of seeds and young pea plants. The students had demonstrated pride in learning about the structure and function of seeds and in getting their seeds to grow.

On this particular Monday, as students were completing the final lab in the series, Ms. Bell circulated throughout the room, acknowledging individual contributions to the groups of four. "I want to tell you how proud I am of your work," she said to the members of one group. "Randolf and Jon, you did especially well in creating hypotheses prior to testing the effects of temperature and light. Your ideas took into account our prior learning and at the same time were creative. Mia and Amy, your work in recording the data for your group is commendable. Your records are easier to read because they are so neatly done."

As Ms. Bell walked away, Jon leaned over to Mia and Amy and quietly said, "I told you that boys were smarter. If we had listened to you two, Ms. Bell would have said our group was stupid." He concluded this statement by giving Randolf a high five. Mia shot back with, "Well at least Ms. Bell can read what we wrote down. You write like a preschooler!"

To the second group, Ms. Bell said, "Rod and Chang, your predictions as to what would happen in all the labs in this unit were right on target! You have a good grasp of the principles of plant growth. And Sonya and Angie, your help in organizing the materials for the experiments and in checking the measurements of the plants was great. Your group couldn't have gotten the correct results without you!"

Ms. Bell moved to the third group. "Peter and José, your data analysis skills were excellent! Mary and Belle, you made some great drawings of the physical changes." The two girls looked at each other and smiled.

Ms. Bell provided similar feedback to the remaining two groups. All the students seemed appreciative of her comments.

About five minutes before the bell was to ring, Ms. Bell reminded the students of their responsibilities for cleanup and the storage of lab materials. "Be sure you water your plants and return them to the window," she said. The students seemed to know their responsibilities, and they moved to store their plants and clear their tables.

Questions for Reflection

1. What was effective about Ms. Bell's feedback to students in this case?
2. Assume that the reinforcement pattern evident in these exchanges is typical of the feedback given by Ms. Bell during the term. Tell what effect Ms. Bell's interaction would have on the following?
   a. Her students' achievements
   b. Their feelings of pride in their work
   c. Their self-expectations for learning in science
   d. The culture for learning in the classroom
3. What could the teacher do to structure the science activities so that they would be more likely to lead to success for both the boys and the girls?
4. What might Ms. Bell have said to a) Jon, and b) Mia, regarding their comments to each other?

Activities for Extending Thinking

1. Teach a lesson in an accessible school. If you are currently in a field experience or are teaching, you may want to teach your lesson in that school. Videotape the lesson and analyze the tape for patterns of teacher–student interaction. Are there individuals and/or groups of students with whom you have more or less interaction? What types of interactions do you have with various individuals and groups (e.g., interactions that stimulate higher levels of thinking)? List the interaction patterns you have identified. Be prepared to share in class.
2. Examine local, state, and/or national standards for teacher education and identify the standards that relate to the key issues in this case.
3. Interview several peers about their own school experiences with gender bias. Summarize key findings from the interviews.

Case 2

Fridays Are Video Days

A teacher attends to student socializing during the Friday video.

It was Friday, and Ms. Hanson loaded another videotape on the Apollo space project into the videocassette recorder. It was her opinion that if the students worked hard all week, they should be rewarded with a video each Friday. In addition to serving as a reward, the videos also gave her a chance to help those who needed it.

Students who were not interested in the Friday video had the option of working on an extra-credit project related to the current unit of study. This month the unit was on mass and volume. On this particular Friday, Jenny, Desweon, and Ann had opted to do extra credit rather than watch the tape. In fact, the same group had chosen to do extra credit for the past three weeks.

This Friday was no different from other recent Fridays in that a group of four or five boys in the back of the room had again begun to talk during the video. For some reason, they had come to equate video watching with socializing.

To curb their talking, Ms. Hanson used proximity. Taking a seat next to the group allowed her to give them her full attention. From her vantage point, she could also see the students working on extra credit. If a student in that group raised his or her hand for help, she could motion to the student to come to her.

When Jenny and Ann raised their hands, Ms. Hanson waved for them to come to her. Jenny pointed to a problem at the end of the chapter. "I don't get number 8," she said. "Me either," added Ann. "Let's take a look," replied Ms. Hanson. "What part *do* you understand?"

As Jenny began to respond, Ms. Hanson interrupted. "Hold that thought." She leaned toward Todd and Tim and, with her finger to her lips, said, "Shhh, please, I've asked you before not to talk during the videos. Every time I have to ask you, it takes away from the time I could be helping someone." She waited until the boys quieted down.

When she turned to Jenny, she apologized. "Sorry. Where were we?" Jenny reminded her and they began again.

Ten minutes later, Teresa raised her hand. Ms. Hanson motioned for her to come over. Teresa complained that Todd was talking so loud that she couldn't hear the video. Ms. Hanson reminded the boys to be quiet again.

That evening, on the way home from school, Ms. Hanson wondered about the Friday arrangement. She thought of the patterns of behavior so typical of Fridays, including having to spend much of the period with the boys in the back of the room. She listed the pros: giving the students choices (to view the video or do extra credit), varying the weekly activity routine, rewarding student work, and giving personal attention to those who need it. Maybe the Friday arrangement was fine after all.

Questions for Reflection

1. Respond to Ms. Hanson's rationale for maintaining Fridays as days that students could choose to either watch an educational video or complete extra-credit work. Do you agree or disagree with her practice? Why?
2. List aspects of Ms. Hanson's Friday instructional plan that you feel are a) beneficial, and b) not beneficial.
3. How could the Friday activities be changed to benefit all students?
4. What moral/ethical issues, if any, are raised in this case?

Activities for Extending Thinking

1. Design a student survey that elicits pupil opinion about the use of a particular classroom activity, such as the "video day" activity. What questions would you ask?
2. List two or three ideas around which you could develop cases (stories with problems) that you could use in classes you might teach. Begin by listing the key information (e.g., about history or biology, or literature) you want students to obtain or develop; then, briefly outline a story that creates students' desire to obtain or construct that information.
3. Examine local, state, and/or national standards for teacher education and identify the standard or standards that relate to the key issues in this case.

Case 3

Developing Skills of Critical Analysis: Exposing the Myths of Films and Fairy Tales*

A teacher guides students in the exposing of myths that perpetuate common societal stereotypes and in using writing and speaking as vehicles for change.

Ms. Christensen wanted her students to develop the tools necessary to critique major ideas in terms of the degree to which they contribute to, or distract from, the building of a just society. To this end, each year her class embarked on a journey of analyzing cartoons, children's movies, and stories.

This year, she planned to begin by reading to the class Ariel Dorfman's *The Emperor's Old Clothes: What the Lone Ranger, Babar, and Other Innocent Heroes Do to Our Minds,* in which the author claims that both popular literature and children's literature perpetuate existing power structures and deny the possibility of greater equality.

Next, as the first step in dismantling old values and constructing more just ones, the class would critique cartoons and children's movies, including *Bugs Bunny, 101 Dalmatians, Pocahontas, The Lion King, Dinosaurs, The Emperor's New Groove, Sleeping Beauty, Cinderella, The Jungle Book,* and *Snow White*. The class would identify roles of people of color, as well as of men and women in the films. They would look at the power relationships among the characters; listen for loaded words, such as *backward, primitive,* and *lazy;* and consider the effect of the story on the self-image of members of a diverse audience.

In the final leg of the journey, students would share their critiques with audiences beyond the classroom. Such a step would suggest to students that their efforts were of larger import and indeed might lead to changes in their school, community, or state. Some students wrote a pamphlet to distribute to parents serving on school advisory boards, whereas others watched Saturday-morning cartoons and wrote a report card for each. (Popeye received an F because of its portrayal of ethnic groups as stupid and Americans as superior, and Teenage Mutant Ninja Turtles received a D because of its focus on using violence to solve problems.)

*Credit for the idea on which this case is based is given to: Christensen, L. (1994). Unlearning the myths that bind us. In *Rethinking our classrooms,* special edition of *Rethinking Schools* (pp. 8–13). Milwaukee, WI: Rethinking Schools Limited.

Ms. Christensen noted that each year most students looked deeper into the issues and understood, for example, the master–servant relationship or how the images affected the dreams and goals of viewers or readers. A few, however, shrugged their shoulders and suggested that being rich or poor is okay, or that kids just read or view fairy tales as fun and do not really internalize the values portrayed. Ms. Christensen recalled occasional statements from students such as "Just because girls see Tinker Bell or Cinderella with tiny waists doesn't mean they'll want one." She wondered, "How can I determine how many of my students hold on to societal stereotypes and how firmly they hold them? How can I assess the degree to which my students are developing the knowledge, skills, and dispositions for thinking critically?"

Questions for Reflection

1. What did you find effective about Ms. Christensen's use of literature and movies to teach about values and character development?
2. How would you address society's perceptions of beauty, age, and personal goals with your students?
3. How can Ms. Christensen determine the degree to which her class believes that stereotypes in media are not harmful, and whether they are improving in their ability to think critically as they participate in this unit of instruction? (Draw on your knowledge about performance assessment, authentic assessment, and portfolios in responding to this question.)
4. Is it appropriate for teachers to challenge students' traditional social and role concepts (e.g., learn alternative gender roles), especially those based on family and religious values? If so, at what ages and by what method?
5. Given the pressures to engage in sexual activity in the preteen and adolescent years, how could you as a teacher help your students come to a clearer and healthier understanding of issues related to sexual activity in school-age youth? Identify any cultural differences related to this issue, e.g., the tradition in certain cultures to begin families at ages 11–13.

Activities for Extending Thinking

1. Discuss with a parent, a teacher, and an administrator his/her philosophy about teaching values, particularly values embedded in traditional fairy tales and children's literature. Discuss both the process (methods) of teaching values and the content of the values themselves. Include the previous "Questions for Reflection" in your discussions.
2. Critique television programs such as *Hannah Montana iCarly, That's So Raven, and Drake and Josh,* and/or commercials for their underlying values. What specific messages are sent to the viewer about gender roles?
3. Discuss with students the impact of fairy tales on conceptualizations about gender in their lives and the lives of people they know. Record your insights, and be prepared to summarize your findings in class.
4. Outline a unit plan or a series of lesson plans that would promote healthy values in a class that you might teach. Relate your product to local, state, and/or national standards for teacher education.

Case 4

Integrating Women's Issues into Curriculum

A student challenges a teacher's assignment that requires them to conduct research on important women in history.

Ms. Williams had just completed teaching her class about how to conduct research using library and Internet resources. So that her students could apply the research skills that they had learned, she devised an assignment about important women in history. Her goals were twofold: first, to learn about the often-overlooked accomplishments of women, and second, to allow students to see firsthand the value of knowing how to apply research skills.

Ms. Williams brought the assignment sheet and the rubric to be used in grading it. She handed out the assignment sheet and explained the requirements for the project. To stimulate interest, she gave diverse examples of important women in history, including Rosa Parks's impact on the civil rights movement, Sylvia Earle's contributions to underwater exploration, Ellen Ochoa's role in space exploration, and Marie Currie's scientific discoveries. She was interrupted by a comment from the back of the room. "No way," said Sam. "I'm not doing a report on a stupid girl!"

"Hey, girls aren't stupid!" Savannah replied.

Other students mumbled as Ms. Williams tried to regain control of her classroom. "That's enough," she said. The room quieted down.

Ms. Williams explained that each student, with no exceptions, needed to pick a woman about whom to do a project. Sam sunk down in his chair with a frown. Ms. Williams finished handing out the papers and excused the students for lunch.

Questions for Reflection

1. What could Ms. Williams have done ahead of time to prevent potential opposition to the assignment?
2. How would you respond to Sam's comment?
3. What message(s) do you think the students got from class that day? How do you think they felt on leaving class?
4. Within your subject matter area, list important contributions of women that you would want your students to know about.

Activities for Extending Thinking

1. Outline a lesson plan in your subject matter major that involves the contributions of a woman or women to your subject matter area. Incorporate in the lesson how you will prevent potential opposition and set the stage for a positive learning experience. Identify the local, state, and national standards your lesson will address.
2. Identify two women from five different racial/ethnic groups that have made important contributions to U.S. history. (List names and respective contributions.)

Design Your Own Case

Gender

Drawing on your personal experiences as a P-12 pupil, or those from a clinical experience in a school, design a case that explores an issue of gender in the classroom. The story can focus on a method or strategy related to a single subject matter area (e.g., English or social studies) or on a more generic method or strategy pertinent to a wider range of subject matter areas. Your issue might also relate to:

- Planning and preparation
- Classroom environment
- Instruction
- Teacher responsibilities*

Include some demographic data that tell a bit about the community, school, classroom, teacher, students, and curriculum. Include at least one problem for which there is no obvious answer. Choose a topic that allows the reader to link theory and practice in the areas of learning, development, teaching, and of course, multicultural/cross-cultural education. Your topic of choice should also invite discussion of multiple perspectives rather that a singular viewpoint. Consider, too, the general level of experience and knowledge of the intended reader (i.e., whether they are in an early stage of the teacher education program or a more experienced/knowledgeable professional.

Use fictitious names of persons and schools to maintain confidentiality. Your case should be approximately two pages in length (typed, double-spaced) and should include three to four Questions for Reflection and one or two Activities for Extending Thinking. Go to Resource C and use the form to design your own case.

*The four categories are from Danielson, (1996). *Enhancing professional practice: A framework for teaching*. Alexandria, VA: Association for Supervision and Curriculum Development.

Readings for Extending Thinking

Alarcon, N., Castro, R., Perez, E., Pesquera, B., Riddell, A.S., & Zavella, P. (Eds.). (1993). *Chicana critical issues*. Berkeley, CA: Third Woman Press.

American Association of University Women. (1996). *Girls in the middle. Working to succeed in school*. Washington, DC: American Association of University Women.

Andersen, M. L., & Collins, P. H. (Eds.). (1995). *Race, class, and gender: An anthology* (2nd ed.). Belmont, CA: Wadsworth.

Baca Zinn, M., & Dill, B. T. (Eds.). (1994). *Woman of color in U.S. society*. Philadelphia: Temple University Press.

Bailey, D. F., & Paisley, P. O. (2004). Developing and nurturing excellence in African-American male adolescents. *Journal of Counseling and Development, 82,* 10–17.

Barbieri, M. (1995). *Sounds from the heart: Learning to listen to girls*. Portsmouth, NH: Heinemann.

Barnett, R. C., & Rivers, C. (2004). *Some differences: How gender myths are hurting our relationships, our children, and our jobs.* New York: Basic Books.

Belenky, M. F., Clinchy, B. M., Goldberg, N. R., & Tarrule, F. M. (1986). *Women's ways of knowing: The development of self, voice, and mind.* New York: Basic Books.

Bilken, S. K., & Pollard, D. (1993). *Gender and education.* Chicago: University of Chicago Press.

Blais, M. (1995). *In these girls hope is a muscle*. New York: Atlantic Monthly Press.

Bly, R. (1990). *Iron John: A book about men*. Reading, MA: Addison-Wesley.

Boyd, H., & Allen, R. L. (Eds.). (1995). *Brotherman: The odyssey of Black men in America—An anthology.* New York: Ballantine.

Brown, L. (1998). *Raising their voices: The politics of girls' anger*. Cambridge, MA: Harvard University Press.

Brown, L., Chesney-Lind, M., & Stein, N. (2006, June 7). What about the boys? *Education Week,* 40.

Brozzo, W. (2006). Bridges to literacy for boys. *Educational Leadership,* 71–74.

Burbridge, L. (1991). *The interaction of race, gender, and socioeconomic status in education outcomes*. Wellesley, MA: Center for Research on Women.

Campbell, P. B., & Sanders, J. (2002). Challenging the system: Assumptions and data behind the push for single-sex schools. In A. Datnow & L. Hubbard (Eds.), *Gender in policy and practice: Perspectives on single-sex and coeducational schooling* (pp. 31–46). New York: Routledge Falmer.

Cassidy, K. W. (2007). Gender differences in cognitive ability, attitudes, and behavior. In D. Sadker & E. S. Silber (Eds.), *Gender in the classroom: Foundations, skills, methods, and strategies across the curriculum* (pp. 33–72). Mahwah, NJ: Erlbaum.

Castillo-Speed, L. (Ed.). (1995). *Latina: Women's voices from the borderlands*. New York: Touchstone/Simon & Schuster.

Chapman, A. (1997). *A great balancing act: Equitable education for girls and boys*. Washington, DC: National Association of Independent Schools.

Cook, G. (2007, April). Boys at risk: The gender achievement gap. *Annual Editions: Education 07–08,* Dubuque, IA: McGraw-Hill, pp. 69–70.

Crawford, S. H. (1996). *Beyond dolls and guns: 101 ways to help children avoid gender bias*. Portsmouth, NH: Heinemann.

Crosnoe, R., Riegle-Crumb, C., Field, S, Frank, K., & Muller, C. (2008, Jan.–Feb.). Peer group contexts of girls' and boys' academic experiences. *Child Development, 79*(1), 139–155.

Cunningham, M. (1999). African-American adolescent males' perceptions of their community resources and constraints: A longitudinal analysis. *Journal of Community Psychology, 27*(5), 569–588.

de la Torre, A., & Pesquera, B. M. (1993). *Building with our hands: New directions in Chicana studies*. Berkeley: University of California Press.

Douglas, S. J. (1994). *Where the girls are: Growing up female with the mass media.* New York: Times Books.

DuBois, E., & Ruiz, V. (Eds.). (1994). *Unequal sisters: A multicultural reader in U.S. women's history* (2nd ed.). New York: Routledge.

Dyer, G., & Tiggemann, M. (1996). The effect of school environment on body concerns in adolescent woman. *Sex Roles, 34*(12), 127–138.

Eagly, A. H., Heall, A. E., & Sternberg, R. J. (Eds.). (2005). *The psychology of gender* (2nd ed.). New York: Guilford.

Eder, D., Evans, C., & Parker, S. (1995). *Schooltalk: Gender and adolescent culture.* New Brunswick, NJ: Rutgers University Press.

Farmer, L., (2008). *Teen girls and technology: What's the problem, what's the solution?* New York: Teachers College Press.

Ferguson, A. A. (2001). *Bad boys: Public schools in the making of Black masculinity.* Ann Arbor: University of Michigan Press.

Fordham, S. (1996). *Blacked out: Dilemmas of race, identity, and success at Capital High.* Chicago: University of Chicago Press.

Fordham, S. (1997). *A low score wins: Is high self-esteem compromising Black girls' academic achievement?* Paper presented at the RISE Conference Proceedings. New Brunswick, NJ: Rutgers University, October 1999.

Frankenberg, R. (1993). *White women, race matters: The social construction of whiteness.* Minneapolis, MN: University of Minnesota Press.

Froschl, M., Sprung, B., & Mullin-Ridler, N. (1998). *Quit it!: A teacher's guide on teasing and bullying for use with students in grades K–3.* New York: Equity Concepts; Wellesley, MA: Wellesley College Center for Research on Women; Washington, DC: NEA.

Garbarino, J. (1999). *Lost boys: Why our sons turn violent and how we can save them.* New York: Free Press.

Gaskell, J., & Willinsky, J. (1995). *Gender informs curriculum.* New York: Teachers College Press.

Gilligan, J. (1997). *Violence: Reflections on a national epidemic.* New York: Vintage.

Gurian, M., & Stevens, K. (2005) *The minds of boys: Saving our sons from falling behind in school and life.* San Francisco: Jossey-Bass.

Guy-Sheftall, B. (Ed.). (1995). *Words of fire: An anthology of African-American feminist thought.* New York: New Press.

Harris, L., & Associates, Inc. (1993). *Hostile hallways: The AAUW survey on sexual harassment in America's schools.* Washington, DC: American Association of University Women.

Herr, K., & Arms, E. (2002). The intersection of educational reforms: Single-gender academies in a public middle school. In A. Datnow & L. Hubbard (Eds.), *Gender in policy and practice perspectives on single-sex and Coeducational schooling* (pp. 31–46). New York: Routledge/Falmer.

Hine, D. C., King, W., & Reed, L. (Eds.). (1995). *We specialize in the wholly impossible: A reader in Black women's history.* Brooklyn, NY: Carlson.

Jones-Royster, B., & Mann-Simplins, A. M., (Eds.). (2005). *Calling cards: Theory and practice in the study of race, gender and culture.* Albany: State University of New York Press

Katz, J. (Ed.). (1995). *Messengers of the wind: Native American women tell their life stories.* New York: Ballantine.

Kivel, P. (1999). *Boys will be men: Raising our sons for courage, caring, and community.* Gabriola Island, British Columbia, Canada: New Society.

Klein, S. S., Richardson, B., Grayson, D. A., Fox, L. H., Kamarae, C., Pollard, D. S., & Dwyer, C. A. (Eds.). (2007). *Handbook for achieving gender equity through education.* New York: Taylor & Frances.

Kleinfeld, J. (1999, Winter). Student performance: Males versus females. *The Public Interest, 134,* 3–20.

Kramer, S. (1988). Sex role stereotyping: How it happens and how to avoid it. In A. O'Brien Carelli (Ed.), *Sex equity in education* (pp. 5–23). Springfield, IL: Charles C. Thomas.

Leach, M. (2005.) Shelby considers same-sex classes. *The Birmingham News,* November 21, 2005. Retrieved November 24, 2005, from: http://www.al.com/news/birminghamnews/

Lee, V. E. (1997). Gender equity and the organization of schools. In B. J. Bank & P. M. Hall (Eds.), *Gender, equity, and schooling: Policy and practice* (pp. 135–158). New York: Garland.

Maher, F. A., & Tetreault, M. K. (1994). *The feminist classroom.* New York: Basic Books.

Meyer, E. J. (2009). *Gender, bullying, and harassment: Strategies to end sexism and homophobia in schools.* New York: Teachers College Press.

Mid-Atlantic Equity Center. (1999). *Adolescent boys: Statistics and trends* (A fact sheet). Chevy Chase, MD: Mid-Atlantic Equity Assistance Center.

Moghadam, V. M. (2005). *Globalizing women: Transnational feminist networks.* Baltimore: Johns Hopkins University Press.

Mosca, G. N., & Shmurak, C. B. (1995). An interdisciplinary, gender equitable mathematics project for the middle school. *Middle School Journal, 27*(1), 26–29.

National Coalition for Women and Girls in Education. (2002, June). *Title IX at 30: Report card on gender equity.* Washington, DC: Author.

National Research Council. (1996). *National science education standards.* Washington, DC: National Academy Press.

Nouraie-Simone, F. (Ed.). (2005). *On shifting ground: Muslim women in the global era.* New York: Feminist Press.

Oakes, J. (1985). *Keeping track: How schools structure inequality.* New Haven, CT: Yale University Press.

Odean, K. (1997). *Great books for girls.* New York: Ballantine.

Orenstein, P. (1994). *Schoolgirls: Young women, self-esteem, and the confidence gap.* New York: Doubleday.

Perry, E. L., Schmidtke, J. M., & Kulik, C. T. (1998). Propensity to sexually harass: An exploration of gender differences. *Sex Roles: A Journal of Research 38*(5–6), 443–460.

Peterson, S. (2002). Gender meanings in eighth grade: Students talk about classroom writing. *Gender and Education, 14*(4), 351–366.

Pipher, M. (1994). *Reviving Ophelia: Saving the selves of adolescent girls.* New York: Ballantine.

Raider-Roth, M., Albert, M., Bircam-Barkley, I., Gidseg, E., & Murray, T. (2008). Teaching boys: A relational puzzle. *Teachers College Record, 110*(2), 443–481.

Ravitch, D. (1996, November 18). Stereotype bashing. *Forbes,* 203.

Rosser, S. V. (1995). *Teaching the majority: Breaking the gender barrier in science, mathematics, and engineering.* New York: Teacher College Press.

Sadker, D. (1999). Gender equity: Still knocking at the classroom door. *Educational Leadership, 56*(7), 22–26.

Sadker, D., & Zittleman, K. (2005, March/April). Closing the Gender Gap—Again! *Principal Magazine, 84,* 18–22.

Sadker, M. P., & Sadker, D. (1994). *Failing at fairness: How America's schools cheat girls.* New York: Scribner's.

Sadker, M. P., & Sadker, D. (2005). *Teachers, Schools and Society* (7th ed.). Boston: McGraw-Hill.

Sadker, M. P., & Sadker, D. M. (2004). Gender bias: From colonial America to today's classrooms. In J. A. Banks & C. A. M. Banks (Eds.), *Multicultural education: Issues and perspectives* (5th ed., pp. 135–163). Hoboken, NJ: Wiley.

Salisbury, J., & Jackson, D. (1996). *Challenging macho values: Practical ways of working with adolescent boys.* London: Falmer.

Sanders, J., & Rocco, S. (1994). *Bibliography on gender equity in mathematics, science, and technology: Resources for classroom teachers.* New York: Center for Advanced Study in Education, CUNY Graduate Center.

Sax, L. (2005). *Why gender matters: What parents and teachers need to know about the emerging science of sex differences.* New York: Doubleday.

Scantlebury, K., Johnson, E., Lykens, S., Bailey, B., Clements, R., Gleason, S., Lewis, R., & Letts, W. (1996, January). *Creating a cycle of equitable teaching.* Paper presented at the annual meeting of the Association for the Education of Teachers in Science, Seattle, WA.

Schiff, K. G. (2006). *Lighting the way: Nine women who changed modern America.* New York: Miramax Books/Hyperion.

Shmurak, C. B. (1994). Girls' high schools—How empowering have they been? *The High School Journal, 78*(1), 1–12.

Shmurak, C. B., & Ratliff, T. M. (1994). Gender equity and gender bias: Issues for the middle school teacher. *Middle School Journal, 25*(5), 63–66.

Silverstein, O., & Rashbaum, B. (1994). *The courage to raise good men.* New York: Penguin.

Simmons, R. (2003). *Odd girl out: The hidden culture of aggression in girls.* New York: Harcourt.

Streitmatter, J. (1994). *Toward gender equity in the classroom.* Albany: SUNY Press.

Titus, J. J. (1993). Gender messages in education foundations textbooks. *Journal of Teacher Education, 44*(1), 38–43.

Tovey, R. (1995, July/August). A narrowly gender-based model of learning may end up cheating all students. *Harvard Education Letter,* 3–6.

Tyson, C. A., & Hinton-Johnson, K. (2003, January/February). Once upon a time: Teaching about women and social justice through literature. *Social Education, 67*(1), 54–57.

U.S. Census Bureau. (2006). *Statistical abstract of the United States: 2007.* (126th ed.). Washington, DC: U.S. Government Printing Office.

Weis, L. (Ed.) (2008). *The way class works: readings on school, family, and the economy.* New York: Routledge.

Wellesley Center for Research on Women. (1992). *How schools shortchange girls: A study of major findings on girls and education.* Washington, DC: American Association of University Women.

Wharton, A. S. (2005). *The sociology of gender: An introduction to theory and research.* Malden, MA: Blackwell.

Internet Sites for Extending Thinking

http://www.aauw.org/
American Association of University Women materials on promoting gender equality.

http://www.aauw.org/research/all.cfm
Gender Gaps Executive Summary for PDF.

http://www.aauw.org/research/upload/forstudents.pdf
Harassment-Free Hallways.

http://www.nmwh.org/
History of women's suffrage.

http://www.greatwomen.org/
Women who have contributed to American society; teaching ideas.

http://www.nwhp.org/
Clearinghouse for women's history; resources, programs, and events.

http://www.looksmart.com/
Type "men's issues" in the "Search the Web" box and click on "Search"—links to library resources, including health and sexuality, publication for men.

http://www.centerforlearning.org/
The Center for Learning
21590 Center Ridge Road
Rocky River, Ohio 44116

http://www.activecitizenship.org/
Center for Multicultural Cooperation
P.O. Box 1385
Coarsegold, California 93614

http://www.charactercounts.org/
Character Counts!
Josephson Institute of Ethics
4640 Admiralty Way, Suite 1001
Marina del Rey, California 90292-6610

http://www.ethicsusa.com/
Character Education Center
P.O. Box 80208
Rancho Santa Margarita, California 92688-0208

http://www.womeninwwii.com/
This Web site has a wide variety of information about women in WWII, both those who served in the war and those who worked at home.

http://www.smartboysbadgrades.com/
This site contains tips for teachers regarding the learning styles of boys, trends in performance of boys and girls in school, and strategies and techniques for helping boys (and girls) learn.

Chapter 3

Ethnicity

Introduction

Ethnicity is used in this text to refer to a group of people of common national origin or origins (Gollnick & Chinn, 2004). Hence, for persons born in America, "American" is one of their ethnic groups. At the same time, however, other national origins are reflected in their ancestors (e.g., French, German, Irish, Italian, Swedish, and the like). Hence, a Black student, if born in America, will be American and may also be (ethnically) French, German, or of another country of origin.

Some scholars view ethnicity as a subgroup of race (e.g., the ethnic groups of Cambodian, Chinese, Japanese, Thai, and Vietnamese are considered subgroups of the Asian racial category; Adams, Bell, & Griffin, 1997). The United States, a country based on principles that welcome diversity, is now comprised of approximately 300 ethnic groups (Gollnick & Chinn, 2009).

Chapter 3 contains cases that help us think about similarities and differences in students related to their ethnic heritage. They also help us recognize possible biases in ourselves and in society that unfairly stereotype persons of particular ethnicities. Exploration of ways in which prejudice and discrimination affect students can help prepare us to take measures to prevent these actions, as well as to respond appropriately when bias is cast on us.

Typically, discussions of important ethnic issues, such as those in this section, include key terms and concepts such as the following.

cultural competence
cultural norms
culture
democracy in the classroom
ethnic group
ethnocentrism
interdisciplinary teaching
learning styles
multiculturalism
rule consequences
social justice curriculum
stereotype

Definitions of key terms are located in the glossary of this text.

Case 5

Let's All Make Up the Rules for Our Classroom

Students are given the opportunity to make real decisions regarding the operation of their classroom by helping to formulate rules for behavior.

It was the first day of the new school year. After greeting his students and describing his course goals, Mr. Chu split the class into small groups. He explained to the students that because this was their classroom as well as his, they could help make a class constitution. He told each group to write out several rules to recommend to the class, as well as a consequence for breaking each rule. He monitored all the groups, making notes on each student's participation. After the groups completed the assignment, he collected their lists.

That evening he reviewed the lists and developed five rules that captured some aspects of each list. He stated the rules positively; for example, if a group had written "Don't be rude," Mr. Chu wrote, "Respect others," and he gave written examples, such as, "Listen when others are talking." He also included the consequence of breaking each rule, such as time-outs, loss of privileges, and detention.

When he had finished compiling the class list, he recalled that a number of the students had not participated in formulating rules and consequences for the class. He had not pressed them to contribute when he monitored the groups, but he was curious why they chose not to help create the rules. He noted further that two of the students were of Russian heritage, one a male and one a female. Another two were female students from Cambodia. Mr. Chu wondered whether cultural values, such as respect for and even dependence on adult authority, might have been the reason for their lack of participation. He would ask them when he had a chance.

The next day, Mr. Chu explained how he had arrived at five collective class rules and consequences. After the class agreed that the list was acceptable, Mr. Chu wrote the rules on a poster and hung it in the front of the room. Each student signed the new constitution. He felt confident that by having ownership in the rules, students would be more likely to follow them.

Mr. Chu reminded the students that the next 10 minutes would be devoted to silent reading. He thought to himself, "Now would be the time to have a friendly chat with each of the four students who did not help make up the class rules." He knew he needed to be clear that he was not disappointed in them, but rather that he merely was interested in understanding why they did not participate.

Questions for Reflection

1. How could Mr. Chu address the nonparticipating students' in a way that would respect their cultural differences?
2. If the students answered, "I don't know," when asked why they did not participate, what would you recommend Mr. Chu say? Is it permissible for these students not to participate in activities like this one?
3. Develop a student behavior management plan that you could implement in your classroom, including the following:
   a. How you would involve all students in developing the rules and procedures for classroom behavior
   b. The rules and procedures that you would hope to develop (with or without student involvement), that is, any nonnegotiable rules
   c. The positive consequences of honoring the rules or procedures
   d. The negative consequences of not honoring the rules or procedures
4. What would you say to students who do not follow their own rules?

Activity for Extending Thinking

1. Interview a school administrator, a school counselor, and a teacher to determine their views on involving students of various ethnicities (some of whom may feel it is not their role to participate) in establishing expectations for classroom behavior. Summarize your findings in writing, and be prepared to share in class.
2. Considering a grade level at which you hope to teach, create an activity for your K–12 students that would help them explore cultural differences in role expectations for teachers and students.

Case 6

A Lesson on Cultural Celebrations of Thanksgiving

Thanksgiving celebrations of five different cultures are compared in a small-group reading activity.

It was mid-November when Mr. Rodriguez began his lesson on "Giving Thanks in Different Lands." He read the lesson objectives from the blackboard to his class: "Today we will learn how people of the United States have celebrated 'Thanksgiving,' as well as how people of other countries give thanks."

"How many of you have ever celebrated Thanksgiving?" he asked. Nearly all the students raised a hand. "Please take out a sheet of paper and write what you know about Thanksgiving celebrations. Your papers will not be graded. I just want to know what you already know about our topic."

After several minutes, it appeared that all had finished writing. Mr. Rodriguez collected the papers and then read a brief story, entitled "The First Thanksgiving," a traditional account of how English settlers in North America gave thanks for their good fortune. Mr. Rodriguez raised a number of questions about the historical accuracy of the account, including whether Native Americans typically would have helped in the celebration.

"Class, now that you have heard the usual story about the 'First Thanksgiving,' I would like to extend our thinking about celebrations of thanks. It turns out that Native Americans actually had such celebrations before the English arrived in this land." For the next two minutes, Mr. Rodriguez read a short story about the first fruits ceremony and the green corn ceremony of the Wampanoags of Plymouth, Massachusetts, noting the cultural significance of each celebration.

Now," he said, "I have stories of how four other cultures gave thanks for what they considered to be important. I have assigned pairs. I will give each pair two stories of Thanksgiving celebrations of people of other lands. I would like each of you to read one story to your partner. Take your time in reading. Your goal is to understand both the stories completely. We will discuss them when everyone is done."

Mr. Rodriguez passed out the stories. They were "First Fruits," a celebration of the African Zulu; "Mid-Autumn Festival," the holiday of many Chinese people in San Francisco's Chinatown; "Día de Gracias," celebrated by native people of Mexico (including the Olmecas, Zapotecas, Mayas, Toltecas, Mixtecas, and Haustecas); and "Sukkot," or "Feast of the Tabernacles," celebrated by Jewish people.

When the students were finished reading to one another, Mr. Rodriguez asked them to share the key aspects of each celebration with the class. He recorded critical elements of each story in four columns on the board.

He then asked, "What are some similarities in how all four groups give thanks?" After listing several, he asked, "What are some differences?" Finally, as the period was drawing to a close, he asked, "What general principles have we learned about different groups of people and how they give thanks for what they have?" Again, he listed student responses on the board.

"What have we learned about broadening our perspectives or extending our understanding of the meaning of 'First' in 'First Thanksgiving'?"

"Tomorrow," he concluded, "We will talk more about how you give thanks, as well as what today's lesson might mean to you personally. Good job today! See you tomorrow."

Questions for Reflection

1. What did Mr. Rodriguez do to extend students' knowledge about Thanksgiving celebrations? List the steps that he had students follow.
2. How would Mr. Rodriguez's method for presenting information help students learn how to think?
3. Describe other kinds of lessons that can contribute to goals of multiculturalism. Give an example of each kind of lesson.
4. If you wanted to teach your students about the injustices against Native Americans, would you include it as part of this lesson or as a separate topic for another time? Briefly explain the rationale for your position.

Activities for Extending Thinking

1. Conduct a simple survey of persons of various ethnicities on the pros and cons of multiculturalism. Be prepared to summarize your findings for the class.
2. Discuss with practicing teachers methods they use for engaging students with content, or as some would say, methods for getting students to "actively construct meaning." For example, in teaching a skill, a teacher might tell about the skill, model (demonstrate) it, have students practice the skill with guidance, and then have students practice the skill independently. In teaching a concept, the teacher might define the concept, give examples and nonexamples of it, have students give examples and nonexamples, and have students demonstrate how to apply the concept. Ask the teachers how, if at all, they modify their teaching strategies to accommodate the needs of students of diverse backgrounds.

Case 7

A Teacher's Answer to "When Will I Ever Use This?"

A teacher designs an interdisciplinary math lesson that not only teaches graphing but also helps raise student awareness of social issues.

Ms. McMullen had taught fifth grade for five years. She was considered a competent teacher by her colleagues and students. One of her favorite subjects was math. She had kept up with developments in the field, including the use of manipulatives to help students engage in concrete activities. Moreover, she could really see that students were learning the content of the subject, and she knew it would be important in their lives as students in school and beyond.

Recently, Ms. McMullen had noticed a news report of a poll on perceptions of whites and blacks about the economic conditions of blacks in the United States. As she began planning for her next unit on constructing and interpreting charts and graphs, she decided that by using the current data from the article, she could teach not only math (graphing), but also a lesson on how math could be used to explore important social issues such as that of race relations.

On the first day of her unit, Ms. McMullen introduced the academic objectives of the math unit, defined some key terms, and outlined the benefits of understanding the charts and graphs. She showed how to represent data in a bar graph, a line graph, and a pie chart.

She then assigned students the task of reading and summarizing the material from a recent study on racial attitudes that was conducted by a leading national newspaper, a well-known foundation, and a nationally respected university. Finally, she informed students that they should present the data in the form of a graph. They could choose any of the charts or graphs she had introduced, but they had to be able to defend their choice. She was curious to hear the rationales they would give.

In their graphs, students were to represent survey respondents in terms of race and to depict what they considered to be key findings of the survey—for example, that 68 percent of blacks surveyed said that racism is a big problem in our society today, whereas only 38 percent of whites thought so; and 46 percent of whites said that blacks on average hold jobs of equal quality to those of whites, whereas government data show that blacks on average earn 60 percent less than whites.

After class, Mary Greencrow asked, "Ms. McMullen, could you find information on racial attitudes of whites compared to Native Americans?"

"Good idea, Mary", I'll look into it."

Questions for Reflection

1. Would you support Ms. McMullen's efforts to integrate the two lessons (graphing and race relations)? Why or why not?
2. Would the cultural makeup of the class—for example, all white students, or a majority of students of color—affect your answer to question 1?
3. Assuming that an introduction to the types of racial attitudes reflected in the poll would have been appropriate, outline briefly how you would design such a contextual introduction.

Activity for Extending Thinking

1. Interview at least two practicing teachers to learn the strategies they use to integrate social justice issues with subject matter content. Be prepared to summarize your findings in class.
2. How might you design a lesson in your subject matter area in which you connect some "traditional" subject matter, such as graphing, reading, writing, or computing, with issues of social justice? Describe the lesson briefly. For example, a biology or health teacher might build a lesson around the Tuskegee Syphilis Experiment in which, between 1932 and 1972, 339 black men were purposely given ineffective treatments for syphilis in a government effort to discover how the disease affected blacks as compared to whites—an activity later called "profoundly morally wrong and clearly racist" by President Clinton. The lesson(s) could focus on both scientific and social justice issues (http://infoplease.com/ipa/A0762136.html).

Case 8

Encountering Art That Contains Stereotypes

A parent criticizes a display of photos of murals from the 1930s for depicting stereotypical images of African-Americans and women.

It was parent conference night, and Ms. Lotzer was saying good night to her last parent visitor when he said to her, "By the way, those large photos with the world maps on the bulletin board, did you know that they contain stereotypical images of Africans in loincloths and 'pickaninny hairstyles'? And one has 'Aunt-Jemima–like' women picking cotton. They are really insulting!"

Ms. Lotzer responded, "You know, I never thought of that. Those are photos of murals that were donated to the school by the city. They're from a collection commissioned during the Depression years to employ out-of-work artists. They were thought to have artistic value. I thought they would be better for the children than blank walls, and they do accurately portray perceptions that existed in the 1930s."

"Well, that's true, but I don't think they send the right message! In fact, in addition to the ethnic stereotypes portrayed, three of them don't depict any female images at all!"

The next day, Ms. Lotzer shared her experience with the school principal. Sympathetic to the parent's concern, the principal ordered the photos covered until it was decided whether they should be permanently removed.

The following day in class, Ms. Lotzer's students asked, "Why are the photos covered?" She told them of the events of the previous day, being careful to maintain the anonymity of the parent involved. She also mentioned that the photos would remain covered until the next faculty meeting. "At that time, I will present the parent's concerns, and I hope we can agree on a reasonable policy, but for now the pictures will be covered," she said.

Some of her students seemed to support the principal's decision, whereas others did not agree with his decision to cover the photos. The students asked Ms. Lotzer, "What do you plan to do?"

"I'm not sure what I'll say," she replied. "It would also be helpful, though, to know what you think—both as individuals and as a class. It would be helpful to know what more parents think," she said. "Perhaps we could devise several survey questions for parents and compile the responses. Then, I can represent not only my own views, but also those of you and your parents. Are you willing to do that?" she asked.

Hearing no objection, Ms. Lotzer asked, "Who can think of a first question that we could include in our survey?"

Questions for Reflection

1. Do you agree or disagree with the principal's decision to cover the photos? Give a brief rationale for your answer.
2. What principles should teachers follow in
   a. Selecting materials for display in their classrooms
   b. Involving students and parents in decisions regarding such issues
   c. Countering stereotypes portrayed in other forms of media, such as television, magazines, newspapers, and electronic media (e.g., the Internet)
3. Did Ms. Lotzer overstep her authority in surveying students and parents without authorization from the principal?
4. What kinds of displays might be culturally acceptable, yet at the same time violate more universal ethical principles (e.g., nudity in art or anthropological pictures)?

Activity for Extending Thinking

1. Examine the classroom bulletin boards and display areas of several classrooms to determine whether their content contributes to the establishment of a multicultural learning environment. In what ways do displayed materials perpetuate or break down cultural stereotypes?
2. List several common stereotypes of traditionally oppressed groups (e.g., racial, ethnic or gender-based groups) and for each, suggest a visual (e.g., a picture, chart, graph) that could be displayed in an effort to counter each stereotype listed.

Case 9

Presidents, Leaders, and Cultures

Several students ask permission to focus their research project on Native American leaders rather than the Mount Rushmore presidents assigned by the teacher.

Ms. Williams was in her third year of teaching, an endeavor that she referred to as "a privilege rather than a job."

She believed deeply in creating and selecting learning activities for students that were based on current events. From a newspaper article on the U.S. government's intention to clean and restore the Mount Rushmore monument (at a cost of $56 million), she designed a group project in which students were to summarize the major accomplishments and admirable traits of a president honored on Mount Rushmore. Ms. Williams thought that the project would not only refine the students' research skills, but it would also give them the opportunity to learn cooperatively.

On the day that she introduced the project to the class, she gave each student a list of the presidents honored on Mount Rushmore: Washington, Jefferson, Lincoln, and Theodore Roosevelt.

After class, Mary Bearrunner and Beth Whiteman, two Native American students, asked Ms. Williams if they could do their project on a Native American chief, such as Crazy Horse. They added that although the presidents on Mount Rushmore had done some good for whites, each had a hand in what some would call racist acts against Native Americans. "For example," said Beth, "Jefferson bought land from France that actually belonged to Native American people, and he laid the groundwork for 'Manifest Destiny,' which justified taking land and other resources without regard to the rights and cultures of others. President Lincoln approved the mass execution of 38 Indians in Mankato, Minnesota. And 10 of our first 12 presidents had slaves."

Ms. Williams praised the girls for their knowledge of history and responded further, "Here's what I propose."

Questions for Reflection

1. Write the verbatim response you would give to Mary and Beth if you were their teacher.
2. To what extent would you explore with your class the "racist acts" of the presidents? Explain your response.

3. To what extent would the ethnic composition of the class affect your response to question 2?
4. List several other issues related to ethnicity you would want to include in your curriculum. How would you go about including these issues?
5. Is Ms. Williams teaching "heroes history"? Should she have taken a broader ("issues") approach? Which, if any, issues would you include in courses you'll teach?
6. Do young people need heroes to develop character and acquire values? Explain.

Activities for Extending Thinking

1. Discuss with three or four students of a variety of ethnic backgrounds how you could better integrate multiethnic content into your curriculum. List the topics and processes that they believe should be included.
2. Discuss with three or four classmates reasons why Mount Rushmore includes the faces of the four presidents it does, and what other presidents, if any, they might think are better selections. Be prepared to share your conclusions in class.

Design Your Own Case

Ethnicity

Based on your personal experience as a statement, or any work in a school as an adult, design a case that explores an issue of ethnicity in the classroom. The story can focus on a method or strategy related to a single subject matter area (e.g., English or social studies) or on a more generic method or strategy pertinent to a wider range of subject matter areas. Your issue might also relate to:

- Planning and preparation
- Classroom environment
- Instruction
- Teacher responsibilities*

Include some demographic data that tell a bit about the community, school, classroom, teacher, students, and curriculum. Choose a topic that allows the reader to link theory and practice in the areas of learning, development, teaching, and, of course, multicultural/cross-cultural education. Your topic of choice should also invite discussion of multiple perspectives rather that a singular viewpoint. Consider, too, the general level of experience and knowledge of the intended reader (i.e., whether they are in an early stage of the teacher education program or a more experienced/knowledgeable professional). Include at least one problem for which there is no obvious answer. Use fictitious names of persons and schools to maintain confidentiality.

Your case should be approximately two pages in length (typed, double-spaced) and should include three to four Questions for Reflection and one or two Activities for Extending Thinking. Go to Resource C and use the form to design your own case.

*The four categories are from Danielson, C. (1996). *Enhancing Professional Practice: A Framework for Teaching*. Alexandria, VA: Association for Supervision and Curriculum Development.

Readings for Extending Thinking

Adams, M., Bell, L. A., & Griffin, P. (Eds.). (1997). *Teaching for diversity and social justice: A sourcebook.* New York: Routledge.

Alba, R. D., & Nee, V. (2003). *Remaking the American mainstream: Assimilation and contemporary immigration.* Cambridge, MA: Harvard University Press.

Banks, J. A. (1997). *Teaching strategies for ethnic studies* (6th ed.). Boston: Allyn & Bacon.

Banks, J. A., & Banks, C. A. M. (Eds.). (1995). *Handbook of research on multicultural education.* New York: Macmillan.

Banks, J. A., & Gay, G. (1978). Ethnicity in contemporary American society: Towards the development of a typology. *Ethnicity, 5*, 238–251.

Bersh, L. C., (2009). Deconstructing whiteness: Uncovering prospective teachers' understandings of their culture: A Latina professor's perspective. *Multicultural Perspectives, 11*(2), 107–112.

Bialystok, E., & Hakuta, K. (1994). *In other words: The science and psychology of second-language acquisition.* New York: Basic.

Chubbuck, S. M. (2004). Whiteness enacted, whiteness disrupted: The complexity of personal congruence. *American Educational Research Journal, 41*(2), 301–333.

Coballes-Vega, C. (1992, January). Considerations for teaching culturally diverse children. *ERIC Digest,* 1–2.

Cornbleth, C., (2008). *Diversity and the new teacher.* New York: Teachers College Press.

Crawford, J. (1992). *Hold your tongue: Bilingualism and the politics of "English only."* Reading, MA: Addison-Wesley.

Delgado, R., & Stefancic, J. (1997). *Critical white studies: Looking beyond the mirror.* Philadelphia: Temple University Press.

Delpit, L. (1995). *Other people's children: Cultural conflict in the classroom.* New York: Cambridge University Press.

Delpit, L., & Dowdy, J. K. (Eds.). (2002). *The skin that we speak: Thoughts on language and culture in the classroom.* New York: New Press.

Feagin, J. R., & Feagin, C. B. (2008). Racial and ethnic relations (8th ed.). Upper Saddle River, NJ: Prentice Hall.

Fine, M., Weis, L., Powell, L. C., & Wong, L. M. (Eds.). (1997). *Off white: Readings on race, power, and society.* New York: Routledge.

Gay, G. (2000). *Culturally responsive teaching: Theory, research, and practice.* New York: Teachers College Press.

Glass, G. V. (2008). *Fertilizers, pills, and magnetic strips: The fate of public education in America*. Charlotte, NC: Information Age Publications.

Gollnick, D. M., & Chinn, P. C. (2004). *Multicultural education in a pluralistic society: Multimedia edition* (6th ed.). Upper Saddle River, NJ: Merrill/Prentice Hall.

Gollnick, D. M., & Chinn, P. C. (2009). *Multicultural education in a pluralistic society: Multimedia edition* (8th ed.). Upper Saddle River, NJ: Merrill/Prentice Hall.

Gordon-Fox, T. (2007, March 12). Behind burqa: Student gets an education in bigotry. *The Hartford Courant*, p. A1.

Green, R. L. (2005). *Expectations: How teacher expectations can increase student achievement and assist in closing the achievement gap*. Columbus, OH: SRA/McGraw-Hill.

Henderson, D. L., & May, J. P. (2005). *Exploring culturally diverse literature for children and adolescents: Learning to listen in new ways.* Boston: Pearson Allyn and Bacon.

Hernandez, D. J. (2004). Children and youth in immigrant families. In J. A. Banks & C. A. M. Banks (Eds.), *The handbook of research on multicultural education* (2nd ed., pp. 404–419). San Francisco: Jossey-Bass.

Hirsch, E. D., Jr., Kett, J. F., & Trefil, J. (2002), *The new dictionary of cultural literacy: What every American needs to know.* Boston: Houghton Mifflin.

Hollins, E. R., (1996) *Culture in school learning: Revealing the deep meaning.* Mahwah, NJ: Erlbaum.

Hollins, E. R., King, J. E., & Hayman, W. C. (Eds.). (1994). *Teaching diverse populations: Formulating a knowledge base*. Albany: State University of New York Press.

Huntington, S. P. (2004). *Who are we? The challenges to America's national identity.* New York: Simon & Schuster.

Irvine, J. J., & York, D. E. (1995). Learning styles and culturally diverse students: A literature review. In J. A. Banks & C. A. M. Banks (Eds.), *The handbook of research on multicultural education* (pp. 484–497). New York: Macmillan.

Jacoby, T. (Ed.). (2004). *Reinventing the melting pot: The new immigrants and what it means to be American*. New York: Basic.

Kailin, J. (1999). How white teachers perceive the problem of racism in the schools: A case study in "liberal" Lakeview. *Teachers College Record, 100,* 724–750.

Kliebard, H. M. (2004). *The struggle for the American curriculum, 1893–1958*. New York: Routledge/Falmer.

Kuper, A. (1999). *Culture: The anthropologists' account*. Cambridge, MA: Harvard University Press.

Ladson-Billings, G. (1994). *The dreamkeepers: Successful teachers of African-American children*. San Francisco: Jossey-Bass.

Ladson-Billings, G. (1995). Toward a theory of culturally relevant pedagogy. *American Educational Research Journal, 32*, 465–491.

Lipsitz, G. (1998). *The possessive investment in whiteness: How white people profit from identity politics*. Philadelphia: Temple University Press.

Manning, M. L., & Baruth, L. G. (1991). Appreciating cultural diversity in the classroom. *Kappa Delta Pi Record, 27*(4), 104–107.

McCall, A. L. (2004). Using poetry in social studies classes to teach about cultural diversity and social justice. *The Social Studies, 95*(4), 172–176.

Nichols, S. L., & Berliner, D. C. (2007). *Collateral damage: How high-stakes testing corrupts America's schools*. Cambridge, MA: Harvard Education Press.

Perez, B. (1992). Cultural and linguistic democracy: A challenge for today's schools. *Curriculum Report (NASSP), 22*(2), 1–4.

Perry, P. (2002). *Shades of White: White kids and racial identities in high school.* Durham, NC: Duke University Press.

Roediger, D. (2002). *Colored white: Transcending the racial past.* Berkeley: University of California Press.

Valdes, G. (2001). *Learning and not learning English: Latino students in American schools*. New York: Teachers College Press.

Wang, M. C., & Gordon, E. W. (Eds.). (1994). *Educational resilience in inner-city America: Challenges and prospects*. Hillsdale, NJ: Erlbaum.

Williams, P. J. (1995). *The rooster's egg: On the persistence of prejudice*. Cambridge, MA: Harvard University Press.

Internet Sites for Extending Thinking

http://asianweek.com/news/
News-oriented, current events; profiles Asian stars, other success stories, and analysis of Asian business trends.

http://hmongstudies.com/LibraryPressReleaseJune07-1.pdf
Web site of the Hmong Cultural Center, in St. Paul, Minnesota, contains links to lists of books, journal articles, and theses on aspects of Hmong culture.

http://www.Indianz.com
Updated news reports on various tribes. Health issues of American Indians and contemporary topics.

http://hanksville.org/NAresources
Links to resources on history, culture, art, language, education, and native nations.

http://www.history.navy.mil/faqs/faq61-2.htm
This Web site has information on the Native American code talkers and about Native American involvement in World War II in general.

http://www.latinolink.com
News, helpful resources in areas such as music and entertainment, business and finance, sports, education, and careers.

http://www.goshen.edu/soan/
Links to race and ethnic relations Web sites, including groups of European-American, African-American, Native American, and Asian-American people, as well as to race and ethnic relations, cultural competence, and professional organization sites (a Web page of Goshen College Department of Sociology and Anthropology).

http://www.rense.com/politics5/code.htm
This Web site is a link to an article about the Navajo code talkers.

Chapter 4

Race

Introduction

Race may be defined as a system of categorization designed to distinguish between groups of persons on the basis of **perceived** physical differences. This taxonomy, developed over a century ago, has been discredited by more recent studies showing that differences within groups based on physical characteristics such as skin color are often greater than differences between groups. For example, groups of color, such as African American, range in skin color from dark brown to white.

Based on studies of genetics, researchers believe the underlying genetic variation and expressed physical traits "do not fracture into races (subspecies)" and that the "demographic units of human societies (and of the U.S. census) are products of social or political rules, not the forces of biological evolution" (Rotimi, 2004). However, most geneticists, and educators alike agree that the nonexistence of races (subspecies) does not mean the nonexistence of racism, "the structured systematic oppression against individuals and groups defined based on (perceived) physical traits" (Rotimi, 2004).

Although most educators today view race as a socially constructed concept, some teachers, students, and parents hold—perhaps subconsciously—to the age-old view of race and, further, to the view that some "races" are inferior to others (Jacoby & Glauberman, 1995). Most also agree that children begin to develop attitudes about race between the ages of two and five, that not talking about race leaves them vulnerable to misinformation and stereotyping, and that children's acceptance of differences among ethnic and racial groups is essential if we are to create a society with freedom and justice for all (Byrnes & Kiger, 2005).

Chapter 4 focuses our attention on important issues of race that may be purposely included in curriculum or that may arise spontaneously from student impetus. Terms and concepts that often are used or may be useful in discussing the issues of race include the following.

access
agent group
classism
equity pedagogy
experiential knowledge
hip-hop culture
institutional racism
knowledge base
oppression
power
prejudice and discrimination (see Chapter 2 glossary)
race as a socially constructed concept
racism
racial identity theories
social action activities
student self-esteem
target group
tracking
white privilege

Definitions of key terms are located in the glossary of this text.

Case 10

Knowledge Base on Diversity: Resources for Teachers

Recognizing the increasing number of students of diverse racial backgrounds in her school, a teacher explores the knowledge base on racial/ethnic diversity as she makes plans for the coming year.

It was August, and Ms. Johnson was beginning to think seriously about beginning another academic year. She had taught five years, all at Washington School, but had noticed a significant change over the past two years in the demographics of the student body. In fact, the proportion of students of color had increased from 12 percent five years ago to a projected 48 percent for the coming fall.

Ms. Johnson had regularly employed principles for building self-esteem in children and youth, both in her home with her own children, as well as at work with her students. The conceptual framework that she attempted to follow included five principles for building self-esteem in students (Anderson, Redman, & Rogers, 1991):

1. Listen to and acknowledge the thoughts and feelings of students.
2. Structure situations so that they will succeed.
3. Give them reasonable feelings of control over aspects of their lives.
4. Reinforce them for being lovable and capable.
5. Model a positive view of self.

Ms. Johnson was pleased with the results from applying the principles to all her students over the past few years, but with the increasing number of students of color in her school, she wondered if she could be doing more for them—perhaps applying the principles in a slightly different way—to better meet the needs of students of color.

She scanned the table of contents of what she considered a reliable resource by Ducette, Sewell, and Shapiro (1996), "Diversity in Education," in Murray, *The Teacher Educator's Handbook: Building a Knowledge Base for the Preparation of Teachers,* to get a sense of current research and recommendations for practice. With respect to diversity based on race, she outlined a number of points that seemed to relate to the self-esteem principles with which she was familiar:

1. In studying predominantly working-class Puerto Rican and African-American students, Fine (1989) found that school administrators often censored rather than facilitated the sharing of students' experiences and ideas. For example, racism

was censored so as not to demoralize students, and dropping out of school could not be discussed because it might give students ideas. Conversely, others call for listening to and acknowledging to students and building on their life histories and microcultural experience (Gollnick & Chinn, 2009).

2. Murrell (1995) suggests that to structure for success for students of color, we might formulate goals that focus more on experiential knowledge in a social context, particularly as it relates to problems of race, class, gender, and culture (p. 206), and Gollnick and Chinn (2009) intimated that critically analyzing oppression and power relationships will help students understand racism, classism, sexism, and bias against the physically challenged, the young, and the aged.
3. The same authors suggest engaging students in collective social action to ensure a democratic society (Gollnick & Chinn, 2009). Others suggest sublimating traditional individualistic reward systems in favor of goals for the collective advancement of the racial/ethnic community at hand (Fordham, 1988). Such rewards may more effectively reinforce students of color as lovable and capable.
4. Others suggest that teachers need to discuss crucial decisions made in people's lives, including difficult topics such as drug use, having a baby, and dropping out of school (Aronowitz & Giroux, 1985).
5. In a study of urban, working-class students, it was found that a group of white students who believed that school would not lead to success were found to be using wealthy, not-well-educated persons in the community as role models (MacLeod, 1987). Perhaps providing more appropriate (e.g., more educated, less wealthy) models would benefit such students.

In previous years of teaching, Ms. Johnson had based her curriculum and instruction on research, theory, and "best practice." As she reviewed her outline of accepted studies on racial/ethnic diversity, she began to envision ways of converting theory to practice in her own classroom. It would again be exciting to try some new ideas, this time with a new and more diverse group of students.

Question for Reflection

1. Design a series of lessons that might serve as an outline of a unit plan in your own subject matter area. For example, a unit on racism might begin:

   Students will better understand the central nature, cause, concept, and effects of racism (objective) and use a mapping strategy to identify prior knowledge of the nature, cause, and effects of this form of bias (activity). You might decide that assessment of this activity will be based on performance on a project as measured by a rubric specifying criteria.

   The unit description might be followed by 8 to 10 lesson plans that would form a general, rough draft outline of a teaching unit based on the concept of racism and related issues.

Objective Activity Assessment Strategy

a.

b.

c.

d.

e

Activity for Extending Thinking

1. How could you translate theory to practice for each of the research-based ideas previously noted? From each of the studies previously outlined, list at least one practical strategy that you could use in your own teaching to address those findings. Identify the grade level and subject matter area for which you intend the curriculum or instructional plan.

   Objective Activity Assessment Strategy

   a.

   b.

   c.

   d.

   e.

2. Using a reputable educational resource such as ERIC, summarize key findings from two articles that give recommendations for teaching students with diverse backgrounds.

Case 11

Students Right an Injustice: A Lesson in Social Action

Students extend and refine reading and writing skills as they engage in a "social action" activity.

Mr. Hultgren's class had been keeping a record of upcoming class events such as field trips, student report days, and quizzes on a commercial calendar. The pictures on the calendar were of children and adolescents—mostly close-ups showing facial expressions such as wonder, excitement, happiness, and awe. On the first day of November, Mr. Hultgren turned the page of the calendar. Hector, an outgoing youth of Mexican heritage, asked his teacher, "Mr. Hultgren, how come none of the pictures on the calendar have any kids that look like me?" Other students of color chimed in, "Yeah, or me?"

Mr. Hultgren had not paid much attention to the pictures on the calendar. "You're right," he replied, looking through the rest of the pages. "There are no children of color in the remaining pictures, either. Can anyone think of anything we could do about this?"

Marty offered a suggestion, "Perhaps we can write to the people who made the calendar and ask them to put in pictures of kids like us in their next one." The class agreed.

Mr. Hultgren briefly explained about calendar publishing companies and how they could find out to whom they should write. He then designed some activities that included prewriting, editing, rewriting, spelling, grammar and usage, and business letter format. For the next week, students devised, edited, and revised a class letter to the calendar company. The letter was sent on Friday. In addition, Mr. Hultgren invited the students to bring in magazine pictures representing children of color to add to the calendar.

Five weeks later, the class received a letter from the calendar company. It said, "Thank you for making us aware of this oversight. We apologize for our mistake, and we plan to add students of color to the calendar next year."

Questions for Reflection

1. What were the strengths of Mr. Hultgren's response to the calendar problem? What else would you have said and done if you had been in his position?
2. List Mr. Hultgren's specific behaviors that likely
   a. Demonstrated teacher and student efficacy
   b. Created an inclusive classroom environment
   c. Enhanced learning of academic material

3. Describe any experiences you have had in which students have taken a social-action approach to solve a real problem in the school or broader community (see "Social Action Approach" in the Banks model, Resource B).
4. Briefly outline an activity that would encourage pupils to discuss the Banks model and to identify social-action issues that they could address. How could you ensure that such a discussion was developmentally appropriate?
5. In a classroom in which you are preparing to teach, how would you handle the issue of mixed race (e.g., if a student asked about referring to President Obama as a "black" president, when he is half white)?

Activity for Extending Thinking

1. Discuss with practicing teachers, students, and parents the social problems and issues that could/should be addressed in the kinds of classes you teach or will teach. For each social problem or issue listed, identify one or two activities that would encourage students to gather relevant data, examine their own values and those of others, and take thoughtful actions to help resolve the problem or issue. (See examples in Resource B, "Social Action Approach.")
2. In a classroom in which you are preparing to teach, how could you approach the issue of stereotyping of races (e.g., that (all) Asian persons have greater intellectual abilities, that African-American youth all like hip-hop)?

Case 12

Use of the N-Word in the Classroom

A teacher considers how to respond to four male friends—three African American and one white—who use the term "nigga" as a term of endearment in her classroom.

Daunte, Denzel, Michael, and Ryan had been inseparable over the past year. They had first become friends through working in small groups in one of their classes and had strengthened the bond of friendship as football buddies and in just "hanging out" after school, enjoying various forms of music, and texting their friends. Most of all they seemed to enjoy having fun taunting one another with friendly quips designed to both show their wit and to affirm their friendship.

Daunte, Denzel, and Michael were of African-American descent; Ryan was white. Often, taunts related to the ancestry of the four friends. "Hey, my nigga" was a greeting often extended by and to the African-American friends; "Hey, my wigga" (the abbreviation for white nigga) was a common greeting for Ryan. For classmates who knew of their close and long-lived relationship, this form of language seemed clearly inclusive and affirming, especially when used in the informal contexts of the neighborhood and the school hallways.

However, their teacher, Ms. Persons, was new to the school and had no knowledge of the friendship of these four students. Her first introduction to their jiving and taunting of one another came toward the end of the morning as the class geared down to get ready for lunch. As students put their papers and books in their bags, Ms. Persons overheard what the four friends thought was a private conversation. She also was sure that several other students overheard them as they gathered to walk together:

"What it is, my nigga?" Ryan asked Denzel.

"Hey, wigga," Denzel replied.

As Daunte approached the two, Ryan smiled. "Yo, bro. I starved—let's get our eat on."

Ms. Persons' ears had begun to burn after the first greeting. Her first thought was that such language should never be tolerated in any classroom. At the same time, the boys did seem to be friendly toward one another; it was obvious that the interaction was not intended to harm. Yet what about the other students who had heard the exchange? Would ignoring the exchange give permission to others in the class to use such terms?

She didn't need this challenge on the first day of class, for she knew that it could have a significant effect on the development of respect and rapport between her and the class and among the students. Knowing she had but a few short moments to respond, she wondered what, if anything, she *should* say.

Questions for Reflection

1. What would you say (verbatim) to the boys?
2. If you thought that because the terms "nigga" and "wigga" were in common use in the school and hence may be used again in your classroom, and if you therefore decided it might be best to discuss the implications of the use of such terms with your class, outline the questions that you would want to ask and the points that you would want to make in the class discussion.
3. What rationale would you use to explain to others (your class, parents of your students, colleagues) your decision to discuss the issue in class?
4. Is it appropriate for a white student who is referred to as a "wigga" by a close friend of color to refer to his friend of color as a "nigga"? If so, when? Is it ever appropriate for a white teacher to use the "er" version of the N-word? If so, when?
5. What other racial epithets might warrant discussion with your classes? List as many such terms as you can.

Activities for Extending Thinking

1. Review current resources on the pros and cons of deconstructing racial epithets such as the N-word. Summarize the key insights you obtain from the readings.
2. Interview two teachers in urban schools who have had encounters such as the one in the story. Summarize their opinions on the issue of responding to the student use of such terms.
3. Interview white students and students of color who have attended urban schools with diverse student populations. Ask them about their views on the use of terms that are sometimes used as terms of inclusivity and at other times as racial epithets. Summarize your findings in writing.
4. Knowing that your students may inadvertently encounter Web sites or print materials that use racial epithets, what preventative measures, if any, would you take to mitigate against such encounters? Would you purposely direct students to such sites so they might formulate ways to counter the effects of the negative messages? Why or why not?

Case 13

Hey, Teach—You Trippin' on Me, but Not on the White Kids!

A teacher is accused of racist behavior by a student in her class.

It was Friday, the sixth week of school, and the day of the big game with the rival school. Excitement was in the air. Ms. Moss's students were caught up in the spirit of the moment as they entered her room, talking and laughing with each other. Ms. Moss liked this class and was pleased about the mutual respect that existed between her and the vast majority of her students.

The bell rang. Ms. Moss and her students had discussed and followed a clear routine for beginning class. It was understood that they had two minutes to complete their conversations, take their seats, assemble their books and papers, and cease talking. Those first two minutes of free time for the students also allowed Ms. Moss to complete attendance and to sign passes for students who were tardy or absent the previous day.

"Okay, class, it's time to begin," she said.

This day, the students were not as responsive as they usually had been in the past. Their conversations trailed on. Several students had not yet taken their seats. "Marty, Willie, Desweon, please, sit down."

When students did not respond, Ms. Moss moved toward the students who seemed to be loudest and least responsive. Her intent was to use proximity—a closer and more personal presence—to get the students' attention.

She spoke more loudly to be sure she was heard. "Desweon, Willie, I asked you to please sit down. It's time to start class."

Desweon turned to Ms. Moss. "Why you be trippin' on us? You didn't say anything to those guys," pointing to three white students across the room. "You trippin' on us' cause we're black!"

"I'm trippin' on you because you're the loudest and the closest. I'm on my way to say the same thing to Marty and Tom. Now you sit down, please." Ms. Moss paused just long enough for a response, and then continued toward the white students, somewhat surprised and disappointed that she had been accused of being racist.

The class began to settle down. Ms. Moss thought to herself, "What other follow-up would be appropriate? Should I talk to Desweon and Willie in the hall? Should I discuss the incident with the class?" She decided to think about it overnight.

That evening as she pondered the questions from the incident that day, she also wondered about other details: Could there have been some underlying negative racial attitudes that affected her response to the class? Why didn't she approach the white students first? She had always tried to be an advocate for students of traditionally oppressed groups; she even voluntarily served as chair of the text-bias review committee for the district. Perhaps even a culturally sensitive teacher could be unknowingly influenced by some underlying attitudes. She began to think about other recent reprimands for indicators of patterns.

Questions for Reflection

1. Assess Ms. Moss's behavior in class. What behaviors, if any, were appropriate? Which, if any, were inappropriate?
2. What else, if anything, would you have done at the time of the confrontation by Desweon?
3. What, if anything, would you do as a follow-up later that day or in the following days?
4. What local, state, and/or national standards for teacher education relate to the key issues in this case?

Activities for Extending Thinking

1. Develop a prevention plan that would minimize the likelihood of being accused of being racist by a student or students.
2. In a school setting—a field experience site or arranged visit—discuss the issue (teacher accused of racism by student) with a teacher and student of color and with a white teacher and student. Record their suggestions for avoiding and for responding to such an accusation.
3. Discuss with colleagues in your teacher preparation program incidents similar to the one described. Record their recommendations for preventing and for responding to this issue.
4. With peers or professional educators, discuss how a teacher might respond if accused by a student of being sexist or biased in terms of socioeconomic status, ethnicity, religion, language, special needs, or sexual orientation.

Case 14

A Lesson on Oppression and Whiteness

White students ask "What's in it for me?" and struggle to identify social group membership in a lesson on social oppression.

For several years Mr. Albornoz had taught children in the early elementary grades. Each year he had taught about discrimination in a concrete way—by replicating the "Blue Eyes/Brown Eyes" activity developed by Jane Eliot. On the first day of this simulation, blue-eyed students were considered "superior," and were given privileges such as extra servings at the cafeteria, use of the drinking fountain, and extra time at recess. On the second day, roles were reversed so that all students could experience feelings related to being inferior as well as superior.

In follow-up discussions of feelings of pupils in the superior and inferior groups, it was clear that they were not ready to discuss the plight of another group, such as African-Americans or gays, without first having talked about their own ethnic group. When he brought up group names like Native American, Latino, Asian, or African American, the white pupils would consistently ask, "What about us?"

With this question in mind, and working this year with older students, Mr. Albornoz sought new ways to begin his lessons on social oppression. He had been impressed with the Oppression Model in a text entitled *Teaching for Diversity and Social Justice* (Adams, 1997). The model is based on helping students identify their own social group membership (gender, class, sexual orientation, physical/developmental/psychological ability, race, religion, and age) and then applying that information. The Oppression Model lists forms of oppression (e.g., racism), the agent group in that form (e.g., Whites), and the target groups of that form of oppression (e.g., Blacks, Latinos, Asians, Native Americans, people of mixed race). Other forms of oppression were sexism, classism, ageism, and bias toward religion, ethnicity, persons of gay/lesbian/bisexual/transsexual (GLBT) orientation, and persons with disabilities. Students are then asked a series of questions related to ease of identifying their status (agent or target) for each group membership. In pairs, students answer questions such as: which group membership(s) were easiest to identify as your own, were hardest to identify as your own, were you least aware of, and would you like to know more about?

On this day, as students began to examine their own social group membership, and more specifically their own ethnicity, Jeremy, a white student of upper-middle economic class parents, stated: "Hey Mr. A., I'm an American; that's my group!" Other white students nodded in agreement. "All white people are American." Mr. Albornoz replied: "Are others in class—our African-American and Latino brothers and sisters—not American?" Jeremy appeared puzzled.

The teacher continued: "And is 'American' an ethnic group?"

Luis responded: "No, I think 'American' is a term that refers to a national group."

"That's right," replied Mr. Albornoz. "It is indeed."

Marie offered her thoughts: "Everyone has an ethnic background—that is, they share a common culture that distinguishes them from other groups, like German or Italian Americans. They have traditions common to their group, but traditions that are different from other groups."

"Very good!" replied Mr. Albornoz. Turning to Jeremy, he continued: "So Jeremy, what ethnic group or groups do you think are part of your heritage?"

Jeremy thought: "Well, I guess my mother is Swedish and my father is German and may be English."

"So if those are your ethnic groups, of what other social groups are you a member?" pressed Mr. Albornoz. "Write them down on your paper—I'll collect them in a few minutes."

Realizing that some students may not know their ethnic heritage, Mr. Albornoz instructed them to write "unknown," until they could talk to their parents. After allowing a couple of minutes for students to write their ethnic and other social groups on their papers, Mr. Albornoz posed a new question. "Looking at our Oppression Model, to which agent (oppressive) groups and which target (oppressed) groups do you belong? Write them down on the same paper." Tomorrow, when he returned the papers, Mr. Albornoz would ask them about stereotypes often assigned to target groups, as well as how members of each agent and target group might interact with a member of another group.

"Can we be a member of both agent and target groups?" asked Kim.

"Yes, most of us are," replied the teacher. "Now," he continued, "what privileges or advantages do people in any of the agent groups have over persons in a target group?"

"What do you mean?" asked one of the students.

"Take for example, those of us who are white—do we have any advantages over persons of color—just because of our skin color?"

"Yeah," stated Will, "We whites don't get harassed with racial profiling—you know, arrested for 'DWB, driving while black.'"

"And we are less likely to be closely watched for shoplifting in stores," added another white student.

"Okay, in your pairs, list a couple of advantages possessed by each agent group, like males, upper-middle economic class people, heterosexuals, Christians, nondisabled persons, and young and middle-aged adults," said Mr. Albornoz.

As the students discussed in pairs, Mr. Albornoz thought about how he would debrief student comments and help students distinguish between forms of oppression—individual, institutional, and societal—and related issues.

Questions for Reflection

1. If some of your students could not recognize the difference between being white and being American, what questions, metaphors, and other techniques could you use to help them differentiate the two?
2. What forms of "white privilege" have you personally observed?

3. How could you teach a similar lesson (on oppression or whiteness) in your own subject matter area (i.e., in what course and unit could you include it)? How would you tie it to your course and unit in your introduction of the lesson?
4. What guidelines or ground rules would need to be established to conduct this lesson?
5. Students of multiple ancestries often face unique problems resulting from being of mixed race. If you have knowledge of or have had prior experiences working with students of mixed race, identify racial issues that might arise in P–12 classrooms. Briefly suggest a way in which teachers could address each of the issues that you have identified.

Activity for Extending Thinking

1. Examine a model of white racial-identity theory (e.g., Helms, 1995) and one of racial identity theory of persons of color (e.g., Hardiman & Jackson, 1992; Helms, 1995; Tatum, 1997). Identify the stage that you feel best matches your attitudes and beliefs. Using the theory that applies to you, write a paragraph describing how operating at your stage of racial identity might affect your interaction as teacher, with students (students of color, or white students) in the classroom.
2. Interview several bi-racial peers to better understand which racial heritage they identify most with, what they believe leads them to identify with that (those) component(s), and how much genetics and environment each play in the formation of their identity.

Design Your Own Case

Race

Design a case that explores an issue of race in the classroom. The story can focus on a method or strategy related to a single subject matter area (e.g., English or social studies) or on a more generic method or strategy pertinent to a wider range of subject matter areas. Your issue might also relate to:

- Planning and preparation
- Classroom environment
- Instruction
- Teacher responsibilities*

In selecting a topic, reflect on recent or current field experiences, personal experiences as a student, or accounts of real classroom incidents. Choose a topic that allows the reader to link theory and practice in the areas of learning, development, teaching, and of course, multicultural/cross-cultural education. Your topic of choice should also invite discussion of multiple perspectives rather that a singular viewpoint. Consider, too, the general level of experience and knowledge of the intended reader (i.e., whether they are in an early stage of the teacher education program or a more experienced/knowledgeable professional). Include some demographic data that tell a bit about the community, school, classroom, teacher, students, and curriculum. Include at least one problem to which there is no obvious answer. Use fictitious names of persons and schools to maintain confidentiality.

Your case should be approximately two pages in length (typed, double-spaced) and should include three to four Questions for Reflection and one or two Activities for Extending Thinking. Go to Resource C and use the form to design your own case.

*The four categories are from *Enhancing Professional Practice: A Framework for Teaching,* by C. Danielson, 1996. Alexandria, VA: Association for Supervision and Curriculum Development.

Readings for Extending Thinking

Adams, M., Bell, L. A., & Griffin, P. (1997). *Teaching for diversity and social justice*. New York: Routledge.

Anderson, E. M., Redman, G. L., & Rogers, C. (1991). Self-esteem for tots to teens. 1480 Arden View Drive, Arden Hills, MN 55112: Parenting and Teaching for Self-Esteem.

Anderson, James D. (1988). The education of blacks in the South, 1860–1935. Chapel Hill: University of North Carolina Press.

Anyon, J. (2005). Radical possibilities: Public policy, urban education, and a new social movement. New York: Routledge.

Apple, M. W. (1997). Consuming the other: Whiteness, education, and cheap french fries. In M. Fine, L. Weis, L. Powell, & L. Wang (Eds.), *Off white: Readings on race, power, and society* (pp. 121–128). New York: Routledge.

Aronowitz, S., & Giroux, H. A. (1985). *Education under siege*. Westport, CT: Bergin & Garvey.

Asante, M. K. (1991–1992). Afrocentric curriculum. *Educational Leadership, 49*(4), 28–31.

Ayers, W., (Ed). (2008). *City kids, city schools: More reports from the front row*. New York: New Press.

Bock, M., Rendon, M., & Kellogg, P. (2000). *Whiteness at work: A positive diversity curriculum*. Minneapolis, MN: Sirius Communications.

Brown, D. L. (1999, January 13). No easy lessons on race: Black parents find new ways to prepare children. *The Washington Post,* p. A-1.

Bush, L. (1996). "The N word." *New Yorker, 72*(10), 50.

Byrnes, D., & Kiger G. (Eds.), (2005) *Common bonds: Anti-bias teaching in a diverse society* (3rd ed.). Olney, MD: Association for Childhood Education International.

Casement, R. (2008). *Black history in the pages of children's literature*. Lanham, MD: Scarecrow.

Clark, C., & O'Donnell, J. (Eds.). (1999). *Becoming and unbecoming white: Owning and disowning a racial identity.* Westport, CT: Greenwood Press.

Copenhaver-Johnson, J. (2006). Talking to children about race: The importance of inviting difficult conversation. *Childhood Education, 83*(1), 12–21.

Council of Economic Advisors. (1998, September). *Changing America: Indicators of social and economic well-being by race and Hispanic origin.* Washington, DC: U.S. Government Printing Office.

Cushner, M., McClelland, A., & Safford, P. (1992). *Human diversity in education: An integrative approach.* New York: McGraw-Hill.

Darling-Hammond, L. (1998, September). Unequal opportunity: Race and education. *Brookings Review,* 28–32.

Delgado, Richard (2007). *Critical white studies: Looking behind the mirror.* Philadelphia: Temple University Press.

Delpit, L. (1995). *Other people's children: Cultural conflict in the classroom.* New York: New Press.

Deyhle, D., & Swisher, K. (1997). Research in American Indian and Alaska Native education: From assimilation to self-determination. In M. W. Apple (Ed.), *Review of research in education* (Vol. 22, pp. 113–194). Washington, DC: American Educational Research Association.

Dovidio, J. F., & Gaertner, S. L. (1998). On the nature of contemporary prejudice: The causes, consequences, and challenges of aversive racism. In J. L. Eberhardt & S. T. Fiske (Eds.), *Confronting racism: The problem and the response* (pp. 3–32). Thousand Oaks, CA: Sage.

Ducette, J., Sewell, T., & Shapiro, J. (1996). Diversity in education. In F. B. Murray (Ed.), *The teacher educator's handbook: Building a knowledge base for the preparation of teachers* (pp. 323–380). San Francisco: Jossey-Bass.

Dunn, R., Gemake, J., Jalali, F., & Zenhausern, R. (1990). Cross-cultural differences in learning styles of elementary-age students from four ethnic backgrounds. *Journal of Multicultural Counseling and Development, 18,* 68–93.

Dupree, D., Spencer, M. B., & Bell, S. (1997). The ecology of African-American child development: Normative and non-normative outcomes. In G. Johnson-Powell, J. Yamamoto, G. E. Wyatt, & W. Arroyo (Eds.), *Transcultural child development: Psychological assessment and treatment* (pp. 237–268). New York: Wiley.

Faung, J., & Lee, J. (2008). *Asian American in the twenty-first century.* New York: The New Press.

Fine, M. (1989). Silencing and nurturing voice in an improbable context: Urban adolescents in public school. In H. A. Giroux & P. McLaren (Eds.), *Critical pedagogy, the state and cultural struggle* (pp. 152–173). Albany: State University of New York Press.

Fine, M. (1991). *Framing dropouts: Notes on the politics of urban high schools.* Albany: State University of New York Press.

Fordham, S. (1988). Racelessness as a factor in black students' school success: Pragmatic strategy or pyrrhic victory. *Harvard Educational Review, 58,* 54–84.

Foster, M. (1991). "Just got to find a way": Case studies of the lives and practice of exemplary black high school teachers. In M. Foster (Ed.), *Into schools and schooling.* New York: AMS Press.

Foster, M. (1997). *Black teachers on teaching.* New York: New Press.

Garibaldi, A. M. (1986). Sustaining black educational progress: Challenges for the 1990s. *Journal of Negro Education, 55*(3), 386–396.

Gibbs, J. T. (1988). *Young, black and male in America: An endangered species.* Dover, DE: Auburn House.

Gollnick, D. M., & Chinn, P. C. (2009). *Multicultural education in a pluralistic society* (8th ed.). Upper Saddle River, NJ: Pearson Education.

Grant, C. A., & Secada, W. G. (1991). Preparing teachers for diversity. In W. R. Houston (Ed.), *Handbook of research on teacher education.* New York: Macmillan.

Hale-Benson, J. E. (1982). *Black children: Their roots, culture, and learning style.* Baltimore: Johns Hopkins University Press.

Hardiman, R., & Jackson, B. W. (1992). Racial identity development: Understanding racial dynamics in college classroom and on campus. In M. Adams (Ed.), *Promoting diversity in college classrooms: Innovative responses for the curriculum, faculty and institutions* (pp. 21–37). San Francisco: Jossey-Bass.

Harvey, K. D., & Harjo, L. D. (1994). *Indian country: A history of native people in America.* Golden, CO: North American Press.

Haviland, V., (2008). Things get glossed over: Rearticulating the silencing power of whiteness in the classroom. *Journal of Teacher Education, 59*(1), 40–54.

Helms, J. E. (1995). An update of Helms' white and people of color racial identity models. In J. P. Ponterotto, J. M. Casas, L. A. Suzuki, & C. M. Alexander (Eds.), *Handbook of multicultural counseling* (pp. 181–198). Thousand Oaks, CA: Sage.

Hill, M. L., (2009*). Beats, rhymes, and classroom life: Hip-hop pedagogy and the politics of identity*. New York: Teachers College Press.

Howard, Gary R. (2006). We can't teach what we don't know: White teachers, multiracial schools. New York: Teachers College Press.

Jacoby, R., & Glauberman, N. (1995). *The bell curve debate: History, documents, opinions.* New York: Times Books.

Joe, J. R. (1994). Revaluing Native American concepts of development and education. In P. M. Greenfield & R. R. Cocking (Eds.), *Cross-cultural roots of minority child development* (pp. 107–113). Hillsdale, NJ: Erlbaum.

Katz, J. (2003). White awareness: Handbook for the anti-racism training. Norman: University of Oklahoma Press.

Kennedy, R. (2002). *Nigger: The strange career of a troublesome word.* New York: Pantheon.

Kirklighter, C., Cardenas, D., Wolf Murphy, S. (Eds.). (2007). *Teaching writing with Latino/a students: Lessons learned at Hispanic-serving institutions* Albany: State University of New York Press.

Kivel, P. (1996). *Uprooting racism: How white people can work for racial justice.* Philadelphia: New Society.

Koppelman, K. L. & Goodhart, R. G. (2011). *Understanding Human differences: Mullticultural education for a diverse America.* (3rd ed.) Upper Saddle River, NJ: Pearson.

Kozol, J. (1992). *Savage inequalities: Children in America's schools.* New York: HarperPerennial.

Kozol, J. (2005). *The shame of the nation: The restoration of apartheid schooling in America.* New York: Three Rivers Press.

Levin, S. (2000). Social psychological evidence on race and racism. In M. Chang, D. Witt, J. Jones, & K. Hakuta (Eds.), *Compelling interest: Examining the evidence on racial dynamics in higher education* (pp. 97–125). Stanford, CA: Stanford University Press.

MacLeod, J. (1987). *Ain't no makin' it: Leveled aspirations in a low-income neighborhood.* Boulder, CO: Westview Press.

Montagu, A. (1997). *Race, man's most dangerous myth: The fallacy of race.* Walnut Creek, CA: Altamira Press. (Original work published 1942)

Murrell, P. C. (1995). What is missing in the preparation of minority teachers? In M. Foster (Ed.), *Into schools and schooling.* New York: AMS Press.

NAACP activists upset over dictionary's definition of the word "nigger." *Jet, 91*(3), 23–24.

The NAEP 1998 reading report card: National & state highlights. (1999). Washington, DC: Office of Educational Research and Improvement, U.S. Department of Education.

Novick, M. (1995). *White lies, white power: The fight against white supremacy and reactionary violence.* Monroe, ME: Common Courage Press.

Orfield, G., & Yun, J. T. (1999). *Resegregation in American schools.* Cambridge, MA: The Civil Rights Project, Harvard University.

Phillips, L. (2004, January–February). Fitting in and feeling good: Patterns of self-evaluation and psychological stress among biracial adolescent girls. *Women and Therapy, 27*(2), 217–236.

Phillips, M., Brooks-Gunn, J., Duncan, G. J., Klebanov, P., & Crane, J. (1998). Family background, parenting practices, and the test score gap. In C. Jencks & M. Phillips (Eds.), *The black-white test score gap* (pp. 103–145). Washington, DC: Brookings Institution Press.

Phillips, M., Crouse, J., & Ralph, J. (1998). Does the black-white test score gap widen after children enter school? In C. Jencks & M. Phillips (Eds.), *The black-white test score gap* (pp. 229–272). Washington, DC: Brookings Institutional Press.

Pollock, M. (2004). *Colormute: Race talk dilemmas in an American school.* Princeton, NJ: Princeton University Press.

Rasool, J. A., & Curtis, A. C. (2000). *Multicultural education in the middle and secondary classrooms: Meeting the challenge of diversity and change*. Belmont, CA: Wadsworth/Thomson Learning.

Roegider, D. R. (2005). *Working towards whiteness: How America's immigrants became white: The strange journey from Ellis Island to the suburbs.* New York: Basic Books.

Robinson-Zañartu, C. (1996, October). Serving Native American children and families: Considering cultural variables. *Language, Speech, and Hearing Services in Schools, 27*(4), 373–384.

Root, M. P. P. (2004). Multicultural families and children: Implications for educational research and practice. In J.A. Banks & C. A. A. Banks (Eds.), *Handbook of research on multicultural education* (pp. 110–124). San Francisco: Jossey-Bass.

Rotimi, C. N. (2004). Observations and recommendations regarding race and genetics by the National Human Genome Center of Howard University. In *Understanding and using human genetic variation knowledge in the design and conduct of biomedical research.* Retrieved March 5, 2007, from http://www.bcm.edu/edict/PDF/Scientific_Rationale.pdf

Suarez-Orozco, M. M., Suarez-Orozco, C., & Qin, D.B. (Eds.). (2005). *The new immigration: An interdisciplinary reader.* New York & London: Routledge.

School superintendent in Nevada under fire for using the word "nigger." (2000, August 28). *Jet, 98*(12), 18.

Shade, B. J. (1989). *Culture and learning style within the Afro-American community.* New York: Stone.

Solorzano, D. G. (1998). Critical race theory, race and gender microaggressions, and the experience of Chicana and Chicano students. *International Journal of Qualitative Studies in Education, 11,* 121–137.

Steele, C. M., & Aronson, J. (1995). Stereotype threat and the intellectual test performance of African Americans. *Journal of Personality and Social Psychology, 69,* 797–811.

Tatum, B. D. (1997). *"Why are all the Black kids sitting together in the cafeteria?" And other conversations about race.* New York: Basic.

Tatum, W. F., IV. (1997). Critical race theory and education: History, theory, and implications. In M. Apple (Ed.), *Review of research in education* (pp. 195–250). Washington, DC: American Educational Research Association.

Watkins, W. H., Lewis, J. H., & Chou, V. (2001). *Race and education.* Boston: Allyn & Bacon.

Watson, D. C. (2009). Historical and contemporary usages of the n-word: Deconstructing the content and context in a multiracial, middle school language arts class. *Language Arts, 87*(2), 99–108.

Wellman, D. (1999). Transforming received categories: Discovering cross-border identities and other subversive activities. In C. Clark & J. O'Donnell (Eds.), *Becoming and unbecoming white: Owning and disowning a racial identity* (pp. 78–91). Westport, CT: Greenwood Press.

West, K. (2005). Gold digger, On *Late Registration* (CD). New York: Roc-A-Fella Records.

Wijeyesinghe, C. L., & Jackson, B. W., III. (2001). *New perspectives on racial identity development: A theoretical and practical anthology.* New York: New York University Press.

Wing, A. K. (Ed.). (1997). *Critical race feminism: A reader.* New York: University Press.

Zirkel, P. A. (1999). The "N" word. *Phi Delta Kappan, 80*(9), 713–715.

African Americans

Baker, L. D. (1998). *From savage to Negro: Anthropology and the construction of race: 1896–1954.* Berkeley: University of California.

Egerton, J. (1994). *Speak now against the day: The generation before the civil rights movement in the South.* New York: Knopf.

Frisby, C. L. (1993). One giant step backward: Myths of black cultural learning styles. *School Psychology Review, 22,* 535–557.

Igus, T. (Ed.). (1991). *Book of black heroes: Great women in the struggle.* New York: Scholastic.

Jarrett, R. L. (1995). Growing up poor: The family experience of socially mobile youth in low-income African American neighborhoods. *Journal of Adolescent Research, 10*(1), 111–135.

Magill, F. N. (Ed.). (1992). *Masterpieces of African American literature.* New York: HarperCollins.

Southern Poverty Law Center. (1989). *Free at last: A history of the civil rights movement and those who died in the struggle.* Montgomery, AL: Teaching Tolerance.

Srickland, D. S. (1994). Educating African American learners at risk: Finding a better way. *Language Arts, 71,* 328–336.

Native Americans

Brown, D. (1970). *Bury my heart at Wounded Knee: An Indian history of the American West.* New York: Henry Holt.

Deyhle, D., & LeCompte, M. (1994). Cultural differences in child development: Navajo adolescents in middle schools. *Theory into Practice, 33,* 156–167.

Jaimes, A. (1992). *The state of Native America: Genocide, colonization, and resistance.* Boston: South End Press.

Kast, S. (1993–1994). Mobilizing and empowering Native American youth. *Children Today, 22*(2), 27–31.

Lomawaima, K. T., & McCarty, T. L. (2006). *To remain an Indian: Lessons in democracy from a century of Native American education*. New York: Teachers College Press.

Nel, J. (1994). Preventing school failure: The Native American child. *The Clearing House, 67,* 169–174.

Reyhner, J. (1994). *American Indian/Alaska Native education.* (Phi Delta Kappa Fastback 367). Bloomington, IN: Phi Delta Kappa.

Riley, P. (Ed.). (1993). *Growing up Native American: An anthology.* New York: Morrow.

Shaffer, D. D. (1993). Making Native American lessons meaningful. *Childhood Education, 69,* 201–203.

Weatherford, J. (1991). *Native roots: How the Indians enriched America.* New York: Crown.

Asian Americans

Chan, S. (1994). *Hmong means free: Life in Laos and America.* Philadelphia: Temple University Press.

Chong, D. (1994). *The concubine's children: The story of a Chinese family living on two sides of the globe.* New York: Penguin.

Donnelly, N. D. (1994). *Changing lives of refugee Hmong women.* Seattle: University of Washington Press.

Feng, J. (1994, June). *Asian-American children: What teachers should know. ERIC Digest,* 1–2.

Hamanaki, S. (1990). *The journey: Japanese Americans, racism, and renewal.* New York: Orchard.

Hong, M. (Ed.). (1993). *Growing up Asian American.* New York: Avon.

Lee, S., (2009). *Unraveling the "model minority" stereotype* (2nd ed.). New York: Teachers College Press.

Okihiro, G. Y. (1994). *Margins and mainstreams: Asians in American history and culture.* Seattle: University of Washington Press.

Salyer, L. E. (1995). *Laws harsh as tigers: Chinese immigrants and the shaping of modern immigration law.* Chapel Hill: University of North Carolina Press.

Siu, S. F. (1994). *Taking no chances: Profile of a Chinese-American family's support for school success.* Boston: Wheelock College.

Takaki, R. (1989). *Strangers from a different shore: A history of Asian Americans.* Boston: Little, Brown.

Trask, H. K. (1993). *From a native daughter: Colonialism & sovereignty in Hawaii.* Monroe, ME: Common Courage Press.

Wise, T. (2007). *White like me: Reflections on race from a privileged son.* Brooklyn, NY: Soft Skull Press.

Yen, C. C., & Lee, S. N. (1994). Applicability of the learning style inventory in an Asian context and its predictive value. *Educational and Psychological Measurement, 54,* 541–549.

Hispanic/Latina(o)s

Augenbraum, H., & Stavans, I. (Eds.). (1993). *Growing up Latino: Memoirs and stories.* Boston: Houghton Mifflin.

Carlson, L. M. (Ed.). (1994). *Cool salsa: Bilingual poems on growing up Latino in the United States.* New York: Henry Holt.

Casteneda, D. M. (1994). A research agenda for Mexican American adolescent mental health. *Adolescence, 29,* 225–239.

Center for Immigration Studies. (2006). *Immigration from Mexico: Costs and benefits for the United States.* Washington, DC: Author.

Cofer, J. O. (1990). *Silent dancing: A partial remembrance of a Puerto Rican childhood.* Houston, TX: Arte Publico Press.

Jimenez, C. M. (1994). *The Mexican American heritage* (2nd ed., rev. and expanded). Berkeley, CA: TQS Publications.

Kanellos, N. (1994). *The Hispanic almanac: From Columbus to corporate America.* Detroit, MI: Visible Ink Press.

Marcell, A. V. (1994). Understanding ethnicity, identity formation, and risk behavior among adolescents of Mexican descent. *Journal of School Health, 64,* 323–327.

Mendoza, J. I. (1994). On being a Mexican American. *Phi Delta Kappan, 76,* 293–295.

Muñoz, V. I. (1995). *Where something catches: Work, love, and identity in youth.* Albany: State University of New York Press.

Padilla, A. (2006). Bicultural social development. *Hispanic Journal of Behavioral Sciences, 28*(4), 467–497.

Southern Poverty Law Center. (2007). *Close to slavery: Guestworker programs in the United States,* Montgomery, Alabama, Southern Poverty Law Center.

Internet Sites for Extending Thinking

http://library.csus.edu/guides/kochism/diversity/div_web.htm
Contains Web sites and directions on diverse populations, including Africans, Asians, indigenous populations, Latin Americans, and Middle Easterners as well as women, GLBT, ability groups, and aging populations.

http://www.altavista.com/
Type "African-American webliography"

http://www.goshen.edu/soan/
Links to race and ethnic relations.

Chapter 5

Socioeconomic Status

Introduction

Socioeconomic status (SES) is a concept that includes one's educational attainment, occupation, and income (U.S. Census Bureau, 1999). "[Socio-economic] class is socially constructed by society and its institutions, determining the relationships between families and persons who have little or limited financial resources and those who are wealthy" (Gollnick & Chinn, 2009, p. 85).

Students often intentionally or unconsciously rank one another on SES factors, resulting in a hierarchy that rewards some and demeans others. Low rankings often result in lower feelings of self-regard, reduced motivation to achieve, and concomitant negative attitudes toward schools, teachers, classmates, and society. Not only are certain SES groups demeaned by classmates, but also teachers and school administrators often misdiagnose them, and in a disproportionate number of cases they even assign low SES students to low-ability groups in elementary and secondary schools.

In addition to being more aware of how socioeconomic class ratings affect how students are treated, teachers need to know how to help our future citizens understand economic and political proposals that differentially affect various socioeconomic groups. "Understanding how social and economic class operates in the United States is important in order for them to be able to participate in these debates in an informed way" (Adams, Bell, & Griffin, 1997, p. 232).

Chapter 5 contains cases that deal with socioeconomic issues that often result in differential and unfair treatment of students. Discussion of the cases in this section often includes references to terms and phrases such as the following.

assessment criteria
behavior modification
effects of child-rearing practices
emotional literacy
establishing incentives
free and reduced-price lunch programs (FRP)
hegemony
high-poverty school
meritocracy
poverty
SES

Definitions of key terms are located in the glossary of this text.

Case 15

A New Student and a Lesson for the Teacher

An experience with a new student reminds a teacher to use caution in relating socioeconomic status to outward appearance.

As are most teachers, Mr. McDonald was dedicated and creative, and he cared about his students. Teaching was his passion. Nearly all the students in his class lived in the economically deprived neighborhood in which the school was located. Only about 15 percent of the 85% FRP (free and reduced-price) student body were of middle-class means. It was the sixth week of school when Peter, an African-American transfer student from Chicago, entered his class. Peter was dressed like many of the other students, with a T-shirt and worn blue jeans. Mr. McDonald welcomed Peter into the class and gave him the usual materials: a text, handouts related to the current unit, and a set of free lunch tickets for the remainder of the week.

"Any questions?" asked Mr. McDonald.

"Yeah," Peter said. "What am I supposed to do with these tickets?"

"Just give them to the woman at the cash register in the lunchroom," replied Mr. McDonald. He then began his lesson on European history. Later in the hour, when he was well into his lesson, Mr. McDonald asked, "Can anyone tell me if one could get to Europe via the North Sea?" Peter quickly shot his hand into the air with confidence. "Yes. Actually I've crossed the North Sea with my family."

Doubting that Peter had ever made such a trip, Mr. McDonald replied, "You're right, Peter. It is possible to reach Europe by the North Sea." As the hour was coming to an end, Mr. McDonald reminded students of the homework for the next day. Just as the dismissal bell rang, he finished giving the assignments.

On his way out of the room, Peter asked Mr. McDonald where he should go to get a bus pass. Mr. McDonald informed Peter that he would not need one—that all the kids walked home. Peter glanced quizzically at his new teacher and then was swallowed by the stream of students.

When Mr. McDonald made his usual stop in the principal's office the next morning to get his announcements and messages, the school secretary reminded him to have Peter pick up his bus pass. Mr. McDonald admitted that he had told Peter to walk home the day before. "Five miles!?" asked the secretary. "You know he lives in Roseville [a middle-class suburb], don't you?"

Mr. McDonald admitted that he had not known that Peter's family lived in the neighboring middle-class community. "That explains Peter's puzzled look when I handed him the free lunch tickets," he thought. Mr. McDonald wondered what he would say to Peter later that day in class.

Questions for Reflection

1. What were Mr. McDonald's assumptions about Peter, and on what did he base them?
2. In your experience as a student, what assumptions have teachers made about you because of your socioeconomic status? About others?
3. What can teachers do to prevent/counter the negative effects of student bias based on socioeconomic status?
4. What kind of background information should teachers obtain about their new students to avoid the kinds of problems in this story? When no background information is available, how can teachers avoid making assumptions?
5. How could you help students in your classes understand the importance of getting to know another person rather than making assumptions based on prejudgments?

Activities for Extending Thinking

1. Talk individually with at least two students of a different socioeconomic background (avoid making assumptions when selecting your students). If you plan to use students from a field-experience placement, be sure to inform your cooperating teacher of your plans. Discuss with each student his or her likes and dislikes with respect to out-of-class activities (e.g., hobbies, sports, pets), as well as in-class preferences for learning. Be prepared to share insights.
2. Review one research-based resource from the "Readings for Extending Thinking" at the end of this chapter or from another text (e.g., a primary course text) that would add to your knowledge about the effects of socioeconomic status on students with whom you work. Summarize key insights in writing, and be prepared to share in class.
3. Discuss with a school administrator or counselor the teaching/learning, human development, legal and/or human-relationship competencies needed by teachers who work with students of various socioeconomic backgrounds.
4. Design a plan for a classroom school essay contest with a theme of personal experience with either (a) being the target of discrimination or (b) being successful in confronting some form of bias. Negotiate to have the winning entries published in the school and community newspaper.

Case 16

Gangs and the Victims of Violence—Writing as a Therapy

Students from an economically deprived neighborhood are given a writing assignment in which they express their feelings about the hurtful effects of gang activity.

Ms. Soltow knew her students well. She was fully aware that many of her students were from homes ravaged by crime and poverty. Gang activity was commonplace. Many students had one parent at home—in most cases, a mother. Many of her students had to work around the house —baby-sitting, cooking, and cleaning, for example—to help their working parent or parents. A number of the students had lost friends or relatives to gang-related activity.

It was week four of school, and as usual Ms. Soltow had established a healthy rapport with her students. In an attempt to address some of their emotional needs, and at the same time to provide an opportunity for them to develop their writing abilities, Ms. Soltow addressed the class: "Often in life we are hurt by others—others who don't mean to hurt us, but nevertheless do. Can anyone give an example of how someone has hurt you?"

Raymond replied, "My brother. He's been shot twice and still hangs with a gang. It hurts me when he gets injured."

Ms. Soltow could see the pain on Raymond's face; tears had welled up in his eyes. "That's a good example of how we can be hurt by someone who doesn't mean to hurt us. I can see why that would cause pain. Does anyone else have a story to share?" she asked so as to give Raymond time to wipe his eyes. Several other students told similar stories.

Ms. Soltow redirected her attention to the rest of the class: "I'd like each of you to take out a sheet of paper and write about how someone has hurt you even though he or she didn't mean to. Be sure you state exactly how you felt at the time and how you feel about it now. I'll come around and help those who might like some assistance. Are there any questions before we start?"

The students wrote for approximately 15 minutes while Ms. Soltow circulated, encouraging them to think further about their feelings and then to express them in writing. She provided time for volunteers to share what they could about their painful experiences. Finally, she provided a list of criteria for judging the expression of ideas in the prewriting samples and allowed the remaining 15 minutes for students to evaluate their own writing on the criteria distributed. She would provide a list of criteria, for evaluating grammar, usage, and spelling on the next rewrite.

Questions for Reflection

1. Assess Ms. Soltow's strategy of having students write about how they had been hurt by someone. Was it a suitable strategy for her students, considering their backgrounds and her instructional (writing) goals? What, if anything, should she have done differently?
2. If this case was set in an economically advantaged neighborhood, would you recommend the use of Ms. Soltow's writing strategy? Why or why not?
3. What could Ms. Soltow have done to follow up with Raymond?
4. To what degree should teachers integrate students' personal feelings and personal lives outside school into their instructional goals to promote emotional literacy in their classes?
5. Briefly outline several ideas for preparing for, and responding to, reports of terrorism and horrific natural disasters in the news. List topics that you could/should address in your teaching.
6. Teachers have a professional responsibility to report student statements suggesting danger to themselves or to others. On the other hand, they also have a responsibility to keep certain disclosures confidential. List one or two criteria you would use to decide to report or keep confidential students' disclosures. Give examples of issues you would report and examples of issues you would keep confidential.

Activities for Extending Thinking

1. Discuss with at least one teacher, one curriculum coordinator, and one parent those factors they believe should be considered when adapting instructional goals for students from lower socioeconomic backgrounds. Be prepared to summarize your findings in class.
2. Share appropriate aspects of your own socioeconomic history with your students. Doing so will help motivate students to do the same.
3. In addition to student needs and the nature of the subject matter, what other factors must a teacher take into account when selecting instructional goals?
4. How could you lead your class in a discussion of the role of gangs in young people's lives and how they might find alternatives to gangs? What strategies could you use to discuss neglect, loneliness, and the subsequent low self-esteem and dependence that might make one more vulnerable to gang membership?
5. In the subject matter area in which you plan to teach, design a lesson plan that would address real socioemotional needs of students. Relate the lesson plan to a local, state, or national standard for teaching.

Case 17

How Should I Grade Danielle?

A student who fails to turn in any assigned homework and contributes little to class, yet consistently gets the highest score on tests and quizzes, causes a teacher to rethink his system for assessing students.

From the first day of the fall term, Danielle, an independent Latina student, had worn black lipstick and long, often-torn shirts with names of hip-hop artists on the back, or, on warm days, tank tops with as much exposed skin as possible. The previous year, she had missed the last two months of school, and rumors spread that it was likely due to pregnancy. She had also missed a number of days, allegedly due to anxiety/depression. As a child of factory workers, Danielle had few friends but was usually cordial to those who approached her. She generally cooperated with her teacher, Mr. Edwards.

In class, Danielle rarely turned in a homework assignment. She worked by herself when she could; when "forced" to work in a small group, she would tend to hold back and let other group members do the talking and the work. She never volunteered to answer any questions in class discussions. When Mr. Edwards would call on her, her answer would always be correct, but short. Nevertheless, she regularly had the highest quiz and test scores. In fact, on occasion she would get a perfect score, even on the larger, more difficult comprehensive unit tests. Her scores on standardized tests from previous years were consistent with her classroom test scores. This combination of behaviors caused a problem for Mr. Edwards. Whereas his posted daily objectives usually required students to demonstrate understanding of concepts in homework assignments or small-group discussions, his grading system was based on achievement as measured by tests. With this system, Danielle would easily earn an 'A' for the term. However, he wondered if Danielle's unwillingness to complete and turn in homework assignments and her reluctance to contribute to small groups and to class discussions should be factored into her grade. Certainly her behavior was not helpful in terms of modeling to other students the behaviors in which he would like them to engage and the behaviors most of them needed to succeed.

To compound his problem, Mr. Edwards would always require self-evaluations at the end of each unit. Students were to assign to themselves some number of points out of 50 and to write a two-sentence rationale for the grade assigned. Mr. Edwards believed that, in general, it was most helpful to him to see how student self-evaluations compared with the grades he was about to assign based on the scores in his grade book. Indeed, sometimes a discrepancy between the two would help him identify an error in his record keeping, perhaps a score that inadvertently he had not recorded. For the third unit of the year, Danielle had again assigned herself a grade of A, using her high test scores as the basis for the grade. Mr. Edwards, a second-year teacher, often took such problems to his mentor teacher, Ms. Sundquist. Ms. Sundquist was in her ninth year as a successful teacher. "I think you need to be clear in your own mind about the outcomes you want for your students," advised Ms. Sundquist. "Your criteria and standards for assessment must be congruent with your instructional goals."

"Well," replied Mr. Edwards, "is it legitimate to have as your goals such things as 'turns in homework' and 'contributes to small- and large-group discussions' and the like? If these are legitimate goals, then Danielle should perhaps get a B or C. But when she has the highest test scores in the entire grade level, I'd have a hard time justifying that to her or her parents!"

"To be fair to students," asserted Ms. Sundquist, "the goals need to be meaningful and the students need to be clear about the criteria on which their performances will be judged. For example, if asked to write a descriptive essay, they need to know if they will be assessed on specifics, such as organization, creativity, grammar and usage, spelling, punctuation, and/or other possible criteria for assessment. Some scholars recommend identifying levels of goal attainment on each of the standards—for example, for organization: What type of response would earn a high grade, an average grade, or a low grade? The literature recommends that assessments be authentic; that is, that they reflect real-world applications whenever possible. I'll show you what I do if you'd like."

"Yes, I'd appreciate that," said Mr. Edwards. "I'd also like to explore strategies for using peer evaluations and portfolios, including electronic portfolios. I hear Mr. Boeck has a computer program for electronic portfolios."

"You have some challenging questions. Let's start with examples of how I design authentic performance assessments for my class. I'll bring some to our mentor–mentee meeting on Friday."

Questions for Reflection

1. What grade should Mr. Edwards assign to Danielle? What is your rationale for assigning that grade?
2. To what extent was your assessment influenced by Danielle's cultural background? What other factors influenced the grade you gave to her?
3. What changes, if any, should Mr. Edwards make in his plan for assessing students? Why are those changes needed?
4. Might a student's social class and economic status affect his or her achievements? If so, in what ways?
5. What assessment techniques might be less fair or more fair to students of lower-income families? Why?
6. What strategies could you as Danielle's teacher use to address the issue of overexposure of body parts (e.g., wearing revealing tank tops to class)?
7. What are the recognizable symptoms of anxiety and depression, and what is a teacher's responsibility in responding to them?

Activities for Extending Thinking

1. Interview at least one experienced, practicing teacher to determine (a) his or her desired student outcomes for a given unit and (b) the standards and criteria for assessing those outcomes. Explore the degree to which the means of assessment are fair and supportive of students of lower-income families.
2. Interview at least one experienced practicing teacher to ascertain how, if at all, the teacher's plan for assessment and grading accommodates students of lower-income status.
3. Outline a plan to involve students in developing criteria to be used in assessing their work.
4. List confidentiality issues related to reporting of grades to students and their parents and guardians, i.e., the more common issues that teachers will likely encounter during a year of teaching.

Case 18

Rewarding Respectful Behavior

A teacher uses a behavior modification plan to encourage two students to become more respectful of classmates.

Ms. Anderson was having trouble with two students of color in her class: Tommy, an energetic student from a low-income, blue-collar home; and Delia, a bright student from an upper-middle-class family. They often called their fellow students names—sometimes even using profanity—and did not seem to care about others' feelings. No matter how many times a day Ms. Anderson reprimanded them, they did not seem to change.

One day she offered them a deal. For every time they were thoughtful of another student—such as when they offered to help another student, when they shared, when they said nice things without name-calling or profanity—they would receive a point. When they reached 20 points, they would be allowed to choose a reward from a predetermined list that Tommy, Delia, and Ms. Anderson made together. The point total would be displayed on a chart at Ms. Anderson's desk for them to see whenever they wished.

Tommy enjoyed the challenge and began to say "please" and "thank you" to fellow students and always asked permission before using what belonged to others. He stopped making rude comments to the other students and even played with them without incident. He seemed to thrive on the positive attention. Ms. Anderson told Tommy she was pleased with the change in his behavior.

Delia, however, continued her disrespectful ways. Ms. Anderson considered contacting Delia's parents, but a rumor that her parents were strict and harsh led her to reconsider. She decided to ask other teachers and counselors for recommendations about handling Delia's rude behavior. Perhaps her colleagues could help.

Questions for Reflection

1. To what extent have you used an incentive/reward system such as the one Ms. Anderson used with Tommy and Delia? How well did it work? Under what circumstances would you use such a system?
2. Some scholars say that low SES students are often influenced or motivated by relationships. Give two verbatim relationship-based responses to students who want to know why you (as the teacher) want them to change this behavior.
3. Identify the strengths of Ms. Anderson's system, as well as the aspects that could be improved.

4. How could you help students understand that the expectations for behavior at school may vary from those in their various homes?
5. How might child-rearing practices in lower-income homes affect student behavior? Should child-rearing practices of parents or guardians affect how a teacher manages student behavior?

Activities for Extending Thinking

1. Interview parents of students of two or three different socioeconomic levels regarding the disciplinary policies and practices they prefer used at school.
2. Read a theoretical or empirical research account of the relationship between socioeconomic status and family approaches to discipline. Be prepared to share key insights with your class.
3. Design a written plan to form a student–faculty committee to write a set of rules for respect for the school. Suggest that the final draft be displayed in all classrooms, the cafeteria, and other key locations.
4. Organize with another school a student exchange program that brings together pupils of different socioeconomic backgrounds.

Design Your Own Case

Socioeconomic Status

Design a case that explores an issue of socioeconomic status in the classroom. The story can focus on a method or strategy related to a single subject matter area (e.g., English or social studies) or on a more generic method or strategy pertinent to a wider range of subject matter areas. Your issue might also relate to:

- Planning and preparation
- Classroom environment
- Instruction
- Teacher responsibilities*

In selecting a topic, reflect on recent or current field experiences, personal experiences as a student, or accounts of real classroom incidents. Choose a topic that allows the reader to link theory and practice in the areas of learning, development, teaching, and of course, multicultural/cross-cultural education. Your topic of choice should also invite discussion of multiple perspectives rather that a singular viewpoint. Consider, too, the general level of experience and knowledge of the intended reader (i.e., whether they are in an early stage of the teacher education program or a more experienced/knowledgeable professional). Include some demographic data that tell a bit about the community, school, classroom, teacher, students, and curriculum. Include at least one problem for which there is no obvious answer. Use fictitious names of persons and schools to maintain confidentiality.

Your case should be approximately two pages in length (typed, double-spaced) and should include three to four "Questions for Reflection" and one or two "Activities for Extending Thinking." Go to Resource C and use the form to design your own case.

*The four categories are from *Enhancing Professional Practice: A Framework for Teaching*, C. Danielson. 1996, Alexandria, VA: Association for Supervision and Curriculum Development.

Readings for Extending Thinking

A common bond. (2005, February). *American Teacher, 89*(5), 13.

Adams, M., Bell, L. A., & Griffin, P. (1997). *Teaching for diversity and social justice: A sourcebook*. New York: Routledge.

Anyon, J. (2005). *Radical possibilities: Public policy, urban education, and a new social movement.* New York & London: Routledge.

Archives, 10 (18). Retrieved February 14, 2003, from http://epaa.asu.edu/epaa/v10n18

Barton, P. E. (2004). Why does the gap persist? *Educational Leadership, 62*(3), 8–13.

Carnoy, M. (1994). *Faded dreams: The politics and economics of race in America.* New York: Cambridge University Press.

Clewell, B. C., & Campbell, P. B. (with Perlman, L.). (2007). *Good schools in poor neighborhoods: Defying demographies, achieving success*. Washington, DC: Urban Institute Press.

Chinyavong. A., & Leonard, J. (1997). *Poverty matters: The cost of child poverty in America.* Washington, DC: Children's Defense Fund.

Cohen, E. G. (2000). Equitable classrooms in a changing society. In M. T. Hallinan (Ed.), *Handbook of the sociology of education* (pp. 265–283). New York: Kluwer Academic/Plenum.

Darling-Hammond, L. (2001). Inequality and access to knowledge. In J. A. Banks & C. A. M. Banks (Eds.), *Handbook of research on multicultural education* (pp. 465–483). San Francisco: Jossey-Bass.

Davis, P. (1995). *If you came this way: A journey through the lives of the underclass.* New York: Wiley.

Eron, L. D., Gentry, J. H., & Schlegel, P. (Eds.). (1994). *Reason to hope: A psychosocial perspective on violence and youth.* Washington, DC: American Psychological Association.

Gans, H. (1995). *The war against the poor: The underclass and antipoverty policy.* New York: Basic.

Gilbert, G., (2008). *Rich and poor in America: A reference handbook.* Santa Barbara, CA: ABC-CLIO.

Gollnick, D. M., & Chinn, P. C. (2009) *Multicultural education in a pluralistic society* (8th ed.). Upper Saddle River, NJ: Pearson/Merrill.

Hochschild, J. (1995). *Facing up to the American dream: Race, class and the soul of the nation.* Princeton, NJ: Princeton University Press.

Hooks, B. (2000). *Where we stand: class matters.* New York: Routledge.

Ingram, M., Wolf, R. B., & Lieberman, J. (2007). The role of parents in high-achieving schools serving low-income, at-risk populations. *Education & Urban Society,* 30(4), 479–497.

Jencks, C., & Peterson, P. E. (Eds.). (1991). *The urban underclass.* Washington, DC: Brookings Institute.

Kincheloe, J. L., & Steinberg, S. R. (2007). *Cutting class: Socioeconomic status and education.* Lanham, MD: Rowman and Littlefield.

Kotlowitz, A. (1991). *There are no children here: The story of two boys growing up in the other America.* New York: Doubleday.

Kozol, J. (1991). *Savage inequalities: Children in America's schools.* New York: Crown.

Kozol, J. (2005). *The shame of the nation: The restoration of apartheid schooling in America.* New York: Crown.

Kunjufu, Jawanza (2007). *An African centered response to Ruby Payne's poverty theory.* Chicago: African American Images.

Marable, M. (1995). *Beyond black and white: Rethinking race in American politics and society.* New York: Verso.

Medcalf, N. A. (2008). *Kidwatching in Josie's world: A study of children in homelessness.* Lanham, MD: University Press of America.

Michaels, W. B. (2006). *The trouble with diversity: How we learned to love identity and ignore inequality.* New York: Metropolitan Books.

Morse, J. F. (2006). A level playing field: School finance in the northeast. Albany: State University of New York Press.

McNamee, S. J., & Miller, R. K., Jr. (2004). The meritocracy myth. Lanham, MD: Rowman & Littlefield.

National Center for Children in Poverty. (2007). *A rapidly changing portrait of fatherhood in America and how the states are responding to it.* Retrieved August 18, 2007, from http://fatherfamilylink.gse.upenn.edu/org/nccp/portrait.htm

National Law Center on Homelessness and Poverty. (2007). *Educating homeless children and youth: The guide to their rights.* Washington, DC: Author.

Neuman, S. B. (Ed.). (2008). *Educating the other America: Top experts tackle poverty, literacy, and achievement in our schools.* Baltimore, MD: Paul H. Brookes.

Oakes, J. (2005). *Keeping track: How schools structure inequality* (2nd ed.). New Haven, CT: Yale University Press.

Oliver, M., & Shapiro, T. (1995). *Black wealth/white wealth: A new perspective on racial inequality.* New York: Routledge.

Payne, R. K. (2003). No child left behind: What's really behind it all? *Part I, Instructional Leader, 16*(2), 1–3.

Payne, R. K. (1995). *A framework: Understanding and working with students and adults from poverty.* Baytown, TX: RFT.

Rank, M. R. (2004). *One nation underprivileged: Why American poverty affects us all.* New York: Oxford University Press.

Reay, D. (2002). Shaun's story: Troubling discourses of white working-class masculinities. *Gender and Education, 14*, 221–234.

Rose, S. J. (2000). *Social stratification in the United States*. New York: New Press.

Timmer, D. A., Eitzen, D. S., & Talley, K. D. (1994). *Paths to homelessness: Extreme poverty and the urban housing crisis.* Boulder, CO: Westview.

Sacks, P. (2007). Tearing down the gates: Confronting the class divide in American education. Berkeley: University of California Press.

U.S. Census Bureau. (1999). Statistical abstract of the United States (119th ed.). Washington, DC: U.S. Government Printing Office.

Van Galen, J. A., & Noblit, G. W. (2007). *Late to class: Social class and schooling in the new economy.* Albany: State University of New York Press.

Internet Sites for Extending Thinking

http://www.ed.gov/offices/OUS/PES/esed/poverty3.html
Academic challenge for the children of poverty report analysis and highlights.

http://www.ed.gov/pubs/urbanhope/
Hope for urban education: A study of nine high-performing, high-poverty urban elementary schools, 1999.

http://extremeinequality.org/Author, IPS 2008 Working Group on Extreme Inequality New England Office of the Institute for Policy Studies, Contains charts and graphs on racial income and wealth divide.

http://dmoz.org/society/issues/poverty/
Contains articles and links on hunger, homelessness, and welfare as well as humanitarian organizations serving individuals, institutions, and society, nationally and internationally.

Chapter 6

Religion

Introduction

For millions of people in this country and around the world, religion or spirituality is a significant part of their lives. Even adults who do not believe in a religion usually admit that religions have long been an important part of the history of the world. Many students, including many immigrant children, have seen their people, even relatives, willing to die for deeply held religious values. To many, religion has been, is, and always will be, a vitally important force in the world.

At the same time, some believe that religion should be relegated to the home and church (Christian), synagogue (Jewish), mosque (Islam), mandir (Hindu), or other place of worship. "Separation of church and state" is a phrase that deters many teachers from the slightest mention of religion in the classroom.

Yet religious issues commonly arise in the classroom, issues such as parents, teachers, or administrators being present in prayer meetings after school, teachers using religious tenets (e.g., the Ten Commandments as a basis for culturally encoded character education), students of a particular faith (Jewish, Christian, etc.) missing school to observe holidays or important religious-based family traditions, and certain groups (e.g., Jehovah's Witnesses) desire to not celebrate birthdays.

Although it is important to recognize that the government protects student rights to freely express themselves religiously in schools, it is also important to remember that educators cannot directly lead their students toward any religion. Schools must allow student-initiated religious clubs, prayer time, released time to attend parochial school off campus for part of the day, and reading of religious texts such as the Bible, Qur'an, and Torah. Further, teachers can not initiate or direct such activities nor can they teach religion (they can, however, teach about religion).

In short, "Public schools can neither foster religion nor preclude it. Our public schools must treat religion with fairness and respect and vigorously protect religious expression as well as the freedom of conscience of all other students. In so doing our public schools reaffirm the First Amendment and enrich the lives of their students" (Secretary of Education Richard W. Riley, 1998, in Robinson, 2003).

The cases in Chapter 6, "Religion," invite inquiry into issues that have ramifications for curriculum content, teaching methods (e.g., teaching about values), scheduling of curricular and extracurricular activities, and classroom and school policies (e.g., dress codes involving religious wear and guidelines for religious activities). Terms and concepts that often arise in the discussion of these cases include the following.

agnosticism
atheism
anti-Semitism
Buddhism
Christianity
Hinduism
Islam
Judaism
provisions of the First Amendment to the Constitution
religious symbols
separation of school and state
Sikhism
spirituality
values

Definitions of key terms are located in the glossary of this text.

Case 19

Isn't the Christmas Tree a Christian Symbol?

A classroom Christmas tree and other winter holiday symbols cause students to question the teacher's intent.

It was the first week of December. The previous day Ms. Halverson had added to her bulletin boards some holiday wishes, including "Merry Christmas," "Happy Hanukkah," and "Happy Kwanza." In addition, she had placed a two-foot-tall Christmas tree in the front corner of the room by her desk.

Several of her students had entered the room a few minutes before class was to begin. The students were of Russian, Chinese, and Egyptian heritage. They made a few comments to one another and then addressed Ms. Halverson: "Ms. Halverson, you told us to let you know if we felt that our classroom was not as inclusive as it could possibly be. Well, isn't the Christmas tree a symbol of the Christian religion?" asked Yen. "And by having a Christmas tree, aren't you emphasizing one religion over another?"

Ms. Halverson nodded as Yen spoke: "Actually, it's a pre-Christian symbol that arose in Europe. But I only meant to acknowledge it as one of the most prevalent historical and cultural symbols in the United States."

Yen responded, "But since we know that's a 'Christmas tree' it seems like you're saying that we should all celebrate Christmas."

"No," replied Ms. Halverson. "But I'm glad that you raised the issue. I now realize that I need to clarify for the class just what my intentions are regarding the tree. Thanks for being sensitive to those who might have other interpretations. It's exactly this kind of feedback that I need to make our class more inclusive! Perhaps you and the class can offer some other suggestions for making our room look more inclusive during the holidays." The students seemed eager to help.

On his way out of class that day Yen asked his teacher: "Ms. Halverson, do you believe in God?" Ms. Halverson was glad that he didn't wait for her answer. She did, however, anticipate that he might ask again the next day.

Questions for Reflection

1. Should Ms. Halverson have placed a Christmas tree in her room? Why or why not?
2. How adequate was Ms. Halverson's explanation of her intent to the students? What, if anything, would make it more adequate?

3. What factors should affect a teacher's decision to display religious symbols?
4. Comment on the relationship between the teacher and Yen. What did Ms. Halverson say, or do that tend to affect her relationship with him?
5. What could Ms. Halverson and her class do to extend their new knowledge beyond their own classroom (i.e., to affect school policy)?
6. How would you as a teacher answer Yen's final question?

Activities for Extending Thinking

1. Discuss with a school administrator the policies in his/her school regarding the use or display of objects that have or could have some religious meaning. Summarize your key insights in writing.
2. List school practices with regard to religion that are allowed by law. List practices not allowed by law. Summarize your findings in writing.
3. Examine the musical selection of school orchestra, band, and choir to determine the degree of cultural diversity represented. Share your findings (in a supportive/ constructive way) with teachers involved with those programs, and submit a 2–3 page paper outlining your findings and the responses of the teachers to each response.

Case 20

My Persuasive Essay Is "Why We Should Follow Jesus"

To foster a feeling of ownership in their persuasive essays, a teacher allows students the opportunity to choose the topic they will present to the class.

Mr. Kauls had taught middle-school English for 10 years. One of his favorite units was persuasive writing. Although students were typically reluctant when it came to talking to the class, they seemed to become very motivated—even excited—to talk about something in which they truly believed. Each year in a letter to parents, Mr. Kauls made it clear that his goal was to actively involve students in the process of writing and speaking persuasively, not to condone the specific topic chosen. How could he? Last year students spoke on "Why Abortion Should Be Available to All," "Eliminating Affirmative Action," "Why Schools Should Put Pop Machines in Each Room," and "Evidence That the White Race Is Superior," and he certainly did not agree with the premise in all those reports.

Of course, Mr. Kauls did his best at structuring the project for students' success. Before they presented, he modeled for the class the presentation of a piece of persuasive writing of two students from a previous year, as well as one of his own. He tried to make the expectations for the project as clear as possible.

In addition, Mr. Kauls collected and made written suggestions on the prewriting phase of each student's persuasive essay. After rewriting, he again collected and graded the second draft. By the time it was their turn to present orally to the class, students knew that Mr. Kauls supported their plan.

Finally, Mr. Kauls made it very clear that classmates must show the presenter the utmost respect. Consequences of showing even a hint of disrespect included detention and a phone call to their parents.

As in previous years, when Mr. Kauls first explained the assignment to the class, he had students write down the topics about which they would like to write and speak. Michael, a capable student respected by classmates for his academic and athletic abilities, as well as for his personal qualities, listed "Why We Should Follow Jesus" as the topic of his persuasive writing and speaking project.

When it was Michael's turn to present, he began by acknowledging that he knew it was risky to write and speak about his selected topic, but that he believed it was so much more important than his alternative, "Why We Should All Visit Alaska." After introductory comments, he outlined his arguments: "First, following Jesus provides a reason for living, a purpose for life, that of caring for others. Second, following Jesus assures us of eternal life, and offers salvation. Third, following Jesus helps us cope with our daily lives. I don't know how persons handle stress without the comfort that comes through prayer." Michael continued, "Because we cannot understand all the mysteries of God, we do at times need a strong faith. Finally, Jesus is a great gift. Although there have been many kings throughout history, Jesus is the only one who died for us." Michael cited what he considered evidence that Jesus had divine power. He paused for a moment, then took his seat. The class applause for his presentation was louder than it had been for the other reports.

Mr. Kauls commented that Michael's report had been well organized and clearly presented and that he had more than satisfied the criteria for a good persuasive essay.

After class Greg and Dion, two students whom Michael knew only slightly, approached Michael with smiles: "I didn't know you were a Christian. We are, too. You did a good job on your report."

"Thanks," replied Michael. "Where do you guys go to church?" They talked as they walked to their lockers. "See you tomorrow," they said as each headed off to a different classroom.

The next morning Mr. Kauls checked his phone messages. One was from Mr. Warren, the father of Billy Warren, one of his students. Mr. Kauls knew that the Warrens were of the Mormon faith. The other message was from Sylvia Bernstein, mother of James. The Bernsteins were Jewish. Mr. Kauls wondered if it was a coincidence that two parents who had never contacted him before were requesting a conference the day after Michael's presentation.

After school that day Mr. Kauls' suspicions were realized. When he returned their calls, both parents questioned the propriety of allowing a student to do a persuasive essay on a religious topic. "I thought that schools were prohibited from evangelism," commented Mr. Warren.

Mr. Kauls reminded them of the letter that he had sent prior to the beginning of the new unit. His conversations with both parents seemed to quell their concerns. Yet, he could not help but wonder what else he might have done to make the persuasive essay activity more satisfactory to both students and parents.

Questions for Reflection

1. What else, if anything, would you have done to prevent or address parental concerns about persuasive essay on religion in the public school classroom?
2. What limits, if any, would you have set on student choice of topic?
3. Construct a verbatim response to the Warrens and the Bernsteins regarding their concerns.
4. The First Amendment provides for the inclusion of certain religious references in the public schools. For example, it provides for books such as the Bible (Christianity), Tanach (Judaism), Qur'an (Islam), or Tripitaka (Buddhism) to be used as historical or literary resources. In what other ways can religion be included in the public school classroom, e.g., in math, science, English, and so on.
5. Identify several lesson plans in your own subject matter area that would draw on religious references.

Activities for Extending Thinking

1. Discuss the issue in this case with a practicing teacher. Elicit ideas for preventing, guiding, and responding to the series of events in the story. Inquire about similar experiences that the teacher may have had. Summarize key insights in writing.
2. Select one of the "Readings for Extending Thinking" at the end of this section. Outline its key claims or assertions in writing, and give a personal reaction to each.
3. Discuss with parents or teachers in your community the issue of diversity within a religion (e.g., Christianity). List areas of potential conflict for students due to such diversity. Give concrete examples of problems and ways they could be addressed in your classroom.
4. Develop a concise list of what the constitution allows, and what it prohibits with respect to religion in the classroom.

Case 21

Planning for Religious Diversity: Special Needs of Muslim Students

In light of increasing numbers of Islamic children in the nation's schools, a local teacher examines the background and special religion-based needs of her Islamic students.

Ms. Bush worked hard to be sensitive to the needs of students of diverse backgrounds. She had become aware that the fastest-growing group of students in her school were of the Muslim faith. She had seen data suggesting that Islam has become the second-largest religion in the United States. She also knew that over one billion people, one-fifth of the world's population, were Muslim, that about 14 percent of all immigrants entering the United States are Muslim, and that although one-third of Muslims living in the United States are African American, several million Americans from various ethnic backgrounds have adopted the religion of Islam within the last quarter-century. She was curious about the special needs and interests that the students in her classroom might have.

Ms. Bush requested and received material from her local Islamic Education Foundation Center. She read from a brochure entitled "You've Got a Muslim Child in Your Room: The Needs of Muslim Children in the Public School" (Islamic Education Foundation, 2000):

> Muslim students have the following needs and requirements: Muslim students, from the onset of puberty, may not sit in close proximity to students of the opposite sex, and they may not interact closely with them. Thus, girls and boys should be assigned to sit near others of their own sex, and should not be assigned to group or partner activities with members of the opposite sex.

Because she was familiar with research on best teaching practice, Ms. Bush had always intentionally created heterogeneous groups with respect to gender, race, learning style, and other factors. She wondered if her students of Muslim Faith would want to follow the guidelines stated in the brochure strictly, and if they did, how she would accommodate them.

As she read further in the brochure, she learned that Muslim students who follow their religious tenets strictly may not participate in plays, social parties, proms, dating, or other such activities that involve close interaction with the opposite sex. In addition, they may not participate in any event or activity related to Halloween, Christmas, Valentine's Day, or Easter because such events have social and religious connotations contrary to the Islamic faith. In addition, they may not pay allegiance to the flag, and they should not be asked to stand and sing the national anthem. The brochure stated also that although well-meaning educators have expressed concern for Muslim students who are "deprived" of participating in activities of their non-Muslim peers, Muslim parents love their children. Therefore, teachers should refrain from expressing well-intended but inappropriate "sympathy" or disapproval of parental requests. Ms. Bush decided that she would refer additional guidelines related to physical education and prayer in the schools to her colleagues who would be most directly affected.

Ms. Bush wondered how she should react to the information she had just read. How should the special needs of her Muslim students affect her planning for the coming fall?

Questions for Reflection

1. If you were Ms. Bush, what questions might you want to ask your Muslim students and/or their parents about the special religious needs stated in the brochure?
2. Assume that certain parents of Muslim students are quite concerned about following the tenets/principles of their faith, and that their child is moderately concerned. How, if at all, would you accommodate the need of that student to be grouped only with persons of the same sex?
3. Would you arrange meaningful alternate activities for Muslim students who could not participate in holidays such as Christmas, Halloween, and so on? If so, what types of activities might you offer?
4. How would you respond if a Muslim parent asked that his or her child not be required to say the pledge of allegiance to the flag and/or sing the U.S. national anthem? State your response verbatim.
5. Identify other religious groups and the special needs that students of each faith might have. How might you alter your curriculum or instruction to accommodate those needs?
6. How could you as a teacher prevent or respond to post–9-11 anti–Middle-Eastern sentiment in your classroom resulting from terrorist acts or threats?

Activities for Extending Thinking

1. Obtain from community agencies and religious organizations information about the religious needs of students in your school. If your school does not have students from a variety of religious backgrounds, obtain information about religions with which your students will likely interact in their lives beyond P–12 schooling. In general, what types of things should students know to interact with others of differing religions?
2. Interview students about how schools and teachers can become more aware of special religious needs of students from diverse religious backgrounds. List practical strategies that teachers can use to accommodate students with special religious needs.
3. Interview school officials in your area about current policies and practices that relate to religious affiliation. Ask about religious issues that tend to arise more frequently (e.g., find out how the school or district conducts winter holiday celebrations [traditionally called "Christmas Programs"]). Do they read scripture, sing religious songs, display traditional and/or nontraditional scenes, etc.? Ask how the school has addressed such issues.
4. How could you integrate information about religious diversity into the discipline(s) you will teach? List specific topics that you might include in certain units you are likely to teach.

Case 22

Faith-Based Teasing, Student Curiosity, and the Question of Infusing Religion into the Curriculum

Given the impact that religion has had on the history of the world, as well as the tendency on the part of many schools to avoid all references to religion in the curriculum, a teacher ponders her personal stance on the issue.

In each of the three years of her work as a teacher, Ms. Vang periodically found herself at a crossroads: to what degree should she and her colleagues, intentionally infuse religious issues into the curriculum? The question had been raised many times over the years, often by students in her classroom or in the hallways of the school. Sometimes, they were teasing classmates, for example, when they taunted students of Hindu faith of "praying to, or honoring cows," or being "reincarnated from a cat," or when they referred to a Sikh student as "Aladdin" because he wore a turban. Indeed, whether Christian, Buddhist, Jewish, Islamic, Sikh, Hindu, atheist, or other, no one was immune to faith-based harassment.

Just last year, a student of Jehovah Witness faith had asked to be excused from class during a birthday celebration for a classmate, because such a celebration was antithetical to his religion. Though Ms. Vang had respectfully excused him, when he returned to class he asked for a cupcake left over from the party. Ms. Vang resisted, reminding him that the dessert was part of the celebration of a birthday, and hence she would not assist him in violating one of his religious tenets.

In addition to the instances of teasing and the birthday celebration incident, the school had faced the usual questions about celebrating "Christmas" as opposed to a "winter holiday." In addition, some of the teachers had talked about commonly used language such as "turning the other cheek," and "good Samaritan," that would affirm those of Christian belief, but that would only marginalize students of other faiths.

With religious issues having been raised so often in the classroom and school, it was no wonder that Ms. Vang had considered on more than one occasion the degree to which she should intentionally integrate lesson plans that would provide opportunities for students to think about and discuss the importance of religion in history, to forms of government, literature, music, art, architecture, and nearly all aspects of human life.

Questions for Reflection

1. List terms or phrases that you personally have heard used by students in teasing others about their religious beliefs.
2. Give two examples of ways that you might infuse religious issues into your curriculum. How likely are you to include these two and other issues in your own teaching? (1 = not likely, 5 = highly likely) Why do you choose that level?
3. How would you respond (verbatim) to:
   a. students teasing classmates as in the beginning of this case?
   b. the Jehovah's Witness student who asked for a birthday treat after returning to class?
   c. those who want to preserve current names of holidays versus broadening them to include others (e.g., "Christmas" to "winter holiday")?
   d. student questions about major leaders of other religions, major cities of religious significance, and major holidays of other religions?
4. Given, on the one hand, the immense impact that religion has had on civilization throughout history and, on the other hand, the desires of some to maintain the separation of church and state, to what degree do you believe students should have opportunities to objectively and responsibly think about religious issues in schools? Give a brief rationale for your position.
5. In light of increased backlash to acts of terrorism (backlash in the form of violence and other forms of discrimination), outline several steps you could take as a teacher to counter negative student attitudes towards persons of Middle Eastern decent.

Activities for Extending Thinking

1. Identify several print or electronic resources related to integrating religion into your curriculum. (Give a full APA citation for each.)
2. Interview two teachers to find their views on infusing religious issues into their classrooms. List what they have done as well as experiences that they might have had with students or parents relative to integrating religion into curriculum.
3. Identify three community resources that could help provide opportunities for students seeking information on faith-based issues.
4. List stereotypes often associated with various religions (e.g., Judaism, Islam, Hindu, Buddhist, Christianity, and Sikhism). After each, list a way by which you could provide evidence that would break down that stereotype.
   Example of stereotypes: "Islam teaches violence, hence, Muslims believe in terrorism," and "Jews are self serving and, therefore are not charitable."
5. Identify major religious texts for each religion named in item #4. Also, identify key holidays, like Holi and Diwali (Hindu) and Ramadan (Islam) and the holiest cities, such as Mecca (Islam) or Varanasi (Hindu), and other key religious terms or phrases.

Design Your Own Case

Religion

Design a case that would help classmates explore issues related to religious diversity. The story can focus on a method or strategy related to a single subject matter area (e.g., English or social studies) or on a more generic method or strategy pertinent to a wider range of subject matter areas. Your issue might also relate to:

- Planning and preparation
- Classroom environment
- Instruction
- Teacher responsibilities*

In selecting a topic, reflect on recent or current field experiences, personal experiences as a student, or accounts of real classroom incidents. Choose a topic that allows the reader to link theory and practice in the areas of learning, development, teaching, and of course, multicultural/cross-cultural education. Your topic of choice should also invite discussion of multiple perspectives rather than a singular viewpoint. Consider, too, the general level of experience and knowledge of the intended reader (i.e., whether they are in an early stage of the teacher education program or a more experienced/knowledgeable professional). Include some demographic data that tell a bit about the community, school, classroom, teacher, students, and curriculum. Include at least one problem for which there is no obvious answer. Use fictitious names of persons and schools to maintain confidentiality. Your case should be approximately two pages in length (typed, double-spaced) and should include three to four "Questions for Reflection" and one or two "Activities for Extending Thinking." Go to Resource C and use the form to design your own case.

*The four categories are from *Enhancing Professional Practice: A Framework for Teaching,* by C. Davidson, 1996. Alexandria, VA: Association for Supervision and Curriculum Development.

Readings for Extending Thinking

Al-Ani, S. H. (1995). Muslims in America and Arab Americans. In C. L. Bennett (Ed.), *Comprehensive multicultural education: Theory and practice* (3rd ed., p. 139). Boston: Allyn & Bacon.

Ayers, S. J., & Reid, S. (2005). Teaching about religion in the elementary school: The experience of on Texas district. *The Social Studies, 96*(1), 14–17.

Black, S. (2003, April). Teaching about religion. *The American School Board Journal, 190*(4), 50.

Bowie, F. (2006). *Anthropology of religion: An introduction.* Oxford: Blackwell.

Crim, K., Bullard, R., & Shinn, L. D. (Eds.). (1981). *The perennial dictionary of world religions.* San Francisco: HarperCollins.

Doerr, E. (2005, March). Much to learn from Newfoundland. *Phi Delta Kappan, 86*(7), 559.

Feingold, H. L. (1995). *Bearing witness: How America and its Jews responded to the Holocaust.* Syracuse, NY: Syracuse University Press.

Finke, R. (2005). *The churching of America, 1776 2005: Winners and losers in our religious economy.* New Brunswick, NJ: Rutgers University Press.

First Amendment to the Constitution of the United States, 1791.

Freitas, D., & Rotherham, A. (2004, January 7). Teaching about religion. *Education Week, 23*(16), 37.

Haltom, B. (2000). I'll keep praying for my football team. *Tennessee Bar Journal, 36*(8), 34–35.

Holliday, L. (1995). *Children in the Holocaust and WWII: Their secret diaries.* New York: Pocket Books.

Islamic Education Foundation. (2000). *You've got a Muslim child in your room: The needs of Muslim children in the public school.* Minneapolis, MN: Islamic Education Foundation.

Kirmani, M. H., & Laster, B. P. (1999). Responding to religious diversity in classrooms. *Educational Leadership, 56*(7), 61–63.

Lustig, A. (1995). *Children of the Holocaust.* Evanston, IL: Northwestern University Press.

Markowitz, R. J. (1993). *My daughter, the teacher: Jewish teachers in the New York City schools.* New Brunswick, NJ: Rutgers University Press.

Marks, J. (1993). *The hidden children: Secret survivors of the Holocaust.* New York: Ballantine.

Marshall, J. M. (2004, January). How teachers can still teach about religion. *The Education Digest, 69*(5), 23–27.

Marty, W. R. (1998). Christians in the academy: Overcoming the silence. *Journal of Interdisciplinary Studies, 10*(1–2), 1–16.

Merino, N., (2007). *Religion in the schools*. Farmington Hills, MI: Greenhaven Press.

Moore, D. L. (2007) *Overcoming religious illiteracy: A cultural studies approach to the study of religion in secondary education.* New York: Palgrave Macmillan.

Not the Last Word. (2000). *America, 183*(2), 3.

Ooka Pang, V., & Barba, R. H. (1995). The power of culture: Building culturally affirming instruction. In C. A. Grant (Ed.), *Educating for diversity: An anthology of multicultural voices* (pp. 345–356). Boston: Allyn & Bacon.

Rabinove, S. (2000). The 10 Commandments and public schools: Shall we post the penalties too? *Church & State, 53*(10), 21.

Robinson, B. A. (2003, February 12). Religion in U.S. public schools. Retrieved October 16, 2005, from http://www.religioustolerance.org/ps_pray.htm

Scherer, M. M. (1998). Linking education with the spiritual. *Educational Leadership, 56*(4), 5.

Smith, J. Z., & Green, W. S. (Eds.). (1995). *The HarperCollins dictionary of religion.* San Francisco: HarperCollins.

Thomas, R. M. (2007). *God in the classroom: Religion and America's public schools.* Westport, CT: Praeger.

Thomas, R. M. (2009). *Religion in schools: Controversies around the world.* Westport, CT: Praeger.

Uphoff, J. K. (1993). Religious diversity and education. In J. A. Banks & C. A. McGee Banks (Eds.), *Multicultural education: Issues and perspectives* (2nd ed., p. 46). Boston: Allyn & Bacon.

Werner, H. (1992). *Fighting back: A memoir of Jewish resistance in WW II*. New York: Columbia University Press.

Wiesel, E. (1986). *Night* (25th anniv. ed.). New York: Bantam.

Young, W. A. (2005). *The world's religions: Worldviews and contemporary issues.* Upper Saddle River NJ: Pearson Prentice Hall.

Internet Sites for Extending Thinking

http://www.nmajh.org/
Virtual tours of online exhibitions, comparative timeline that tracks U.S. history, U.S. Jewish history, and world Jewish history.

http://www.clsnet.org/
Christian Legal Society Web site on religious expression in public schools.

http://www.nsba.org/
National School Board Web site on religious expression in schools.

http://www.academicinfo.net/religindex.html
Libraries, directories, and other resources on a wide variety of religions.

http://www.academicinfo.net/Religiontolerance.html
References on religious tolerance/freedom.

http://www.looksmart.com/
Click on "Religion & Belief," click on "Islam," click on "Education," and finally click on "Online Courses."

http://www.edweek.org/tm/vol-07/06relig.h07
An excellent article that includes an overview of the issue and highlights the author's visits to classrooms where teaching about religion is incorporated into the curriculum.

http://www.cie.org/
The Council on Islamic Education's mission is to support public education, with lessons, teaching units, and other resources for educators.

http://www.teachingaboutreligion.org/
This site provides academic information and materials for educators, especially on teaching about religion in social studies and religious studies.

http://www.adl.org/adl.asp
The Anti-Defamation League provides materials on anti-Semitism, civil rights, extremism, the Holocaust, Israel, interfaith, and curriculum development.

Chapter 7

Special Needs

Introduction

In this text, the area of special needs or exceptionality includes students who are identified as gifted or talented as well as students with disabilities. Disability in its broadest sense includes perceptual challenges (e.g., visual and hearing), as well as learning disabilities; illness-related (e.g., multiple sclerosis, AIDS); physical (e.g., cerebral palsy); developmental (e.g., Down syndrome); psychiatric (e.g., chronic depression, bipolar); mobility (e.g., quadriplegia, paraplegia); and environmental (e.g., asthma and sensitivities to allergies; Adams, Bell, & Griffin, 1997).

Discrimination against students with disabilities (also called "ableism") takes many forms in schools, including the use of the terms *retard* or *retarded* as a pejorative, teasing or bullying, telling jokes about persons with disabilities, and excluding exceptional students from groups, activities, and events.

Special-needs or exceptional students are those who require attention from teachers and schools that is beyond that and/or different from attention needed by students without special challenges. As in the case of other oppressed groups, special-needs students often come to feel that others view them as less worthy. Such perceptions often lead to feelings of low self-worth, resulting in reduced interest in school academic and social endeavors.

A key issue related to the education of exceptional students is that of confidentiality. Special-needs student have the same rights to confidentiality of information as all other students. The Family Educational Rights and Privacy Act (FERPA; 20 U.S.C.*1232g; 34 CFR Part 99) is the law that protects the privacy of students' academic records. This law also states that schools must have written permission from a parent or guardian to release any information from a student's school records. Hence, teachers should not reveal any information about a student's disability without consent of a parent or guardian.

Discussion of cases in Chapter 7 often results in the use of the following terms and concepts.

ableism
accommodation
culturally and linguistically diverse (CLD)
disability
FAPE (Free and Appropriate Paid Education)
FERPA (Family Educational & Privacy Act)
grouping strategies
Individualized Education Program (IEP)
Individuals with Disabilities Education Act (IDEA)
Individuals with Disabilities Education Improvement Act (IDEIA)
learning disabled
mainstreaming
Section 504

Definitions of key terms are included in the glossary of this text.

Case 23

We Only Meant It as a Joke

Several students "play a joke" on a female classmate by telling a male learning-disabled pupil that she has a crush on him.

Mr. Carr consistently demonstrated respect for all his students. All students, including special-needs students, had a chance to work in heterogeneous, cooperative groups, share leadership roles, and generally contribute equally to classroom life. Mr. Carr was careful to praise and encourage all students equally.

One of the classroom procedures posted on the front wall was "Respect others." Students understood what this meant—they had been given numerous specific examples on the first day of class.

For the first six weeks of the term, Mr. Carr's students honored the procedures listed. Then one day, several students were moved to have what they considered fun with Mia, one of their classmates. They suggested to Mike, a learning-disabled student, that Mia had expressed an interest in him and that he should ask her to be his girlfriend. They intended that the "joke" would be on Mia. At lunch that day, Mike asked Mia if she would be his girlfriend. Mia politely replied that she did not want a boyfriend.

When Mr. Carr heard what had happened, he immediately thought about how he would enforce the classroom rule that students respect others. Of course, the perpetrators would have to pay the consequences established on the first day of school. Mr. Carr believed in being consistent in maintaining standards for behavioral conduct. Now he was faced with the question of how to best make this situation a learning experience.

Questions for Reflection

1. Is it possible for a teacher to establish, ahead of time, rules and consequences for an offense such as the one in this case? If so, how?
2. What consequence(s) would be appropriate for the students who created the problem for Mike and Mia?
3. What might you say to Mike that would be helpful to him? What would be some responses that you would not want to make?
4. What would you say to Mia? What would be some responses you would not want to make?
5. What could Mr. Carr do to help all his students be more respectful of those with special needs?
6. Should the teacher's response have been different if this had transpired between regular education students? If so, in what way?

Activities for Extending Thinking

1. Discuss with at least one special-education teacher the types of conflicts that most often occur between students with special needs and (a) teachers and (b) regular education students. What can teachers do to prevent such problems?
2. Discuss with a special-needs student what he or she would like general education teachers to do to improve interaction between special-needs students and (a) non-special-needs students and (b) teachers. Summarize your findings in writing and be prepared to share in class.
3. In consultation with teachers and administration, design an orientation program that addresses the needs of students with mental, physical, or sensory challenges. If such a program already exists, in consultation with special-needs students, assess its adequacy and suggest improvements.

Case 24

Structuring for Success in a Mainstreamed Classroom

By employing a number of special instructional strategies, a teacher tries to ensure that students with learning disabilities will succeed.

Mr. French believed that mainstreaming students with mental and physical disabilities would benefit not only those with the disability but the nondisabled as well. Over the past four years, he had given much thought to how best to arrange his instruction to ensure that both groups of students would have access to the curriculum and the opportunity to learn. With the disabled students, for example, he regularly limited problems so that they focused their learning on a single concept, included in assignments only material that was essential to the task at hand, and collected student work as soon as it was completed so that he could give immediate feedback. In addition, he held frequent, short, one-on-one conferences in which he asked each student to restate his or her responsibilities with respect to the assignment. Finally, he had a corner of his room set aside for students so that they could choose to work in a quiet area, and they frequently took advantage of the opportunity he provided.

On the third day of school, Mr. French was planning his lesson for the next day. His goal was to have students learn a number of social skills that they could use in his class, as well as in others. He would begin with listening skills and skills for asking questions, for these were two skill groups with which *all* students often had trouble. He would have students work in groups of five. There were five learning-disabled students in his class this term, and he would have them form one group. Mr. French reasoned that having them work together would give each student a feeling of support, knowing that each had a learning disability, and no one would make fun of them. Once the groups were formed, he would briefly define and model for them one of the four good listening skills: paraphrasing, empathizing, asking open questions, and asking clarifying questions, and then he would allow them to practice each skill through role-play. If he modeled one skill at a time, students would be able to focus on that skill and not be confused with too many new concepts at once. After the groups were finished practicing the skills, the class as a large group would discuss the effects of the role-play—for example, whether it was easier or harder to use the skills than they had expected and what problems they had experienced.

Each previous year, the students had seemed to enjoy the role-play activity. Mr. French always believed that students had achieved their goals in the activity.

Questions for Reflection

1. Which of the learning activities used by Mr. French would you support as being consistent with his goal of maximizing learning for both the disabled and nondisabled students? Why? Which would you oppose? Why?
2. Was Mr. French's grouping strategy appropriate for both disabled and nondisabled students? Provide a brief rationale to support your answer.
3. Identify 2-3 special needs (e.g., ADHD, autism, visually challenged, etc.) that may be present in any given classroom. For each type, list a way that teachers could organize the physical space in the classroom to facilitate learning for a diverse student population? Consider factors such as arrangement of furniture, use of teaching aids (e.g., overheads, flip charts, and computer presentation programs), and student accessibility to learning resources.
4. What else could Mr. French do to be sure that all students would feel equal in his classroom?

Activities for Extending Thinking

1. Discuss with at least two special-education teachers pedagogical techniques appropriate for students with various types of special needs. List grouping strategies, common sources of student error, and proven subject-based pedagogy for each kind of special need. In addition to identifying patterns of learning for each group, identify individual differences within those patterns. Provide demographic data on the number of students in special education in their school, including the number of males, females, students of color, and bilingual students, as well as the number mainstreamed.
2. Using written resources or special-education teachers, identify strategies for assessing and grading special-needs students. Summarize your findings in two to three pages.
3. Identify steps that teachers and other school personnel could take to advocate for students whose parents refuse to have them tested and/or admitted into a special-needs program.

Case 25

Inaccessibility of Web Sites to Students Who Are Blind

A student who is blind finds it impossible to access Web sites designed to take advantage of the graphic capabilities of browsers.

Amanda was a bright, creative, and cooperative student. Blind from birth, she had faced and overcome the many physical, intellectual, and social challenges she encountered. Usually optimistic, she could, like many sighted students, have days when she felt like a victim of circumstance. Today was one of those days. Mr. Grant, Amanda's social studies teacher, had taken the class to the computer lab to give them the opportunity to locate Internet resources for their assigned projects. When Amanda raised her hand for help, Mr. Grant responded.

"Yes, Amanda? May I help you?" he asked.

"I'm having trouble with some of the Web sites. The ones with text are accessible—my computer can read the responses aloud. However, those with graphical Web browsers are inaccessible—my computer can't report pictures. I get lost!" she said with frustration in her voice.

"I understand," replied Mr. Grant. "Tai is working on a related topic, and in fact, she has collected nearly all the citations that she will need for her project. I'll ask her to help you, if that's okay with you."

"I get so frustrated! But that's okay," said Amanda. "We get along well, and I'm sure it won't take long. I already have several text-based sites that I can use."

"You may want to start with the Web page 'Bobby.' As you know, it will display the page and highlight the features that would be difficult or impossible for a person who is visually disabled to use," added Mr. Grant.

"I will. I've used it before. Thanks for your help," said Amanda appreciatively.

Tai accepted Mr. Grant's request that she help Amanda. She was proud to have been selected to play the role of teacher.

Questions for Reflection

1. Assess Mr. Grant's response to Amanda's problem. How, if at all, would you change it?
2. What other technological challenges exist for students with special needs? (For example, in the future, people who are deaf may have trouble using full-motion video transmission over the Internet unless text captions are included on the screen along with the images.)

3. Design a social-action activity through which your students attempt to rectify a technology-based injustice toward students with special needs. (For example, communicate with the World Wide Web Consortium [www.w3.org] in Cambridge, England, or directly with designers to ensure that standards are in place to protect persons with special needs.)

Activities for Extending Thinking

1. Select a resource from the "Readings for Extending Thinking" list at the end of this section or from another source, such as your primary text. Summarize key insights related to the use of technology with special-needs students.
2. Interview a special-education resource teacher or a computer resource teacher regarding programs he or she would recommend for the special-needs students you teach (or will teach). List at least three recommended programs, and cite their strengths, weaknesses, and how they relate to general course goals.
3. Interview a teacher in your licensure area about ways in which, using computers, he or she accommodates students at varying levels of knowledge and skill. List several guidelines that you could recommend to your classmates. Summarize your findings in writing (one to two pages).

Case 26

Modifications for Special Students: Autism Spectrum Disorder

A teacher contemplates how to respect the confidentiality of a disruptive autistic student.

Thao had been diagnosed with autism spectrum disorder at age 3. Thao's struggles were amplified by the fact that English was his second language. He had very low language abilities in both his first language and in English, primarily due to his autism.

The special-education teacher and regular education teacher had come together to create some supports for Thao. They taught him to utilize a visual schedule, cue cards, taking breaks, and a paraprofessional. Thao was able to make it through most class periods. Sometimes he would get frustrated and need to take a break. He often used the cue cards to signal when he needed a break and when he was ready to come back to class. At times his frustration got the best of him, and he was unable to control his own behavior.

Partway through the school year the two grade-level teachers, Mr. Leon and Ms. Xiong, decided to split their classes and form a high and low math class. Thao remained with Mr. Leon, but because of this change, Thao and the new group of students were exposed to each other for the first time.

The first day Thao was overwhelmed with all the changes. About five minutes into the lesson, he began screaming and clearly needed a break. The teacher acknowledged Thao's frustration and reminded him to signal when he was ready to come back, as stated in his Individualized Educational Plan.

The new student sitting next to Thao took inventory of the situation and began screaming. Mr. Leon responded to Chong with confusion. "What is going on Chong?" "I need a break too," he said. As far as Mr. Leon knew, Chong was not a special needs student. Mr. Leon thought about how he would respond, keeping in mind important student confidentiality issues.

Questions for Reflection

1. How should Mr. Leon respond to Chong? How should he respond to Thao following the outburst by Chong?
2. Should Mr. Leon address the entire class? If so, how, in keeping with the FERPA laws, should he address the class? Should he address—the behavior; the condition (autism)?
3. How could the classroom be better prepared to prevent this situation?

Activities for Extending Thinking

1. Identify ways in which teachers can use appropriate sensory stimuli to address issues related to autism.
2. Examine the spectrum of characteristics and behaviors of students with autism and Asperger syndrome, and suggest how teachers might respond to students at various levels of each.

Design Your Own Case

Special Needs

Design a case that would help classmates explore issues related to exceptionality in schools. The story can focus on a method or strategy related to a single subject matter area (e.g., English or social studies) or on a more generic method or strategy pertinent to a wider range of subject matter areas. Your issue might also relate to:

- Planning and preparation
- Classroom environment
- Instruction
- Teacher responsibilities*

In selecting a topic, reflect on recent or current field experiences, personal experiences as a student, or accounts of real classroom incidents. Choose a topic that allows the reader to link theory and practice in the areas of learning, development, teaching, and of course, multicultural/cross-cultural education. Your topic of choice should also invite discussion of multiple perspectives rather that a singular viewpoint. Consider, too, the general level of experience and knowledge of the intended reader (i.e., whether they are in an early stage of the teacher education program or a more experienced/knowledgeable professional). Include some demographic data that tell a bit about the community, school, classroom, teacher, students, and curriculum. Include at least one problem for which there is no obvious solution. Use fictitious names of persons and schools to maintain confidentiality. Your case should be approximately two pages in length (typed, double-spaced) and should include three to four "Questions for Reflection" and one or two "Activities for Extending Thinking." Go to Resource C and use the form to design your own case.

*The four categories are from *Enhancing Professional Practice: A Framework for Teaching*, by C. Danielson, 1996, Alexandria, VA: Association for Supervision and Curriculum Development.

Readings for Extending Thinking

Adams, M., Bell, L. A., & Griffin, P. (1997). *Teaching for diversity and social justice: A sourcebook.* New York: Routledge.

Al-Hassan, S., & Gardner, R., III. (2002). Involving immigrant parents of students with disabilities in the educational process. *Teaching Exceptional Children, 35*(2), 12–16.

Anderson, N. B., & Shames, G. H. (2006). *Human communication disorders: An introduction* (7th ed.). Boston: Allyn & Bacon.

Artiles, A. J., Trent, S. C., & Palmer, J. (2004). Culturally diverse student in special education: Legacies and prospects. In J.A Banks & C. A. M. Banks (eds.) *Handbook of research in multicultural education* (2nd ed., pp. 716–735). San Francisco: Jossey-Bass.

Artiles, A. J., & Trent, S. C. (1994). Overrepresentation of minority students in special education: A continuing debate. *Journal of Special Education, 27,* 410–437.

Bauer, A. M., & Brown, G. M. (2001). *Adolescents and inclusion: Transforming secondary schools.* Baltimore: Paul H. Brookes.

Billingsley, B. S. (2005). *Cultivating and keeping committed special education teachers: What principals and district leaders can do.* Thousand Oaks, CA: Corwin Press.

Burkhardt, S. A., Obiakor, F. E., & Rotatori, A. F. (Eds.). (2004). *Current perspectives on learning disabilities.* Boston: JAI.

Carrasquillo, A. L., & Rodriguez, V. (1995). *Language minority students in the mainstream classroom.* Bristol, PA: Taylor & Francis.

Cerney, J. (2007) Deaf education in America: Voices of children from inclusion settings. Washington, DC: Gallaudet University Press.

Correa, V. I., & Heward, W. L. (2000). Special education in a culturally diverse society. In W. L. Heward, *Exceptional children: An introduction to special education* (6th ed., pp. 82–114). Upper Saddle River, NJ: Merrill/Prentice Hall.

Ford, D. Y., & Harris, J. J., III (1999). *Multicultural gifted education.* New York: Teachers College Press.

Ford, D. Y. (1998). The underrepresentation of minority students in gifted education: Problems and promises in recruitment and retention. *Journal of Special Education, 32,* 4–14.

Fuchs, D., & Fuchs, L. S. (1995). Sometimes separate is better. *Educational Leadership, 52*(4), 22–25.

Fuchs, D., & Fuchs, L. S. (2003). Inclusion versus full inclusion. In W. L. Heward, *Exceptional children: An introduction to special education* (7th ed., pp. 80–81). Upper Saddle River, NJ: Merrill/Prentice Hall.

Giangreco, M. F. (2003). Moving toward inclusion. In W. L. Heward, *Exceptional children: An introduction to special education* (7th ed., pp. 78–79). Upper Saddle River, NJ: Merrill/Prentice Hall.

Giangreco, M. F., Cloniger, C. J., & Iverson, V. S. (1998). *Choosing options and accommodations for children: A guide to educational planning for students with disabilities* (2nd ed.). Baltimore: Paul H. Brookes.

Gottlieb, J., & Atter, M. (1995). *Overrepresentation of children of color referred to special education.* New York: New York University Department of Teaching and Learning.

Hammer, M. R. (2004). Using self-advocacy strategy to increase student participation in IEP conferences. *Intervention in School and Clinic, 39,* 295–300.

Heward, W.L. (2006). *Exceptional children: An introduction to special education* (8th ed.). Upper Saddle River, NJ: Merrill/Prentice-Hall.

Hill, J. L. (1999). *Meeting the needs of students with special physical and health care needs*. Upper Saddle River, NJ: Merrill/Prentice Hall.

Individuals with Disabilities Act of 1990. (1990). P. L. No 101-476, 20 U.S.C. 1400–1485.

Janney, R. E., Snell, M. E., Beers, M. K., & Raynes, M. (1995). Integrating students with moderate and severe disabilities into general education classes. *Exceptional Children, 61*(5), 425–439.

Kauffman, J. M. (2005). *Characteristics of emotional and behavioral disorders of children and youth* (8th ed.). Upper Saddle River, NJ: Merrill/Prentice-Hall.

Kauffman, J. M., & Hallahan, D. K. (1995). *The illusion of full inclusion: A comprehensive critique of a current special education bandwagon.* Austin, TX: PRO-ED.

Klinger, J. K., Vaughn, S., & Boardman, A. (2007) *Teaching reading comprehension to students with learning disabilities.* New York: Guilford.

Kohl, H. R. (1994) I won't learn from you: And other thoughts on creative maladjustment. New York: New Press.

Meyer, L. H., & Park, H. S. (1999). Contemporary most promising practices for people with disabilities. In J. S. Scotti & L. H. Meyer (Eds.), *Behavioral intervention: Principles, models, and practices* (pp. 25–45). Baltimore: Paul H. Brookes.

Milner, H. R., & Ford, D.Y. (2007). Cultural considerations in the underrepresentation of culturally diverse elementary students in gifted education. *Roeper Review 29,* 166–172.

Ohoven, M., Stern, S., Stipe, M., Vince, W. (Producers), & Dannelly, B. (Director). (2004). *Saved!* [Motion picture]. United States: United Artists.

Oswald, D. P., Coutinho, M. J., Best, A. M., & Singh, N. N. (1999). Ethnic representation in special education: The influence of school-related economic and demographic variables. *Journal of Special Education, 32,* 194–206.

Purcell, J. H., & Eckert, R. D. (Eds.). (2006). Designing services and programs for high-ability learners: A guidebook for gifted education. Thousand Oaks, CA: Corwin Sage.

Rainforth, B., York, J., & MacDonald, C. (1992). *Collaborative teams for students with severe disabilities: Integrating therapy and educational services.* Baltimore: Paul H. Brookes.

Ryba, K., Selby, L., & Nolan, P. (1995). Computers empower students with special needs. *Educational Leadership, 53*(2), 82–87.

Sapon-Shevin, M. (1999). *Because we can change the world: A practical guide to building cooperative, inclusive classroom communities.* Boston: Allyn & Bacon.

Smith, D. D., & Tyler, N. C. (2010). *Introduction to special education: Making a difference* (7th ed.). Upper Saddle River, NJ: Pearson/Merrill.

Sternberg, R. J. (2007). Cultural dimensions of giftedness and talent. *Roeper Review, 29,* 160–165.

Trent, S. C., Artiles, A. J., & Englert, C. S. (1998). From deficit thinking to social constructivism: A review of theory, research, and practice in special education. In *Review of research in education, 23,* 277–307. Washington, DC: American Educational Research Association.

Turnbull, R., Huerta, N., & Stowe, M., (2009). *What every teacher should know about the individuals with disabilities education act as amended in 2004* (2nd ed.). Upper Saddle River, NJ: Pearson/Merrill.

Turnbull, A., & Wehmeyer, M. L., (2010). *Exceptional lives: Special education in today's schools* (6th ed.). Upper Saddle River, NJ: Pearson/Merrill.

Yell, M. L. (1995). Least restrictive environment, inclusion, and students with disabilities: A legal analysis. *Journal of Special Education, 28,* 389–404.

Internet Sites for Extending Thinking

http://www.autism-society.org/
This site is run by the Autism Society of America. Includes resources on what autism is, as well as ways to address autism in its various stages, and research and programs for individuals and families dealing with autism.

http://ericec.org/
Sponsored by the Educational Resources Information Center (ERIC), this site is a clearinghouse for data on the disabilities and gifted education. The site features links to Web pages containing fact sheets, digests, laws, research, and other subjects, as well as to online discussion groups, an FAQ, and databases relevant to the subject.

http://www.ldonline.org/
This site, run by the Learning Project at WETA, offers a wealth of information, via internal links to numerous data pages, on various LDs themselves, the issues surrounding LD in education, and other information. In addition, you can take part in online discussion, sign up for a free online newsletter, or submit questions about LDs.

http://seriweb.com/
Billed as "Special Education Resources on the Internet," SERI is basically an extensive page of links to more links, covering almost every aspect of special education. From legal issues to definitions of various disabilities, discussion groups, organization listings—if there's a Web site covering some aspect of special education, you will doubtless find it here on one of the many secondary pages.

http://www.educationworld.com/special_ed/
Education World brings you this megasite, which contains a vast assortment of special-education information that is both wide and deep: articles (including an archive), reviews, resource listings, databases, reference centers, and more. The site is a breeze to navigate and easy to read.

http://www.cec.sped.org/index.html
Council for Exceptional Children site includes publications and products, professional standards, discussion forums, a link to ERIC Clearinghouse on disabilities and gifted education, career connections, and professional development training events, all on topics relating to exceptionality.

http://hoagiesgifted.org/
Click on "educators" for information on books, programs, curriculum, and theories on gifted education.

Chapter 8

Sexual Orientation

Introduction

Some, including this writer, prefer the term "affectional orientation" because it places emphasis on aspects of the self beyond the sexual aspect, that is, it highlights more of the whole person, rather than only the sexual aspect. Others, however, have noted that "sexual orientation" is a more commonly used and easily recognized term, and that we should indeed focus on the key difference between straight and gay orientation.

Local and national policies recognize the importance of raising the awareness of and sensitivity to sexual orientation. Such policies are reflected in statements of the National Education Association, the National School Boards Association, the Child Welfare League of America, the American Academy of Pediatrics, the American Federation of Teachers, and the American Psychological Association (Horowitz & Loehnig, 2005). At the same time, throughout the nation, negative attitudes toward persons of differing sexual orientation linger.

As microcosms of society, schools often reflect matters of national interest. Issues such as gay marriage have brought increasing national attention to matters of sexual orientation. Whether teacher advocates are proactive in addressing such issues, or whether these issues are brought to the fore by students, matters of sexual orientation commonly arise in the school and classroom.

As in many areas of diversity education, terminology is important and often challenging. In the area of GLBT studies, microcultures in one geographical area may use certain terms to define their sexual orientation and related situations, whereas in other areas, those same terms may be viewed as irrelevant or even offensive. (This concept was introduced in Chapter 4 as it relates to race.) Understanding terminology that is acceptable is a key to addressing core issues of sexual orientation.

Chapter 8 introduces a number of real situations that may help elevate the dialogue regarding gay, lesbian, bisexual, and transgender (GLBT) issues. Inquiry into these cases may be aided by a clearer understanding of the following terms and concepts.

bisexual
family
gay
gender dysphoria
GLBT
heterosexism
heterosexual
heterosexual privilege
homophobia
homosexual
inclusive language
internalized homophobia
intersexed individuals
lesbian
LGBT
LGBTQI
out
partner/significant other
pink triangle
queer
questioning
sexual orientation
transgender
transsexual
transvestite
xenophobia

Definitions of key terms are included in the glossary of this text.

Case 27

Not in My Group—He's Gay!

A student publicly objects to the inclusion of a classmate in his small group because, he claims, the classmate is "gay."

Ms. Collins was a firm believer in multicultural education that has the potential to lead to social reform. She organized her curriculum around issues of race, gender, class, disability, language, and sexual orientation. She used the lives of students in her classes as the starting point for addressing such issues.

On this day Ms. Collins' students were busily engaged in small-group discussions about their family heritage projects. She had asked students to share the information about their ethnic heritage that they had obtained from their parents or guardians the night before. Ms. Collins hoped that not only would the small-group discussions give her pupils opportunities to express themselves, but they might also help identify differences and similarities among classmates. Further, she thought the discussions would help them be more thoughtful about what else they would need to find out to make their projects more complete.

As she moved to the small group of students in the rear of the room, Xeng, a Hmong student new to the class, said to her as he pointed to a classmate named Kim, "I don't want him in my group. He's gay!" The other group members covered their mouths and laughed.

Ms. Collins was caught by surprise. Consistent enforcement of class rules established at the beginning of the school year had prevented the use of such labels in her class until today. She noticed that Kim appeared embarrassed by Xeng's accusation.

"Do you know what 'gay' means?" she asked, in an effort to determine if Xeng was just repeating something he had heard someone else say, without knowing what it meant.

"Yeah," replied Xeng. "It's when one dude wants to get with another dude."

Ms. Collins was baffled. She thought to herself, "Should I ask if Xeng is sure that Kim is gay? Should I ask Xeng if he is angry with Kim, and, if so, why? Should I reprimand Xeng for making his judgment public? How should I respond to Kim?"

Ms. Collins was aware of the tremendous controversy over the inclusion in many schools across the country of GLBT (gay, lesbian, bisexual, transgender) issues in the classroom. She would review the school policy and would discuss the matter with the principal.

Questions for Reflection

1. List possible factors that may have motivated Xeng to say what he said about Kim.
2. Write several sentences illustrating how you would respond to the students in this situation. Would you respond differently (a) if Xeng were not a new student, or (b) if Xeng had personal problems at home?

3. Knowing that the word *gay* is often used as a derogatory term, under what conditions, if any, would you involve the class in a discussion of this issue? Write down the actual opening statements/questions you would use to introduce such a discussion.
4. What other incidents regarding sexual orientation have you observed in schools? How were they addressed? How should they have been addressed?
5. What district and state policies and practices exist that relate to sexual orientation in the school, that is, are there any statutes that require a safe environment for GLBT students?

Activities for Extending Thinking

1. Discuss with an experienced practicing teacher the strategies he or she uses to create and maintain a safe classroom environment for all students. List those strategies in writing and be prepared to share in class.
2. Interview an advocate for gay, lesbian, bisexual, and transgender students to identify key issues and specific strategies that classroom teachers can use to create a safe, inclusive environment.
3. Talk with a gay, lesbian, bisexual, or transgender student regarding classroom incidents experienced by him or her, or by friends who are GLBT. Elicit recommendations for preventing negative experiences and encouraging positive ones.
4. Discuss with a principal or superintendent the school and district policies regarding the inclusion of GLBT issues in his or her school(s).

Case 28

Homosexuality and Religion: "In Islam, Homosexuality Is a Sin and a Crime"

A student confides in her class that she is lesbian, and a Muslim student states that homosexuality is a sin and a crime in Islam.

Ms. Elness worked hard to develop an inclusive classroom. She believed in honoring cultural diversity, in designing multicultural curricula, and in general, running a student-centered classroom. Because they knew she cared about all students, her pupils trusted her.

As part of her service to the school, Ms. Elness served as faculty sponsor of the Gay, Lesbian, Bisexual, Transgender (GLBT) support group that met after school. She recalled that three years ago when she volunteered to sponsor the group, she had been nervous. Each year, however, her work as an advocate for students in the GLBT group had become more and more gratifying.

In addition to providing a forum for GLBT students to socialize and to discuss important issues, Ms. Elness would meet with other faculty to help them understand the general and specific needs of students in the group. Each year, on the first day of class, in her own classes she would discuss her work with the group so that students would know of her belief in the importance of creating a safe environment for all.

It was the sixth week of the school year. Ms. Elness had distributed newspapers and asked students to read and summarize for the class a news report of a current event. Tyrone reported an incident on a local university campus in which a number of students had harassed and physically beaten a student because he was gay.

Robert responded to the report, "I don't think that happens that much anymore. Most people are more accepting of people who are different."

Margie raised her hand. "I disagree," she said. "I'm a lesbian, and when people find out, they often look at me funny or avoid me entirely."

Ms. Elness was somewhat surprised. Margie had not confided in her or, as far as she knew, in anyone else in the school about her sexual orientation.

Before Ms. Elness could respond, Fahid, a Muslim student, said in a calm, informing tone of voice, "In Islam, it is a sin and crime to practice homosexuality. Those who believe in Islam know they will be punished if they are found to be homosexual."

Ms. Elness sensed that Fahid was intending merely to describe a belief system held by Muslim people, not to demean Margie. At the same time, his comments seemed ill timed, for Margie had taken a risk to share her secret with the class, only to be informed that her disposition was considered a sin and a crime by a formidable group of people. Several students rolled their eyes, as if to suggest that Fahid was expressing a narrow point of view, was being intolerant, and was out of line. Mark verbalized their dissatisfaction in a disgusted tone of voice: "That's only the opinion of one religion—it doesn't mean it actually is a sin or a crime—only that one religion thinks it is."

Jennifer cautioned Mark and the others who had rolled their eyes, "Let's remember now that Fahid is describing for us another cultural perspective. We ought not judge him for helping us to understand another point of view."

Noting that there was only a minute left in the period, Ms. Elness interrupted, "Yes, I appreciate the comments of both Margie and Fahid. And Jennifer is right—we must acknowledge the rights of both Margie and Fahid to hold the beliefs that they hold." She had barely finished when the bell rang.

As the students filed out, she wondered, "How should I follow up with Fahid, Margie, Mark, and Jennifer? Should we follow up in class tomorrow, or go on with the next lesson in the unit plan?"

Questions for Reflection

1. In your opinion, how should Ms. Elness follow up with
   a. Margie?
   b. Fahid?
   c. Mark?
   d. Jennifer?
   e. the class?
   f. others? (identify)
2. Views opposing homosexuality are made clear by Fahid. What, if anything, should the teacher have done to represent the views of those who support it?
3. What assumptions had Mark made about Fahid's comments? Do they seem warranted?
4. What, if any, are the positive aspects of this case?
5. If you were the teacher, what might you have done differently to prevent, guide, or correct inappropriate student behaviors?

Activities for Extending Thinking

1. Discuss with a gay, lesbian, bisexual, or transgender student his or her school experiences. Inquire about what the school is currently doing and what else, if anything, it could do to provide a safe, inclusive environment for GLBT students.
2. List specific steps you can take to better advocate for a safe environment for all students, particularly those who are GLBT or questioning.
3. Develop a list of curriculum resources that include gay, lesbian, bisexual, or transgendered persons and issues that could be used at the grade level at which you teach. Include several nonfiction and fiction resources.
4. Discuss with a school administrator (a principal, or superintendent) her or his school and district policies on GLBT issues.

Case 29

"Lesbian!": Dealing with the Interaction of Sexuality, Special Needs, and Culture

A teacher considers the difficulties in dealing with multiple issues with sensitivity toward each.

Ms. Green's students were returning from lunch. The aide who had lunch duty popped her head in the classroom to give Ms. Green a "heads-up" that a couple of students seemed to be having problems on the playground. Ms. Green asked who the students were but before the aide could respond, two girls, Sophia, a recent European immigrant, and Leyla, told Ms. Green that Paul, a student with severe ADHD, was teasing them during recess. Ms. Green knew that it was difficult for Paul to control his impulses.

The two girls explained that they were doing laps around the playground talking and holding hands when Paul ran up behind them yelling, "Lesbians! Lesbians!" The girls made note that they were not lesbians but they were holding hands as friends. Sophia added that in France it was common for girls who were friends to hold hands, and "it wasn't a big deal."

This incident reminded Ms. Green of a news article she had read about a seven-year-old student who had told a classmate that his mother was gay. A teacher who overheard the remark scolded him, telling him that *gay* was a bad word and he shouldn't call people gay. As punishment he had to stay in at recess and copy the phrase, "I will not use the word *gay* in school again." Ms. Green also recalled that the American Civil Liberties Union demanded that the school apologize to the boy and his mother.

It was apparent to Ms. Green that this would be a sensitive subject to tackle. She wanted to be sure to communicate to the students that the act of teasing was not appropriate. She also knew that she had to be cautious dealing with special-education confidentiality issues. She knew the whole class was waiting for a response, and she had to reply with caution.

Questions for Reflection

1. Should the teacher in this situation simply treat the incident simply as a case of student behavior management (teasing), or should she, in addition, address with the class the sexual orientation aspect of the incident? Give a brief rationale for your answer.
2. How can Ms. Green address Paul's behavior without violating confidentiality laws?
3. In what situations have you heard someone use a term of sexual orientation as a means to degrade another?

4. What is the best way to deal with the confusion between the social norms of different countries (e.g., France, as in this case) toward sexuality?
5. Examine your own personal opinions about sexual orientation and reflect on how they may affect your own teaching process.
6. What types of consequences would be appropriate for Paul in light of his ADHD?

Activities for Extending Thinking

1. Review and report research findings on the relation of rates of verbal abuse, assaults, depression, and suicide in adolescents of heterosexual and GLBT backgrounds.
2. Identify three or four local community resource centers that provide advocacy/support for students of GLBT orientation. Contact at least one of them and report on the nature and scope of their service (e.g., how many students do they serve, what is the racial/ethnic makeup of the constituency). Include all contact information (e.g., phone number, e-mail address, and street address).
3. Develop an outline of a unit plan or a series of lesson plans in your own subject matter area that would help your students learn about GLBT needs, interests, and lifestyles.
4. The following possible responses to homophobic remarks made by students are suggested by Alan Horowitz, a program specialist for the St. Paul Public Schools Out for Equity program:

   Name it: "That is homophobic harassment (or an age-appropriate alternative)."

   Claim it: That is not permitted in this classroom (or school) because it is disrespectful."

   Stop it: "It won't happen again. If it does (state consequences)."

   Critique this response. Suggest changes, if any. Provide clear, age-appropriate alternative language for younger pupils. (From What to Say to "That's So Gay," by A. Horowitz, *Minnesota Educator*, p. 3, December 17, 2004.)
5. From the following sample book list, read one text and briefly describe how it could be integrated into your curriculum.

   Freymann-Weyr, G. (2002). *My Heartbeat*. New York: Penguin. As she tries to understand the closeness between her older brother and his best friend, 14-year-old Ellen finds her relationship with each of them changing.

   Hartinger, B. (2003). *Geography Club*. New York: HarperCollins. A group of gay and lesbian teenagers find mutual support when they form the "Geography Club" at their high school.

   Levithan, D. (2003). *Boy Meets Boy*. New York: Knopf. A story of a sophomore in a high school like no other: the cheerleaders ride Harleys, the homecoming queen used to be a guy named Daryl (she now prefers Infinite Darlene), and the gay–straight alliance was formed to help straight kids learn how to dance.

   Matthews, A. (2003). *The Flip Side*. New York: Delacorte Press. Robert, a British 15-year-old, is confused when he plays the part of Rosalind while studying Shakespeare in school and discovers parts of his personality that he did not know existed.

Myracle, L. (2003). *Kissing Kate.* New York: Dutton. Sixteen-year-old Lissa's relationship with her best friend changes after they kiss at a party and Lissa does not know what to do, until she gets help from an unexpected new friend.

Newman, L. (2009). *Heather has two mommies: 20th anniversary edition,* Boston: Alyson Books. Preschooler Heather who has two moms, discovers that some of her friends have different family structures. The teacher, encourages them to draw pictures of their families as a way of promoting a sense of celebration of diversity.

Peters, J. A. (2003). *Keeping You a Secret.* New York: Little, Brown. As she begins a very tough last semester of high school, Holland finds herself puzzled about her future and intrigued by a transfer student who wants to start a Lesbigay club at school.

Peters, J. A. (2004). *Luna.* New York: Little, Brown. Fifteen-year-old Regan's life, which has always revolved around keeping her older brother Liam's transsexuality a secret, changes when Liam decides to start the process of "transitioning" by first telling his family and friends that he is a girl who was born in a boy's body.

Polacco, P. (2009). *In our mother's house.* New York: Philomel Books. The narrator, an African-American girl describes how her two Caucasian mothers adopted her, her Asian brother, and her red-headed sister. Eventually they all grow up, marry heterosexual spouses, and return home to visit their aged parents.

Sanchez, A. (2001). *Rainbow Boys.* New York: Simon & Schuster. Three high school seniors, a jock with a girlfriend and an alcoholic father, a closeted gay, and a flamboyant gay rights advocate, struggle with family issues, gay bashers, first sex, and conflicting feelings about each other.

Sanchez, A. (2003). *Rainbow High.* New York: Simon & Schuster. Sequel to *Rainbow Boys.* Follow three gay high school seniors as they struggle with issues of coming out, safe sex, homophobia, being in love, and college choices.

Taylor, W. (2003). *Pebble in a Pool.* Los Angeles: Alyson Books. Two popular high school students enter their senior year full of confidence. After a gruesome accident, the outpouring of grief in their school starkly contrasts with a decidedly more muted reaction to the gay-bashing murder of another student.

Williams, D. (2009). *The boy in the dress.* New York: HarperCollins. Dennis, a 12-year-old boy meets Lisa a popular 14-year-old fashion aficionado. Humor abounds as soccer-star Dennis allows Lisa to convince him to come to school as "Denise" a French exchange student.

Winthrow, S. (2001). *Box Girl.* Toronto: Groundwood Books. Gwen's mother communicates with her, promising a reunion, through postcards with French stamps and no return address. Gwen plans to be a loner until she meets Clara.

Case 30

A Paperwork Problem: A Transgendered Student Teaches about Gender Identity

A teacher learns how student names and nicknames often reflect their gender identity.

Micky was excited for his first day of school. He had spent all summer getting to know the kids in his new neighborhood. He liked to ride bikes with Marcus who lived across the street and practice soccer with Ely and Yeng. He liked his new neighborhood, and he was excited to start the new school year with his new friends.

Arriving at school, Micky eagerly searched for his classroom and sat down in an empty desk. His face illuminated when he saw the neighborhood boys walk into the same classroom. The boys all sat together and waited for class to start.

Mr. Manowicz was excited to get the day started and began taking attendance. "Ely Alverez?" Ely raised his hand and replied, "Here." "Samantha Botwin?" "Sam, my friends call me Sam." Mr. Manowicz looked up at Sam, carefully outfitted in her pink dress and matching pink bow. "Okay Sam. Michelle Carerra, Michelle?"

A silence fell over the room. Micky's heart began to race. "No, no, no," he thought. His mom filled out the paperwork using his "old" name. No one had called Micky Michelle at his old school because everyone had known that she really felt like she was a boy. She grew up as a boy. Micky's mom had been into his old school and talked to his teachers but apparently hadn't spoken with his new teacher yet.

Before he could stop himself, Micky corrected Mr. Manowicz. "It's Micky," he said in his most masculine voice. Mr. Manowicz looked at the paperwork again. It clearly said Michelle Carerra, female. Mr. Manowicz could see he did not have a Michelle in front of him. He could also see the boys around Micky starting to raise their eyebrows while quizzically looking at each other. Mr. Manowicz knew he needed to say something quickly.

Questions for Reflection

1. How should Mr. Manowicz respond in the moment?
2. What follow-up is needed? With the class? Micky? Micky's family? Administration?
3. How can teachers prevent this from occurring in the classroom?

Activities for Extending Thinking

1. Using print or Internet sources, locate stories of incidents that have taken place within the past several years in which GLBT issues have arisen in the schools. Identify the issue(s), the ways in which the issue was handled by the teacher and/or the school, and ways in which the issue(s) could have been handled more sensitively and effectively.
2. In your community, identify resources that are available to GLBT students and families. List the location, contact information, and types of services provided.

Design Your Own Case

Sexual Orientation

Design a case that explores an issue of sexual orientation in the classroom. The story can focus on a method or strategy related to a single subject matter area (e.g., English or social studies) or on a more generic method or strategy pertinent to a wider range of subject matter areas. Your issue might also relate to:

- Planning and preparation
- Classroom environment
- Instruction
- Teacher responsibilities*

In selecting a topic, reflect on recent or current field experiences, personal experiences as a student, or accounts of real classroom incidents. Choose a topic that allows the reader to link theory and practice in the areas of learning, development, teaching, and of course, multicultural/cross-cultural education. Your topic of choice should also invite discussion of multiple perspectives rather that a singular viewpoint. Consider, too, the general level of experience and knowledge of the intended reader (i.e., whether they are in an early stage of the teacher education program or a more experienced/knowledgeable professional). Include some demographic data that tell a bit about the community, school, classroom, teacher, students, and curriculum. Include at least one problem for which there is no obvious solution. Use fictitious names of persons and schools to maintain confidentiality. Your case should be approximately two pages in length (typed, double-spaced) and should include three to four "Questions for Reflection" and one or two "Activities for Extending Thinking." Go to Resource C and use the form to design your own case.

*The four categories are from *Enhancing Professional Practice: A Framework for Teaching*, by C. Danielson, 1996, Alexandria. VA: Association for Supervision and Curriculum Development.

Readings for Extending Thinking

Alexander, L. B., & Miselis, S. D. (2007, Spring). Barriers to GLBTQ collection development and strategies for overcoming them. *Young Adult Library Services*, 43–49.

Bass, E., & Kaufman, K. (1996). *Free your mind: The book for gay, lesbian and bisexual youth—and their allies*. New York: HarperPerennial.

Berzon, B. (Ed.). (2001). *Positively gay: New approaches to gay and lesbian life.* Berkeley, CA: Celestial Arts.

Bilodeau, B. L., & Renn, K. A. (2005). Analysis of LGBT identity development models and Implications for practice. *Wiley Periodicals,* 25–39.

Butler, K. L., & Byrne, T. J. (1992). Homophobia among preservice elementary teachers. *Journal of Health Education, 23*(6), 357–358.

Cass, V. C. (1984). Homosexual identity formation: testing a theoretical model. *The Journal of Sex Research, 20*(2), 143–167.

Cowan, T. (1992). *Gay men and women who enriched the world*. Boston: Alyson.

Daniel, P. L. (2007). Invitation to all: Welcoming gays and lesbians into my classroom and curriculum. *English Journal, 96*(5), 75–80.

Ellis, V., & High, S. (2003). Something more to tell you: Gay, lesbian, or bisexual young people. *British Educational Research Journal, 30,* 213–225.

Elze, D. E. (2003). Gay, lesbian, and bisexual youths' perceptions of their high school Environments and comfort in school. *National Association of Social Workers,* 225–239.

Evans, K. (2002). *Negotiating the self: Identity, sexuality, and emotion in learning to teach*. New York: Routledge.

GLSEN. (2003). *School-related experiences of LGBT youth of color: Findings from the 2003 National School Climate Survey.* New York: GLSEN.

GLSEN. (2003). *The 2003 national school climate survey.* New York: GLSEN.

GLSEN & Harris Interactive. (2008). *The principal's perspective: School safety, bullying and harassment, A survey of public school principals*. New York: GLSEN.

Harbeck, K. M. (Ed.). (1992). *Coming out of the classroom closet: Gay and lesbian students, teachers, and curricula*. Binghamton, NY: Haworth.

Herdt, G., & Boxer, A. (1993). *Children of horizons: How gay and lesbian teens are leading a new way out of the closet*. Boston: Beacon.

Horowitz, A., & Loehnig, G. (2005). *Safe schools manual.* St. Paul, MN: Out for Equity of the St. Paul Public Schools.

Human Rights Watch. (2001). *Hatred in the hallways: Violence and discrimination against lesbian, gay, bisexual, and transgendered students in U.S. schools.* New York: Author.

Hutchins, L., & Kaahumanu, L. (Eds.). (1991). *Bi any other name: Bisexual people speak out*. Boston: Alyson.

Jennings, K. (1994). *Becoming visible: A reader of gay and lesbian history for high school and college students*. Boston: Alyson.

Jennings, T., & Sherwin, G. (2007, April). *Sexual orientation curriculum in elementary teacher preparation: Programs, content and priorities from across the United States.* Paper presented at the annual meeting of the American Educational Research Association, Chicago.

Johnson, D. (1996). The developmental experience of gay/lesbian youth. *Journal of College Admission, 152*, 38–41.

Johnson, E. P. (2008). *Sweet tea: Black gay men of the south, an oral history.* Chapel Hill: University of North Carolina Press.

Kissen, R. (Ed.). (2002). *Getting ready for Benjamin: Preparing teachers for sexual diversity in the classroom.* Lanham, MD: Rowman & Littlefield.

Kosciw, J. G., & Diaz, E. M. (2006). *The 2005 National School Climate Survey: The experiences of lesbian, gay, bisexual, and transgender youth in our nation's schools.* New York: Gay Lesbian Straight Education Network.

Krutky, Judy B. (2008, March). Inter-cultural competency—preparing students to be global citizens: The Baldwin-Wallace experience. *Effective Practices for Academic Leaders,* 3.

Lipkin, A. (2005). Secondary curriculum. In J. T. Sears (Ed.), *Youth, education, and sexualities: An International encyclopedia* (pp. 241–245). Westport, CT: Greenwood.

Lugg, C. (2003). Sissies, faggots, lezzies, and dykes: Gender, sexual orientation and the new politics of education. *Educational Administration Quarterly, 39*(1), 96–134.

Macgillivray, I. K. (2005). Using cartoons to teach students about stereotypes and discrimination: One teacher's lessons from South Park. *Journal of Curriculum and Pedagogy, 2*(1), 133–147.

Macgillivray, I. K. (2007). *Gay-straight alliances: A handbook for students, educators, and parents.* Binghampton, NY: Haworth Press.

MacIntosh, L. (2007). Does anyone have a band-aid? Anti-homophobia discourses and pedagogical impossibilities. *Educational Studies, 41*(1), 33–43.

Mayberry, M. (2006, July/August). School reform efforts for lesbian, gay, bisexual, and transgendered students. *The Clearing House, 79*(6), 262–264.

Mayo, C. (2004). Queering school communities: Ethical curiosity and gay-straight alliances. *Journal of Gay and Lesbian Issues in Education, 1*(3), 23–35.

McCready, L. T. (2004). Some challenges facing queer youth programs in urban high schools: Racial segregation and denormalizing whiteness. *Journal of Gay and Lesbian Issues in Education, 1*(3) 37–51.

McFarland, W. P., & Dupuis, M. (2001). The legal duty to protect gay and lesbian students from violence in school. *Professional School Counseling, 4*(3), 171–179.

Minor, R. N. (2001) Scared straight: Why it's so hard to accept gay people and why it's so hard to be human. St. Louis, MO: HumanityWorks!

Minor, R. N. (2003) Gay & healthy in a sick society: The minor details. St. Louis, MO: HumanityWorks!

Mock, B. (2007). Face right: Black religious opposition to gays rising. *Intelligence Report, 125,* 19–23.

National Education Association. (2006). *Strengthening the learning environment: A school employees' guide to gay, lesbian, bisexual, and transgender issues* (2nd ed.). Washington, DC: Author.

Oswald, R. F. (2001). Religion, family, and ritual: the production of gay, lesbian, bisexual and transgender outsiders-within. *Review of Religious Research, 43,* 39–50.

Rasmussen, M. L. (2005a). *Becoming subjects: Sexualities and secondary schooling.* Oxford, UK: Routledge.

Rasmussen, M. L. (2005b). Safety and subversion: The production of sexualities and genders in school Spaces. In M. L. Rasmussen, E. Rofes, & S. Talburt (Eds.), *Youth and sexualities: Pleasure, subversion, and insubordination in and out of schools* (pp. 131–152). New York: Palgrave Macmillan.

Remafedi, G. (Ed.). (1994). *Death by denial: Studies of suicide in gay and lesbian teenagers*. Boston: Alyson.

Rogers, J. B. (2006). *Jesus, the Bible, and homosexuality: Explode the myths, heal the church*. Louisville, KY: Westminister John Knox Press.

Rosario, M., Schrimshaw, E. W., Hunter, J., & Braun, L. (2006). Sexual identity development among lesbian, gay, and bisexual youths: consistency and change over time. *Journal of Sex Research, 43*(1), 46–58.

Rosick, C. H., Griffith, L. K., & Cruz, A. (2007). Homophobia and conservative religion: Toward a more nuanced understanding. *American Journal of Orthopsychiatry, 77*(1), 10–19.

Ryan, D., & April, M. (2000). Lesbian, gay, bisexual and transgendered parents in the school systems. *School Psychology Review, 29,* 207–216.

Smith, G. W. (1998, Spring). The ideology of "fag": The school experience of gay students. *The Sociological Quarterly, 39*(2), 309–335.

Williams, K., Doyle, M., Taylor, B., & Ferguson, G. (1992). Addressing sexual orientation in a public high school. *Journal of School Health, 62*(4), 154–156.

Internet Sites for Extending Thinking

http://www.createdgay.com/

Menu includes topics such as "what is homosexuality," homosexuals and the bible, Christianity and homosexuality, understanding transgender, and book reviews.

http://www.glsen.org/

Site of national organization fighting to end antigay bias in K–12 schools.

http://www.pflag.org/

Links to resources on relationships, antigay hate crimes; bibliography—by Parents, Families, and Friends of Lesbians and Gays.

http://www.project10.org/

Provides educational assistance for GLBT and questioning youth in public schools, including "Tips for Teachers" and "Tips for Administrators" sections.

http://www.safeschoolscoalition.org/

Resources, including handouts and publications, for teachers, students, and others. Some site features are in both English and Spanish.

http://www.gayscape.com/

A search tool for over 102,000 gay, lesbian, and bisexual Web sites, allowing searches by country or topic.

www.deafqueer.org/

A national nonprofit resource and information center for, by, and about the Deaf Lesbian, Gay, Bisexual, Transgender, Intersex, and Questioning communities.

www.ifge.org

The International Foundation for Gender Education advocates for freedom of expression of all people. The site has information on conferences, scholarships, and resources, including links to electronic sites, books, book reviews, and the like.

www.lamdalegal.org

Lambda Legal is a national organization committed to achieving full recognition of the civil rights of lesbians, gay men, bisexuals, transgender people, and those with HIV through impact litigation, education, and public policy work.

www.iglhrc.org

The site for the International Gay and Lesbian Human Rights Commission, whose mission is to secure the full enjoyment of the human rights of all people and communities subject to discrimination or abuse on the basis of sexual orientation or expression, gender identity or expression, and/or HIV status.

http://www.amnestyusa.org/outfront/index.do

The site of Amnesty International USA, which works to end abuse of LGBT persons, and protect and promote human rights of LGBT people within the United Nations (UN) and other international governmental bodies.

http://glaad.org/
The Gay and Lesbian Alliance Against Defamation, a national media organization, whose mission is to encourage accurate, fair, and inclusive lesbian and gay images in all forms of media.

http://www.ellabakercenter.org/
The Ella Baker Center for Civil Rights has programs and resources for mobilizing and challenging human rights abuses, advocating community based activism, and promoting policy reform.

http://www.alp.org/
The Audre Lorde Project is a GLBT, Two Spirit, People of Color Center for community organizing focusing on the New York City area.

http://www.binetusa.org
BiNet USA is an organization that offers resources to help promote understanding of bisexuality.

http://www.ngltf.org/
The National Gay and Lesbian Task Force is a leading organization supporting LGBT civil rights.

www.teachingtolerance.org/magazine
Lesson plans and other resources—including "A Rose for Charlie," a true story about a gay man who was killed in a hate crime in the 1980s.

www.pbs.org/wgbh/pages/frontline/shows/assault/
The PBS program *Frontline* explored the murder of Billy Jack Gaither in "Assault on Gay America."

www.challenginghomophobia.net/ch/rec_hp.asp
Allport's scale of prejudice, available (with case studies).

Chapter 9

Language

Introduction

Language is an integral part of culture and values, and as such, it has a profound impact on the daily lives of children and youth. Indeed, how teachers handle language issues will often affect the personal and cultural identity, as well as the academic success, of both native English-speaking students and English language learners (ELL students).

With increasing immigration comes an increasing need to be aware of real classroom issues of language acquisition and use. Many large urban school districts report upward of 60 or more languages spoken in the schools. The majority of schools in most areas of the country are experiencing an increase in numbers of ELL students.

A fundamental challenge for everyone, child or adult, is to understand other people's perspectives and expectations. Part of addressing this challenge is acknowledging that individuals whose cultures are different often have different rules for language use. The specific challenge for any educator is to adapt to diverse communicative needs and expectations in the classroom. This is no easy task, but it is a task that recognizes the crucial importance of effective communication. If it is left undone, the role of the teacher in enhancing the teaching and learning enterprise is substantially compromised (Garcia, 2002).

Knowing that ELL students have a limited amount of time in which to become English proficient puts added pressure on regular classroom teachers. Most regular classroom teachers can no longer rely on programs in which students are pulled out of their classes to learn English. In most schools, it is now up to teachers of social studies, science, math, and the other subjects offered to teach English. Adding to that pressure are the requirements that all students pass standardized tests to graduate.

The following terms and concepts may help in discussing the cases in Chapter 9.

bilingual
bilingual programs
Black English vernacular/Ebonics
culturally and linguistically diverse (CLD)
English language learners (ELL)
English as a second language
L1 (first language)
limited English proficiency (LEP)
low-incidence population

Definitions of key terms are included in the glossary of this text.

Case 31

You'll Need Both Black Vernacular and Standard English

A teacher considers varying opinions from colleagues regarding the acceptance of student use of Ebonics.

Mr. Drake had corrected the creative writing homework assignment from the previous day. He had wrestled with one particular paper written by Matt Williams, an African-American student who was new to the school. Mr. Drake was unsure how to handle Matt's use of Black English Vernacular (BEV). Throughout the paper were statements in which "be" was used as a finite verb, statements such as "He be happy and nice," and "When they both be home, they usually be working around the house." And there were other differences in the use of grammar, differences such as using "done" to note that an action had been completed, as in "She done finished it"; the use of double or triple negatives, as in "They ain't got no car"; and the use of *f* for *th* as in *wif* for *with*.

At lunch, Mr. Drake approached Ms. Grover, a trusted colleague in the classroom next to him. He showed her Matt's paper. Ms. Grover read several paragraphs and said, "If I were you, I'd tell him that if I accepted this form of language, he would never learn to operate in society—that he would be at a disadvantage when applying for jobs. Moreover, I'd tell him that Black English Vernacular is a deviation from correct, standard English." Mr. Drake thanked her for her advice.

Mr. Drake also shared his problem with Ms. Manning. He knew she was taking a continuing education course on sociolinguistics at a nearby college. She was interested in his dilemma.

"Would you like to hear a few lines about dialects from our course text?" she asked. Mr. Drake nodded affirmatively. Ms. Manning read from her textbook:

> The fact is, however, that standard English is only one variety among many, although a peculiarly important one. Linguistically speaking, it cannot even legitimately be considered better than other varieties. The scientific study of all language has convinced scholars that all languages, and correspondingly all dialects, are equally "good" as linguistic systems. All varieties of a language are structured, complex, rule-governed systems that are wholly adequate for their speakers. . . . There is nothing at all inherent in non-standard varieties that makes them inferior. Any apparent inferiority is due only to their association with speakers from underprivileged, low-status groups.*

**Socio linguistics: An Introduction to Language and Society,* by P. Trudgil, 1984, New York: Penguin Books, p. 20.

When she had finished reading, she told Mr. Drake of three students in her classes, each of whom used a different form of BEV. She explained to him that Amy, from New York, might say, for example, "Let's get ready to roll to the store," whereas Darnelle, a white student from Georgia, might say, "Let's be fiddin [fixing] to go to tha sto," and Dion, from Louisiana, would likely say, "We goin' to make groceries." It was clear to Mr. Drake that Black English varied by region, depending on the cultural context in which it was learned and used.

Mr. Drake thanked Ms. Manning for her comments. On his way home from school, Mr. Drake wondered how he should respond to Matt's use of Black English in his paper.

Questions for Reflection

1. What other information, if any, would you need to decide how you would respond to Matt?
2. Write verbatim how you would begin a conversation with Matt about his use of BEV. Include specific comments about how his use of BEV will affect his grade on this assignment and on other work in your class in the future. Include elements of good feedback (i.e., it is specific, constructive, substantive, and accurate).
3. How might your response affect Matt's learning, his sense of self-worth, and the socioemotional climate of your classroom?
4. What limits, if any, would you establish regarding the use of nonstandard English in your classroom?
5. How does the cultural context of the class, school, and community affect how you would respond to Matt?

Activities for Extending Thinking

1. Discuss with parents and teachers, including parents and teachers of color, the issue of allowing or encouraging the use of dialects in the classroom. Elicit their opinions regarding your policies and practices, as well as how flexible and responsive a teacher should be in accepting the use of dialects. Summarize your discussions in writing.
2. In thinking about how language might affect your plans for assessment, develop a list of guidelines that you feel would be assessment practices that would be fair to both the English language proficient and students who are not proficient in English. Further, review the FERPA (see Glossary) guidelines and tell how they might affect the assignment and reporting of grades to students.

Case 32

They Speak English and Spanish Well, but a Learning Disability Creates Problems in Reading and Writing

A teacher and principal discuss programs and resources for two Hispanic students, each of whom has a learning disability and limited language proficiency.

Ms. Perez was regarded by students and colleagues as a hardworking and well-respected first-year teacher at Central. She loved kids and wanted them to enjoy learning. She was warm and compassionate, had a good sense of humor, and at the same time, was clearly in charge of her classroom. She acted quickly and fairly when her young students needed guidance or correction. She spoke both English and Spanish fluently.

Ms. Perez was committed to designing lessons that were developmentally appropriate and that reflected the culturally diverse society in which her students would live. She learned quickly about the characteristics, needs, interests, and abilities of her students, and although she admitted to not having great knowledge about the many ethnicities, special abilities, and language acquisition needs of children, she worked hard at identifying resources that might supplement her knowledge. She attempted to motivate her students by helping them see the benefits of learning English, by structuring her activities so that students would experience success, and by providing models of community persons who confirmed her belief in the importance of the venture.

Two of Ms. Perez's Hispanic students, Rita and Ramona, in their third year in an English-speaking school, possessed highly developed conversational language skills in both English and Spanish and a learning disability (LD) resulting in limited reading and writing abilities. Ms. Perez had made certain that the learning disability had been properly diagnosed, for she knew that it takes much longer to learn academic English than conversational English and that sometimes educators assume that any reading and writing problems are LD problems. Both of the girls had been similarly diagnosed in the Spanish-speaking school they had attended before coming to Central.

Ms. Perez aggressively supported a more holistic, student-centered collaborative approach in which the girls would be placed in a general-education setting, experience an oral-based bilingual curriculum, and work on developing reading and writing in the content areas. Ms. Perez contacted special-service program personnel in bilingual and English as a Second Language (ESL) programs, special education, and counseling and worked with friends and colleagues to identify bilingual community members who could tutor the girls after school. She was indeed an advocate for culturally and linguistically diverse (CLD) students in her room.

It was in the fourth month of school when Ms. Perez had an idea that she felt needed to be discussed with the principal. One day during lunch break, she encountered Ms. Williams, the principal, in the cafeteria.

"Ms. Williams, I was wondering if it would benefit our staff and students if we were to offer some parent training programs that would improve parents' ability to help their children in reading, writing, and speaking," began Ms. Perez. "We could focus on practical interaction skills for building self-esteem and on positive approaches to learning to read and write. What do you think?"

"Sounds like a great idea!" replied Ms. Williams. "Mr. Lopez would have a lot to offer in the area of self-esteem, and we could identify other Latino role models as speakers. We could also see if those who come to the first session or two would want to establish support groups—perhaps neighborhood based—to conduct ongoing discussions of our sessions and of personally relevant problems. I think it could work!"

"I think so, too," said Ms. Perez. "And perhaps later on there will be opportunities to encourage parent input on making curriculum more culturally relevant and more accessible to all students. It might be one good way to empower parents."

"Let's bring it up at the next faculty meeting and see what we can do to move ahead. I'm all for it!" said Ms. Williams. She continued, "On a related topic, I've been wondering if Rita and Ramona should be moved to a self-contained classroom for learning-disabled students. They would be with students with similar needs, and the instruction would be in English, the language in which they need the most work. What do you think?"

Ms. Perez had always thought that the current general-education arrangement was the best for the two girls. At the same time, on other issues, she had usually agreed with Ms. Williams, whom she considered to be a wise administrator. She began to wonder: Would moving the girls from their current general-education program into the special-education class be good for them?

Questions for Reflection

1. What thoughts do you have about Ms. Perez's dilemma about a general versus special-education placement for Rita and Ramona?
2. How would you respond to the principal's proposal to move the girls to a self-contained special-education classroom? Provide a rationale for your response.
3. What other school and community resources for teachers would be helpful in dealing with CLD students?
4. What other school and community resources for CLD students would be helpful?
5. What suggestions would you have for modifying or expanding Ms. Perez's plan for a parent-education program?

Activities for Extending Thinking

1. Identify specific school and community resources available in a school in your area (perhaps a school in which you are currently involved in a field experience, or in which you are teaching) for CLD students and for students of other traditionally underrepresented groups.
2. Identify language and cultural-related parent-education programs in a local school (perhaps a school in which you are in a field experience or in which you are teaching). Briefly describe their goals, methods, and evidence of progress toward their goals.
3. Identify and interpret legal aspects of bilingual and special education, including major civil rights legislation, the Bilingual Education Act (also known as Title VII), the Individuals with Disabilities Education Act of 2004, and related case law.
4. On the Internet, explore state resources (e.g., state departments of education) and national resources for teachers and for students (e.g., U.S. Department of Education: www.ed.gov/index.html) that would serve you in curriculum planning in the future. Develop a list of other Web sites, such as Administration for Children and Families (www.acf.hhs.gov). Identify and explore other such general sites as well as those more specific to the instruction of CLD students. (Because URLs are subject to change, be prepared to search for the organizations themselves.)
5. Participate in an education listserv and/or newsgroup. Keep a journal of your participation.
6. Interview a parent of a CLD student to ascertain his or her views on how the school can provide better services for the child.

Case 33

A Bilingual Teacher's Aide Assesses His New School

A bilingual teacher's aide ponders specific strategies for helping teachers better understand their ESL and bilingual students' abilities, interests, prior knowledge, and individual needs.

It was the first day of school, and Andy Seng, a bilingual teacher's aide with 10 years of experience, entered his new school building. He was excited to meet the staff and students.

He had been pleased when he attended the workshop week prior to the first week of actual classes. He had seen "welcome" signs in several different languages posted above the doors. He had been greeted by bilingual volunteers, some of whom were students and some of whom were community members. He had noticed universal symbols and photos over important places, such as the bathrooms, cafeteria, library, and school office. Classrooms appeared to be good examples of text-rich environments with most items in the rooms labeled. He had also seen that many of the classrooms contained resource books in a number of different languages, and he had talked to teachers who said that they encouraged journal writing in the students' first language. All these factors, he thought, would help to develop a positive atmosphere for English as a Second Language (ESL) and bilingual students.

He and the principal had decided during workshop week that it might be useful for him to shadow one or two ESL students during the first day to get an idea of school and classroom policies and practices relative to ESL and bilingual pupils. On his first day, he followed two Vietnamese students, one throughout the morning, the other during the afternoon. Both had been placed in mainstreamed classrooms taught only in English.

At the end of each half day, he spoke with each student. "How did you like your morning?" he asked the first student, whose name was Hung. "It was confusing," Hung replied. "My teacher talked so fast and had the class work in small groups. Because I didn't know what to do, I just watched the other students. And later on the playground, the teacher had us play softball. She thought we'd all know how, but I had never heard of softball before. I was embarrassed."

When Andy asked Chau, the student he followed during the afternoon, Chau responded, "I think my teacher thinks I'm not as smart as the others. He gave me problems that were much simpler than those he gave to the other students." Chau paused. "After class some of the kids made fun of the lunch I brought from home—that made me feel bad."

Andy had worked as a teacher's aide for five years in each of two other schools. He knew that most teachers accepted, appreciated, and supported ESL and bilingual students. However, he had also seen a few teachers who had expectations that were either much too low or much too high for such students. Stereotypically, most cases of too-high expectations involved female students of Asian heritage; cases of too-low expectations usually involved Latino or African-American students. Based on his past experience, then, Chau's situation was an exception to the rule. Andy thanked both Hung and Chau for their responses and promised both of them that he would support them and other ESL and bilingual students throughout the term.

After school that day, Andy pondered ways that he might help teachers know more about the abilities, interests, and needs of each of their ESL and bilingual students. He knew that just telling teachers in a memo or even personally would not necessarily result in their knowing students better. He knew his goal was to be an advocate for students; now he just had to identify the strategies.

Questions for Reflection

1. Andy noted some positive steps the school and some individual teachers had taken to make students of other cultures feel more at home. What were they? What else could the school have done?
2. The students also mentioned some teacher behaviors that had a detrimental effect on student morale. What behaviors did they note? What would you have done differently in each case?

Teacher behaviors with detrimental effects	What I would have done
a.	a.
b.	b.
c.	c.

3. What kinds of information should teachers have about students in their classes? From what sources could they obtain each type of information?
4. Consider a school situation involving two students of another culture or of two different cultures—for example, two Russian students, or a Muslim and an Arab student, or a Native American and a Hispanic student. What cultural conflicts might arise?
5. What actions would you recommend that Andy take to address the problems he has encountered with Hung's and Chau's teachers? What cultural attributes must be taken into account when making these recommendations?

Activities for Extending Thinking

1. Discuss with officials of a local school the language diversity within that school. List the different languages spoken and the services for students who speak them. Include bilingual, ESL, and limited-English-proficiency (LEP) services and programs.

2. Talk with a bilingual and an ESL teacher to identify methods they use to promote academic learning and language development in their classrooms. Discuss what regular-education teachers can do to help ESL, bilingual, and LEP students achieve their course goals.
3. Talk with an ESL/ELL (English language learner) teacher about how to address issues of working in groups, accessing prior knowledge, accommodating different learning styles, and assessment as they pertain to LEP students. Summarize your key insights in writing (one to two pages).

Case 34

Computers and Culturally Diverse Learners

A teacher considers ways in which she can integrate computer technologies and cultural and individual preferences to more effectively meet the socioemotional and academic needs of her students.

Ms. Wright was pleased that for each of the past five years, the school had significantly increased the number of computers and software programs available to students. She believed, however, that neither computers nor software were culturally neutral, that they reflect the assumptions, expectations, and learning styles of their creators (usually white and male), and so she constantly looked for ways to integrate computer culture with the culture of individual students and the culture of the classroom.

To improve cross-cultural skills and intercultural understandings, Ms. Wright had developed an ongoing activity in which each of her students identified and communicated with a pen pal from another country. She was pleased that her classes were enthusiastic about using telecommunications technology to learn about the beliefs, behaviors, and values of persons of other cultures.

In activities involving research on the Internet, Ms. Wright encouraged multidirectional learning. She was as eager to learn from students as she was to have them learn from her. In addition, she encouraged students to help one another whenever possible.

Ms. Wright made every attempt to use computer technology to support a variety of individual and cultural differences. For example, she used visual and graphic representations preferred by some Native American students as a way of understanding; she established pairs and trios at computers as a way to meet the preference for cooperative learning of many black, Asian, and Hispanic students; and she provided an overview and review of material, thereby adding a more global, less-fragmented view preferred by many of her culturally diverse students. In each of her classes, Ms. Wright had several limited English proficiency (LEP) students of Russian, Croatian, and Puerto Rican heritage. Although her LEP students had demonstrated remarkable adaptability, their limited English proficiency kept them a bit behind the other students in learning course content. To accommodate her LEP students' need to learn English, Ms. Wright would often allocate the last 15 minutes of class for the LEP students to complete computer drill-and-practice programs on English grammar, usage, and punctuation. During this same time, non-LEP students would engage in enrichment computer programs requiring creative problem solving in the course content. Ms. Wright believed that this was the best way to attend to the particular needs of both groups of students. By the fifth week of the term, Juan and Vicki, two of her LEP students, had politely reported that the grammar and usage worksheets on the computer were "boring."

"We are learning some English, I guess," said Juan, "But I get tired of doing the same thing almost every day."

Ms. Wright replied, "I think that using technology to help me meet the differing needs of two groups of students is effective and efficient. This way I'm able to help you as well as the other students."

Juan and Vicki appeared unconvinced.

Questions for Reflection

1. What do you consider to be the strengths of Ms. Wright's attempts to use a variety of software programs to address the different learning styles of her diverse student body?
2. What would you change, if anything, about her approach?
3. Identify other modes of learning common to certain cultures, e.g., storytelling of many Somali groups, learning through observation common to certain Native American tribes, etc. How can educational technologies help address these cultural-related modes of learning?
4. What biases might be inherent in computer and related technologies? How would you adapt your approach to using computer technologies so as to eliminate such biases?
5. What other issues must teachers confront to achieve technology equity in their classrooms? For each issue identified, suggest a promising strategy, technique, or approach for addressing the issue.

Activities for Extending Thinking

1. Discuss with female students and students of color their assessment of the degree to which software on the Internet, on disk, and on CD-ROM is bias free and compatible with their styles of learning. Summarize key findings in writing.
2. Design a classroom activity in which students question software developers (programmers and designers) about the degree to which their products address cultural differences in users. Summarize your findings in writing.

Design Your Own Case

Language

Design a case that explores an issue of language diversity in the classroom. The story can focus on a method or strategy related to a single subject matter area (e.g., English or social studies) or on a more generic method or strategy pertinent to a wider range of subject matter areas. Your issue might also relate to:

- Planning and preparation
- Classroom environment
- Instruction
- Teacher responsibilities*

In selecting a topic, reflect on recent or current field experiences, personal experiences as a student, or accounts of real classroom incidents. Choose a topic that allows the reader to link theory and practice in the areas of learning, development, teaching, and of course, multicultural/cross-cultural education. Your topic of choice should also invite discussion of multiple perspectives rather that a singular viewpoint. Consider, too, the general level of experience and knowledge of the intended reader (i.e., whether they are in an early stage of the teacher education program or a more experienced/knowledgeable professional). Include some demographic data that tell a bit about the community, school, classroom, teacher, students, and curriculum. Include at least one problem for which there is no obvious solution. Use fictitious names of persons and schools to maintain confidentiality. Your case should be approximately two pages in length (typed, double-spaced) and should include three to four "Questions for Reflection" and one or two "Activities for Extending Thinking." Go to Resource C and use the form to design your own case.

*The four categories are from *Enhancing Professional Practice: A Framework for Teaching*, by C. Danielson, 1996, Alexandria, VA: Association for Supervision and Curriculum Development.

Readings for Extending Thinking

Alim, H. S., & Baugh J., (2007). *Talkin black talk: Language, education and social change*. New York: Teachers College Press.

Arias, A., Jr., & Bellman, B. (1990). Computer-mediated classrooms for culturally and linguistically diverse learners. *Computers in the schools, 7*(1–2), 227–241.

Artiles, A. J., & Trent, S. C. (1994). Overrepresentation of minority students in special education: A continuing debate. *Journal of Special Education, 27,* 410–437.

Baca, L. M., & Cervantes, H. T. (1989). *The bilingual special education interface* (2nd ed.). Upper Saddle River, NJ: Merrill/Prentice Hall.

Banks, J. A. (2006). *Cultural diversity and education: Foundations, curriculum, and teaching* (5th ed.). Boston: Allyn & Bacon.

Brinton, D., Goodwin, J., & Ranks, L. (1994). Helping language minority students read and write analytically: The journey into, through, and beyond. In F. Peitzman & G. Gadda (Eds.), *With different eyes* (pp. 57–88). Reading, MA: Addison Wesley Longman.

California Department of Education. (1990). *Bilingual education handbook: Designing instruction for LEP students*. Sacramento: Author.

Center for Multilingual, Multicultural Research. (n.d.). *Language policy and language rights*. Retrieved July 8, 2007, from http://www-rcf.usc.edu/~cmmr/Policy.html

Chan, J., & Chips, B. (1989). Helping LEP students survive in the content-area classroom. *Thrust, 18*(6), 49–51.

Chipongian, L. (2000). The cognitive advantages of balanced bilingualism. Retrieved May 5, 2005, from http://www.brainconnection.com/topics/printindex.php3?main=fa/cognitive-bilingualism.

Clark, K. (1999). *From primary language instruction to English immersion: How five California districts made the switch*. Washington, DC: READ (Institute for Research in English Acquisition and Development).

Cummins, J. (1994). From coercive to collaborative relations of power in the teaching of literacy. In R. M. Ferdman, R. M. Weber, & A. G. Ramírez (Eds.), *Literacy across languages and cultures* (pp. 3–29). Albany: State University of New York Press.

Cummins, J. (1996). Primary language instruction and the education of language minority students. In *Schooling and language minority students: A theoretical framework* (2nd ed., pp. 3–46). Los Angeles: Evaluation, Dissemination and Assessment Center, School of Education, California State University, Los Angeles.

Cummins, J. (1999). Alternative paradigms in bilingual education research: Does theory have a place? *Educational Researcher, 28*(7), 26–34.

Cummins, J. (2000). Beyond adversarial discourse: Searching for common ground in the education of bilingual students. In C. J. Ovando & P. McLaren (Eds.), *The politics of multiculturalism and bilingual education: Students and teachers caught in the cross fire* (pp. 126–147). Boston: McGraw-Hill.

Delgado-Gaitan, C., & Trueba, H. (1991). *Crossing cultural borders*. New York: Falmer Press.

Díaz, S., Moll, L. C., & Mehan, H. (1996). Sociocultural resources in instruction: A context-specific approach. In *Beyond language: Social and cultural factors in schooling language minority students* (pp. 187–230). Los Angeles: Evaluation, Dissemination and Assessment Center, School of Education, California State University, Los Angeles.

Díaz-Soto, L. (1991). Understanding bilingual/bicultural young children. *Young Children, 46*(2), 30–36.

Echevarria J. A., Vogt, M. J., & Short, D. J. (2010). *Making content comprehensible for elementary English teachers: The SIOP model*. Upper Saddle River, NJ: Pearson Allyn & Bacon.

Ferdman, B. M., & Weber, R. M. (1994). Literacy across languages and cultures. In B. M. Ferdman, R. M. Weber, & A. G. Ramírez (Eds.), *Literacy across languages and cultures* (pp. 3–29). Albany: State University of New York Press.

Gándara, P., Maxwell-Jolly, J., García, E., Asato, J., Gutiérrez, K., Stritkus, T., & Curry, J. (2000). *The initial impact of Proposition 227 on the instruction of English learners*. Davis: University of California Linguistic Minority Research Institute.

Garcia, E. (2000). *Student cultural diversity: Understanding and meeting the challenge* (3rd ed.). Boston: Houghton Mifflin.

Garcia, E. (2005). *Teaching and learning in two languages: Bilingualism and schooling in the United States*. New York: Teachers College Press.

Genishi, C., & Haas, A., (2009). *Children, language, and literacy*. New York: Teachers College Press.

Gersten, R. (1999). The changing face of bilingual education. *Educational Leadership, 56*(7), 41–45.

Gonzales, V., Brusca-Vega, R., & Yaukey, T. (1997). *Assessment and instruction of culturally and linguistically diverse students*. Boston: Allyn & Bacon.

Gottlieb, J., & Alter, M. (1995). *Overrepresentation of children of color referred to special education*. New York: New York University Department of Teaching Learning.

Griego-Jones, T. (1991). Rethinking programs for language minority students. *Journal of Educational Issues of Language Minority Students, 9,* 61–74.

Gunderson, L. (1991). *ESL literacy instruction: A guidebook to theory and practice*. Englewood Cliffs, NJ: Regents/Prentice Hall.

Hoover, J. J., Klinger, J. K., Baca, L. M., & Patton, J. M. (2008). *Methods for teaching culturally and linguistically diverse exceptional learners*. Upper Saddle River, NJ: Pearson.

Horowitz, E. K. (2007). *Becoming a language teacher: A practical guide to second language learning and teaching*. Boston: Allyn & Bacon.

Hughes, A. (2003). *Testing for language teachers*. New York: Cambridge University Press.

Joyce, B. (Ed.). (1990). *Changing school culture through staff development*. Alexandria, VA: Association for Supervision and Curriculum Development.

Kopcha, T. J., Grover, J. R., & Julian, M. F. (2007). *Six steps to ELL lesson design*. Retrieved from http://edweb.sdsu.edu/People/tkopcha/ELL%20website/index.html

Kriteman, R. (2008). *Teaching English language learners using equal doses of scaffolding and common sense*. Albuquerque, NM: Dual Language Education of New Mexico.

Kuhlman, N., & Murray, D. E. (2000). Changing populations, changing needs in teacher preparation. In M. A. Snow (Ed.), *Implementing the ESL standards for pre-K–12 students through teacher education* (pp. 33–48). Alexandria, VA: Teachers of Speakers of Other Languages.

Kumaravadivelu, B. (2008). *Cultural globalization and language education*. New Haven, CT: Yale University Press.

Ladson-Billings, G. (2005). *Beyond the big house: African American educators on teacher education*. New York: Teachers College Press.

Lee, C. D. (2007). *Culture, literacy, and learning: Taking bloom in the midst of the whirlwind*. New York: Teachers College Press.

Lucas, T., Villegas, A. M., & Freedson-Gonzalez, M. (2008). Linguistically responsive teacher education. preparing classroom teachers to teach English language learners. *Journal of Teacher Education, 59*(4), 361–373.

MacSwan, J. (2000). The threshold hypothesis, semilingualism, and other contributions to a deficit view of linguistic minorities. *Hispanic Journal of Behavior Sciences, 20*(1), 3–45.

May, S. (2008). *Language and minority rights: Ethnicity, nationalism and the politics of language*. New York: Routledge.

Minami, M., & Ovando, C. J. (2004). Language issues in multicultural contexts. In J. A. Banks & C. A. M. Banks (Eds.), *Handbook of research on multicultural education* (2nd ed., pp. 567–588). San Francisco: Jossey-Bass.

Moegher, M. E. (1995, October). Learning English on the Internet. *Educational Leadership, 53*(2), 88–90.

National Council for Languages and International Studies. (2004). *Language competence and cultural awareness in the United States*. Pamphlet. Washington, DC: Author.

National Forum on Personnel Needs for Districts with Changing Demographics. (1990, May). *Staffing the multilingually impacted schools of the 1990s*. Washington, DC: U.S. Department of Education.

Nielsen, D. (1998). *Second language acquisition and its effects on the social and emotional development of immigrant teens in a small midwestern middle school*. Unpublished doctoral dissertation. University of Nebraska, Lincoln.

Nieto, S. (1992). *Affirming diversity: The sociopolitical context of multicultural education*. New York: Longman.

OELA (Office of English Language Acquisition). (2004). National Clearinghouse for English Language Acquisition and Language Instruction Education Programs. Retrieved August 8, 2004, from www.NCELA.gwu.edu.

Ogbu, J. U. (1999). Beyond language: Ebonics, proper English, and identity in a Black-American speech community. *American Educational Research Journal, 36*(2), 147–184.

Ovando, C., Collier, P., & Coombs, M. C. (2003). *Bilingual and ESL classrooms: Teaching in multicultural contexts* (3rd ed.). New York: McGraw-Hill.

Ovando, C. J., & McLaren, P. (2000). *The politics of multiculturalism and bilingual education: Students and teachers caught in the cross fire*. Boston: McGraw-Hill.

Peregoy, S. F., & Boyle, O. F. (1993). *Reading, writing, and learning in ESL*. Reading, MA: Longman.

Peregoy, S. F., & Boyle, O. F. (2005). *Reading, writing, and learning in ESL*. (4th ed.). Boston: Pearson.

Plaut, S., (2009). *The right to literacy in secondary schools: Creating a culture of thinking*. New York: Teachers College Press.

Porter, R. P. (1999–2000). The benefits of English immersion. *Educational Leadership, 57*(4), 52–56.

Rothenberg, C. (2007). *Teaching English language learners*. Upper Saddle River, NJ: Pearson.

Salas, G. (2008). *Increasing reading literacy performance with at-risk elementary students through increased access to fiction/non-fiction resources and incorporating reader's theater.* Chicago: Saint Xavier University & Pearson Achievement Solutions. (ERIC Document Reproduction Service No. ED501061)

Smitherman, G. (1999). *Talkin that talk: Language, culture, and education in African America*. New York: Routledge.

Smitherman, G., & Villanueva, V. (2003). *Language diversity in the classroom: From intention to practice.* Carbondale: Southern University Press.

Snow, M. A. (Ed.). (2000). *Implementing the ESL standards for pre-K–12 students through teacher education*. Alexandria, VA: Teachers of Speakers of Other Languages.

Todd, L. (1997). Ebonics: An evaluation. *English Today, 13,* 13–17.

Tokuhama-Espinosa, Tracey. (2008). Living languages: multilingualism across the lifespan. New York: Praeger.

U.S. English, Inc. (2004, August). *States with official English laws*. Retrieved August 27, 2004, from http://www.us-english.org.

Internet Sites for Extending Thinking

http://www.eslpartyland.com/
Lesson plans, quizzes, discussion forums, and other engaging resources.

http://www.nabe.org/
National Association for Bilingual Education.

http://www.ncela.gwu.edu/
National Clearinghouse for English Language Acquisition.

http://www.cal.org/
Center for Applied Linguistics.

http://www.co-operation.org/
Cooperative Learning Center.

Chapter 10

Ageism

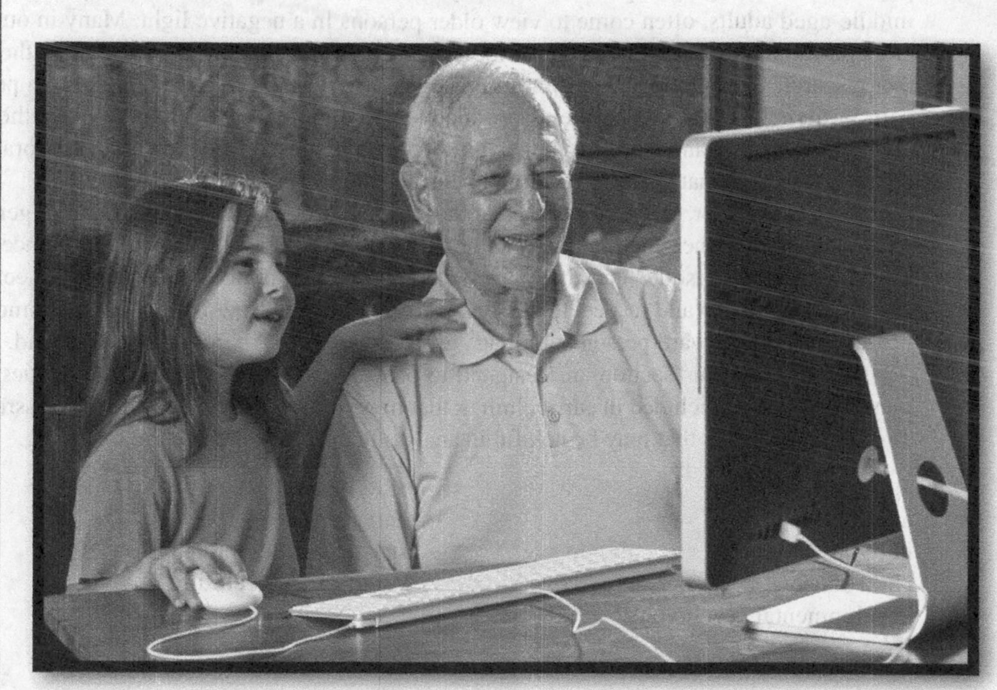

Introduction

Ageism, or bias toward persons of a particular age group, involves stereotypical thinking of persons of particular age groups. The two most commonly targeted groups are (1) adolescents and (2) the elderly (i.e., those over age 65).

Adolescents face many challenges, including neglect, abuse, substance abuse, anxiety, depression and suicide, poverty, sexual behavior issues, and violence, to name a few. At the same time, they often are stereotyped as irresponsible and self-centered and as druggies, gang-bangers, dumb jocks, nerds, and the like. Values, norms, and expectations of adolescents vary by race, gender, social class, and the like. For example, in some cultural groups, pregnancy at the chronological age of 12 or 13 is perfectly acceptable—even encouraged—whereas in other cultures, it is judged to be inappropriate and unacceptable. Adolescents are exposed to an often confusing variety of values and societal/cultural expectations.

In addition to working through their own often confusing and otherwise difficult age-related issues, children and adolescents develop thoughts, opinions, and values related to persons in other age groups. Influenced by others, including the media, they, as well as middle-aged adults, often come to view older persons in a negative light. Many in our society promote the notion that aged or elderly persons cannot be productive, despite the fact that research shows they have lower absentee and accident rates, are more likely to persevere in their job, and indeed are as productive as young workers (Schultz & Salthouse, 1999). Although many learn to view adulthood as a process of decline and deterioration, research suggests that sometimes aging opens new doors and invites new interests.

As noted earlier, views of persons of various age groups will vary by culture, gender, social class, and other such factors. Some cultures view their elderly with reverence, acknowledging the wisdom that they have to offer the community. Other cultures seem to give less admiration and respect to persons who are older. Teachers can assist in promoting healthy attitudes toward persons of all age groups, regardless of cultural background.

The cases in this section are designed to provide examples of age-related issues that may be purposely included in curriculum or that may occur spontaneously in the classroom. Terms and concepts that may be helpful in analyzing the cases include the following.

aged
ageism
bullying
child abuse
developmental psychology
elderly
harassment
stages of development
youth-oriented culture

Definitions of key terms are located in the glossary of this text.

Case 35

Age as a Factor in Bullying and "Cyberbullying"

A teacher responds to instances of older students harassing younger students.

"Word has it that peer mediation has solved your problem with the older girls on the volleyball team—is that true?" Ms. Wheeler asked Tanisha, a younger and new member of the team. "Yep—I guess. As long as Becky and Liz keep their end of the bargain. They're not to pick on me and my friends anymore, just 'cause we're new to the team and just 'cause they're older." "I'm glad to hear you've agreed to get along," said Ms. Wheeler.

Ms. Wheeler knew both the older and the younger group of girls. Each group was diverse in many ways, including race, ethnicity, socioeconomic status, and language. Hence, she had concluded that the key factor in this conflict between the groups was age. Ms. Wheeler knew that the harassment had been extended beyond school hours through the use of the Internet on sites such as MySpace, Facebook, and Twitter. She knew all too well that e-mail messages and Web logs enabled intimidating messages to be more humiliating, as gossip, ugly epithets, and even embarrassing pictures are circulated more widely and are less apparent to adults.

In fact, she had recalled in talking with the school psychologist about "cyberbullies" that several factors—the distance between the bully and the victim, the typical lack of impulse control of young students, and underdeveloped empathy skills—seemed to converge, often resulting in particularly brutal harassment. The psychologist had shared knowledge of cases at other schools in which students had been identified as "sexually active," "boring," "racist," and the like. She was even aware of an instance where a young male student had made a video of himself singing to a girl he liked, who immediately posted it all over the Internet. Cell phones with photo and video capabilities brought a similar set of potential problems.

Ms. Wheeler recalled, too, that when she had taught another grade level, similar harassment problems had occurred, albeit with two groups of boys. In those situations too, each group had noticeable diversity except for age. Age seemed to be a factor in a number of situations of which she was familiar.

Questions for Reflection

1. Identify issues or conflicts that you've experienced as a student that may be age related. What teacher behavior may help prevent such conflicts?

   Conflict or Issue — Teacher Preventative

   a.

   b.

2. Once age-related conflicts have occurred, what conflict mediation strategies might you recommend for addressing each issue? Integrate research on best practice as you respond to this question.

   Conflict — Response

   a.

   b.

   c.

3. Think about question #2 in terms of technology-related issues (e.g., MySpace, Facebook, cell phones, video technologies). Identify conflicts and responses that you know about or that you can imagine.

   Conflict — Response

   a.

   b.

   c.

4. In your subject matter, identify resources (e.g., children's or adolescent literature sources, videos/DVDs) that could be used to support lessons that deal with age. (Topics may include early or middle childhood, adolescent development, drug use, anxiety, depression and suicide, dating, and others.)

   Resources for Students

   a.

   b.

   c.

   d.

   e.

5. How important is it to help students think about issues related to age—issues such as age stereotyping, sexual harassment, drug and alcohol use, anxiety, depression and suicide, bullying/"cyberbullying," and care for the aged? Which of these and what other topics would you be able to address in your subject matter area?

Subject Matter Area Topic

a.

b.

c.

Activities for Extending Thinking

1. Using professional standards from teacher education or standards from your subject matter area, outline (on one page) general ideas for a project on an age-related issue that you could assign in a class that you will likely teach.

   Identify several Internet sites that deal with an age-related issue and provide a one-paragraph description of each site. Identify two to three print resources and two to three videos or DVDs (media products) that appear to be appropriate for your project and provide a one-paragraph description of each.

   Internet Site Description

   a.

   b.

   c.

   Print Resource Description

   a.

   b.

   Media Resource Description

   a.

   b.

2. Discuss with local school officials steps they have taken or steps they feel should be taken to prevent technology-related harassment among students, both during and after school hours. Include interview questions related to developing a positive classroom/school climate, student and staff training, support of the victims, identification of and consequences for bullies, and related issues. List steps taken and those that they would recommend.

   a. Steps taken

      1.

      2.

   b. Steps they would recommend

      1.

      2.

Case 36

The Wages We Will Get as Adults Will Pay for the Elderly? What's Up with That?

A lesson on Social Security causes students to wonder why they must pay for someone else's support.

"You say that when we are working the government will take money from our wages to pay for the care of old people? That's not fair! Why don't their wages cover them and ours cover us? If we work for it, we should get it when we're older!" asserted Dominique. Several others added their usual, "Yeah, what's the deal?" A final somewhat muffled comment came from the back of the room—"Yeah, what the f_ _ _"

Mrs. Bonds replied, "You know the generation of folks behind you will contribute a part of their wages to support you when you are older. So in that way, everyone wins, right?"

"I'd rather not support people I don't even know. And how do we know they won't change the system by the time we're old—maybe we won't get anything," chimed Michael.

Mrs. Bonds recognized the "What's in it for me?" orientation of her students. She thought to herself— they're at the third stage of moral reasoning—OK, we can work with that.

Mrs. Bonds altered her approach. "Actually your grandparents, parents, and their friends as well as some of your neighbors are in the group that you'll support. Does that make a difference? Would you be more willing to support relatives through Social Security?"

The class was quiet for a moment—they seemed to be considering Mrs. Bonds' comment.

"Well, if I knew my money was going for their care, I guess it'd be OK," replied Juan.

"Yeah," said Mai, "my folks and grandparents deserve good care, and I'd be happy to contribute."

Questions for Reflection

1. Should Mrs. Bonds have expanded the discussion of social/cultural values of the aged, e.g., the high value placed on youth culture in this country? Why or why not?
2. What additional questions or comments could Mrs. Bonds have made to expand student thinking about societal values regarding care for the aged?
3. What lessons could you design in your subject matter area that would help students consider social/cultural attitudes and/or values on aging?

4. List two to three alternative responses that a teacher could use in responding to profanity such as expressed in this case. Each response should represent a slightly different approach and/or draw on a variety of strategies for addressing the issue of profanity in the classroom.

Activities for Extending Thinking

1. Outline requirements/guidelines for a P–12 student project that involves student interviews of older members of your culture regarding the care of the elderly. Specify a general interview topic and write out three to four sample interview questions on that topic. Identify two to three student resources for students to examine.
2. Outline requirements for a P–12 student project similar to that in activity #1, but which involves age-related practices of members of a culture other than that of the students' own.

Case 37

You're Teaching Our Kids to Disrespect the Elderly?

Parents misinterpret a teacher's intent in a lesson on age and culture.

"I understand you taught a lesson last Friday in which you suggested that the elderly are of little value to anyone—that they can be disregarded—indeed *should* be disregarded in certain situations," asserted a parent on the phone.

The teacher, Ms. Rice was stunned. "No, honestly, I would never do that," she replied. "The lesson was about certain groups of nomadic Eskimos who often travel great distances with limited supplies of food. It's a fact that when faced with only enough food left to feed part of the group, that it was understood as a cultural norm, that the oldest would volunteer to be left in the wilderness to perish. We did not suggest that in our culture we should also follow that practice. In fact, a number of students stated how gratifying it was to know that our culture does so much to provide for the elderly with nursing homes, in-home care, and other support for the elderly. In the final analysis, I feel that there was unanimous agreement that we should continue and even expand the resources to provide for our aged," explained Ms. Rice.

"I doubt if that point got across to many of the students. My son certainly didn't hear it that way." replied Ms. Carroll. "The way my son stated it was, 'If you have to make such hard decisions, the Eskimos have a good point—favor the young who have more strength to continue and ensure the survival of the species.' That's not promoting the welfare of the older citizens, is it? Why even bring up the survival problems of nomadic people? That'll never happen to us," complained the caller.

"I feel students need to understand the dilemmas, customs, and values of other cultures. Moreover, wrestling with moral dilemmas helps them clarify their own thinking about such important issues. Perhaps some day they'll advocate expanded care for the aged."

"Well, I don't like it, and neither do the other parents I've talked to. We don't want you planting seeds that are contrary to our beliefs. We're contacting Principal Hunter to have this curriculum modified. I'll ask that she have you drop any materials and all lessons that may mislead students regarding social values on aging."

After the phone conversation, Ms. Rice reflected on the surprising call. She recalled that in previous years, student evaluation forms had high ratings for the set of lessons on Eskimo culture. She remembered that in addition, a number of students had told her that the readings and discussion had really made them think and that they felt they and the class had more compassion for people—especially older people—as a result of their study. She headed for her evaluation file to gather the data she'd need to support her case with the principal.

Questions for Reflection

1. Might there have been steps Ms. Rice could have taken to prevent such parent misunderstanding?
2. What should she do now that a number of parents have misunderstood her intent?
3. What lessons in your subject matter area(s) might be useful lessons on culture and age? List three potential lesson topics.

Subject Matter Area	Lesson Topics
a.	a.
b.	b.
c.	c.

Activities for Extending Thinking

1. Design a student project in your subject matter area in which P–12 students research how age relates to another diversity area (e.g., race, gender, religion). Provide two to three project goals and two to three activity ideas in outline form.
2. Identify commonly held stereotypes of teenagers.

a.	d.
b.	e.
c.	f.

   List ways you as a teacher could counter these stereotypes in a course that you may teach.
3. Identify commonly held stereotypes of the elderly (those over 70 years of age).

a.	d.
b.	e.
c.	f.

   List ways you as a teacher could counter these stereotypes in a course that you might teach.
4. Conduct a research study on a culture that honors its elderly. Summarize key points to share with the class.

Case 38

Age-Related Cultural Needs of Children and Youth

A teacher reflects on the various age-related needs of her students and wonders which needs might be culturally based.

It was the half-way through fall term, the time of year that Ms. Middleton usually assessed the degree to which she had been meeting her students' needs. At the beginning of the year she had reviewed her personal collection of teacher education materials and had identified what she felt were the most prevalent cognitive, emotional, physical, social, and moral needs of her students. She had checked various developmental theories, in an attempt to identify the stages at which her students might be operating, always keeping in mind that some students may be at a different stage than that of most students of a particular age. Just this morning she had told her student teacher: "I've found developmental theories to be helpful in predicting the usual stages and behaviors of students, but I also have known individuals who were exceptions to what the theories predict."

Her students did, indeed, seem to fit the profiles suggested by scholars. She observed physical changes in size and strength; cognitive changes in ability to do some abstract thinking, question adult values, and increased daydreaming; and socioemotional shifts including increased sensitivity to criticism, moodiness, heightened self-consciousness, disturbances in self-esteem, and the need for both privacy and, at the same time, the need to be understood. She had also seen social needs in play, such as the increase in peer influence and the strong need for peer relationships. Furthermore, Ms. Middleton sensed the interaction of these age-related changes with other diversity areas such as race, ethnicity, gender, and the like. She believed, for instance, that members of target groups, such as students of color, of a GLBT orientation, and so on, would have experienced the same types of criticism experienced by white, straight students, as well as criticism related to their race and/or gender orientation group membership. She wondered if such additional negativity would tend to lead to lower self-esteem, with concomitant reduction in motivation, and academic and social success.

When Ms. Middleton thought about cultural needs of students, she thought first of general notions about target groups, or as she often thought of them, as "microcultures." Her impression was that members of microcultures often tend to be more group (e.g., family, neighborhood) oriented, more cooperative (versus competitive), and more relationship or socially oriented. She thought, for example, of many of her Hispanic/Latino students who came to school expecting shows of affection from teachers like those they experienced at home.

In addition to the general cultural needs about which she needed to know, Ms. Middleton sought to learn more specifics about age-related cultural needs of her students. For example, on this Monday morning in October, she had asked her students: "What cultural history, heritage, or culture do you feel you want or need to know more about?"

Marcela replied: "I would like to do a project on contributions of Hispanic/Latino people to the history and culture of the United States of America." Gloria, stated: "I would like to identify positive models representing my Japanese heritage." Others gave similar responses related to learning about their cultural heritage. Even white students wanted to learn more about their distinct cultural origins and the contributions that their ethnic groups have made to society.

The comments from the students seemed to correspond to the work of a scholar (Manning, 2000), whose workshop she had attended recently. At that workshop, three culturally related developmental characteristics were identified. First, young adolescents form cultural identities; second, they form close friends, social networks, and opinions of the similarities and differences of others; and third, they develop a sense of justice and fairness related to how people should be treated. Ms. Middleton pondered, "How can I be developmentally and culturally responsive to my students?"

Questions for Reflection

1. Identify four to five multicultural educational experiences that the teacher in this story can use to meet the cultural and developmental needs of her young adolescent students.
2. Considering the age of the students you hope to teach (or do teach), what developmental needs do they have in general? (You may want to use the groupings of K–3, 4–6, 7–9, and 10–12, or similar groupings.)
3. What more specific culturally related developmental needs do they possess? For example, if you anticipate teaching students of African-American descent, what age-related needs do you expect them to have, and how might you address those needs?
4. What are some techniques for dealing with differing age-related views within a specific culture, for example, a traditional view in which marriage partners are arranged by the adults in the family, versus the view in which the individual selects his/her partner? Identify 2–3 issues with differing views, and suggest an approach/strategy with which you could address each issue in your classroom.

Activities for Extending Thinking

1. Discuss the issues in this case and the "Questions for Reflection" above with K–12 students. Summarize your findings in writing.
2. Explore the work of other scholars on cultural/developmental needs of students. Summarize your findings in writing.
3. Discuss with other experienced teachers and/or administrators, the issues in this case. Summarize your findings in writing.

Design Your Own Case

Ageism

Design a case that would help classmates explore issues related to diversity in age. The story can focus on a method or strategy related to a single subject matter area (e.g., English or social studies) or on a more generic method or strategy pertinent to a wider range of subject matter areas. Your issue might also relate to:

- **Planning and preparation**
- **Classroom environment**
- **Instruction**
- **Teacher responsibilities***

In selecting a topic, reflect on recent or current field experiences, personal experiences as a student, or accounts of real classroom incidents. Choose a topic that allows the reader to link theory and practice in the areas of learning, development, teaching, and of course, multicultural/cross-cultural education. Your topic of choice should also invite discussion of multiple perspectives rather that a singular viewpoint. Consider, too, the general level of experience and knowledge of the intended reader (i.e., whether they are in an early stage of the teacher education program or a more experienced/knowledgeable professional). Include some demographic data that tell a bit about the community, school, classroom, teacher, students, and curriculum. Include at least one problem for which there is no obvious answer. Use fictitious names of persons and schools to maintain confidentiality. Your case should be approximately two pages in length (typed, double-spaced) and should include three to four "Questions for Reflection" and one or two "Activities for Extending Thinking." Go to Resource C and use the form to design your own case.

***The four categories are from *Enhancing Professional Practice: A Framework for Teaching*, by C. Danielson, 1996, Alexandria, VA: Association for Supervision and Curriculum Development.**

Readings for Extending Thinking

Allen, S. D., Runell, M., Varghese, R., Williams, T. O., Adams, M., & Whitlock, E. R. (2004). Review of the year's publications for 2003: Social justice education. *Equity & Excellence in Education, 37*(4).

Atchley, R., (2009). *Spirituality and aging: Expanding the view*. Baltimore: Johns Hopkins University Press.

Bayor, R., (2004). *Columbia documentary history of race and ethnicity in America*. New York: Columbia University Press.

Bonnie, R. J., & Wallace, R. B. (Eds.). (2003). *Elder mistreatment: Abuse, neglect, and exploitation in an aging America*. Washington, DC: National Academies Press.

Brown, H. (2003). Schools take on studies of child labor. *Education Week, 22*(31), 1–14.

Centers for Disease Control and Prevention, National Center for Health Statistics. (2005). *Vital and health statistics,* Series 13. Washington, DC: U. S. Government Printing Office.

Chittister, J. (2008). *The gift of years: Growing older gracefully*. New York: BlueBridge.

Crawford, P. A. (2000). Crossing boundaries: Addressing ageism through children's books. *Reading Horizons, 40*(3), 161–174.

Diamond, P. A., & Orszag, P., (2004). *Saving social security: A balanced approach.* Washington DC: Brookings Institution.

Edwards, C. H. (2005). *Teaching and learning in middle and secondary schools*. Upper Saddle River, NJ: Pearson Merrill/Prentice Hall.

Forman, B. I. (1985). Addressing ageism in the schools. *Curriculum Review, 25,* 10–12.

Fried, S. B., & Mehrotra, C. M. (2000). *Teaching diversity and aging through active learning strategies: An annotated bibliography*. Parkville, MO: Park College & Duluth, MN: The College of St. Scholastica. (ERIC Document Reproduction Service No. ED437572)

Gelofand, D., (2003). *Aging and ethnicity: Knowledge and services,* New Your: Springer.

Gullette M. M. (2004). *Aged by culture*. Chicago: University of Chicago Press.

Helman, R., VanDerhei, J., & Copeland, C. (2008, April). *2008 retirement confidence survey: Americans much more worried about retirement, health costs a big concern.* EBRI Issue Brief 316, 1–22.

Jakobi, P. (1999). Using the World Wide Web as a teaching tool: Analyzing images of aging and the visual needs of an aging society. *Educational Gerontology, 25*(6), 581–593.

Johnson, S., (1994). *Book of elders: The life stories of great American Indians*. San Francisco: Harper.

Judd, A. (2007). *The value of later life: Deconstructing the idea of aging as decline.* Paper presented to Macalester College Psychology Department, St. Paul, MN.

Kellough, R. D., & Kellough, N. G. (2003). *Teaching young adolescents: A guide to methods and resources* (4th ed.). Upper Saddle River, NJ: Merrill/Prentice Hall.

Kitwana, B. (2005). *Why white kids love hip-hop: Wangstas, wiggers, wannabees, and the new reality of race in America.* New York: Basic Civitas Books.

Kroger, J. (2007). *Identity development: Adolescence through adulthood.* Thousand Oaks, CA: Sage.

Krout, J. A., & Wasyliw, Z. (2002). Infusing gerontology into grades 7–12 social studies curricula. *Gerontologist, 42*(3), 387–391.

Kupetz, B. N. (1994). Ageism: A prejudice touching both young and old. *Day Care and Early Education, 21,* 34–37.

Langer, N. (1999). Changing youngsters' perceptions of aging: Aging education's role. *Educational Gerontology, 25*(6), 549–554.

Larue, G. A., & Seymour, R. (2005). *Teaching respect: Giving children an understanding of their elders.* Kingston, RI: Papier-Mache Press.

Manning, M. L. (2000, April). *Developmentally responsive multicultural education for young adolescents.* Paper presented at the Association for Childhood Education International, Baltimore, MD.

Martin, L. G., & Soldo, B. J. (Eds.). (1997). *Racial and ethnic differences in the health of older Americans,* Washington DC: National Academy Press.

McGuire, S. L. (1993). Reduce ageism in kids by screening what they read. *Educational Digest, 59*(4), 63.

McGuire, S. L. (2003). Growing up and growing older: Books for young readers. *Childhood Education, 79*(3), 145–151.

National Institute of Mental Health. (2008). *Older adults: Depression and suicide facts.* Washington, DC: Author.

Nelson, T. (Ed.). (2002). *Ageism: Stereotyping and prejudice against older persons.* Cambridge, MA: MIT Press, Bradford Books.

Peacock, E. W., & Talley, W. M. (1984). Intergenerational contact: A way to counteract again. *Educational Gerontology, 10*(1–2), 13–24.

Population Reference Bureau. (1999). *Aging in the United States: An education module.* Washington, DC: Author.

Schultz, R., & Salthouse, T., (1999). *Adult development and aging: Myths and emerging realities* (3rd ed.). Upper Saddle River, NJ: Prentice Hall.

Scott, T., Minichiello, V., & Browning, C. (1998). Secondary school students' knowledge of and attitudes toward older people. *Ageing & Society, 18*(2), 167.

Sheldon, J. P. (1998). Addressing stereotypes and ageism in a life span development course. *Teaching of Psychology, 25*(4), 291–293.

Sorgman, M. I., & Sorenson, M. (1984). Ageism: A course of study. *Theory into Practice, 23*(2), 117.

Stevenson, C. (2002). *Teaching ten to fourteen year olds* (3rd ed.). Boston: Allyn and Bacon.

Thornton, J. E. (2002). Myths of ageing or ageist stereotypes. *Educational Gerontology, 28*(4), 301–302.

Wircenski, M., Walker, M., Allen, J., & West, L. (1999). Age as a diversity issue in grades K–12 and in higher education. *Educational Gerontology, 25*(6), 491.

Yee, B. W. K. (1992, Summer). Elders in Southeast Asian refugee families, *Generations,* 24–27.

Zembeck, B.A., and Singer, A., (1990). The problem of defining retirement among minorities: The Mexican Americans, *The Gerontologist, 30*(6): 749–757.

Internet Sites for Extending Thinking

Anxiety, Panic Disorder, Depression

http://www.adaa.org
Anxiety Disorders Association

http://www.nasponline.org/resources/cyberbullying/index.aspx
The National Association of School Psychologists and CyberSmart! provide K–12 lessons free to schools wanting to prevent cyberbullying at the classroom level and offer outreach to families and the community. Also contains related links.

http://www.nlm.nih.gov/medlineplus/copyright.html
Federal government Medline Plus

http://en.wikipedia.org/wiki/Ageism
Examples, responses, and links to further reading on ageism (from Wikipedia)

http://www.webster.edu/~woolflm/ageismlist.html
Includes theoretical basis, relationship of ageism to self-concept, gender and ageism, cross-cultural perspectives, and psychology and ageism (by L. Woolf, Webster University)

http://www.csriu.org
Offers strategies to help young people behave in a responsible, legal, and safe manner when using technology

http://www.wiredsafety.org
Provides information to internet and mobile device users of all ages, including to related sites, help with identity and credential theft, online fraud and cyberstalking, hacking, and malicious code attacks

Resource A

Creating Additional Context for a Given Case

It is important to bring your own knowledge and personal purpose to the analysis of a given case. Hence, the context of each case has not been highly prescribed. For example, the cases do not indicate grade level, thereby allowing a variety of readers to bring their own grade-level context to the case.

Therefore, prior to analyzing a given case, you are invited to modify its context. Your instructor will help decide which cases might be modified and the extent of the modifications and will direct you to do so individually, in small groups, or as a class.

When so directed by your instructor, include factors that make the case richer, more authentic, or more personally meaningful to you, your small group, or your class. You may want to re-create a context that resembles a school in which you are currently completing a field experience or in which you are teaching, or you may want to create a setting representing the type of school that you hope to work in some day. Include one or two factors from the following categories.

Characteristics of the community. You might include such factors as proportion of socioeconomic, ethnic, and religious groups, etc., as well as the sociopolitical attitudes of various community groups.

Characteristics of the school. You might include demographics related to the ethnic, religious, special needs, etc.; makeup of the student body; curricular and extracurricular emphases of the school; and recent school reform efforts.

Nature of the characters and the classroom. You might include information such as student characteristics (e.g., physical appearance, social abilities, mannerisms and behavioral habits, intellectual abilities, and teaching or learning styles) or grade level of the class, physical arrangement of the classroom, type of curriculum, and daily schedule of the classes.

In summary, prior to analyzing each case assigned by your instructor, take a few minutes to list two or three additional contextual variables that you believe are important.

Possible Cultural Contexts

Each of the cases will generate a richer and more meaningful discussion if it is set in an authentic educational and cultural context. To that end, several options are possible:

Scenario 1. Decide that the school and classroom in which the case takes place are very diverse—with high proportions of students of color, lower socioeconomic status, disability, and the like greater than those of the general population. (See Table 1.1 and Table 1.2 for estimated populations of minority groups in the United States.)

Scenario 2. Specify that the diversity in the community, school, and classroom in which the case takes place is equal to that of the general population.

Table 1.1 Estimated Population of Ethnic Groups in the United States, According to Race and Hispanic, Jewish, and Muslim Origins, 1990

Race	***Percentage***
All Persons	***100.0***
White Americans	80.3
African Americans	12.1
American Indians, Eskimos, or Aleuts	0.8
American Indians	0.8
Aleuts	0.0
Asians or Pacific Islanders	2.9
Chinese Americans	0.7
Japanese Americans	0.3
Asian Indians	0.3
Korean Americans	0.3
Vietnamese	0.2
Native Hawaiians	0.1
Samoans	0.0
Guamanians	0.0
Other Asians or Pacific Islanders	0.3
Other	3.9
Hispanic Origin	
All persons	***100.00***
Hispanic Origin	9.0
Mexican	5.4
Puerto Rican	1.1
Cuban	0.4
Other Hispanic	2.0
Not of Hispanic Origin	91.0
Jewish and Muslim Origin	
All Persons	***100.0***
Jewish	2.8
Muslim	2.1

Source: Bennett, C. L. *Comprehensive multicultural education: Theory and practice* (3rd ed.). Copyright © 1995 by Allyn & Bacon. Reprinted/adapted by permission.

Table 1.2 Estimated Percentage of Children in Poverty; with Disabilities and of Gay/Lesbian/Bisexual Orientation

Poverty	***Percentage***
Children under the age of 18 who are poor (Reed & Sautter, 1990)	20
Exceptionality	
Children identified as having disabilities for purposes of special education services (U.S. Department of Education, 1994)	7.4
Sexual Orientation	
Persons of gay/lesbian/bisexual orientation (Kalota et al., 1994)	10

Scenario 3. Specify that the diversity in the case school is equal to that of the school in which you are completing or have completed a field experience. It is recommended that this option be selected only when a specific and significant need suggests it. For example, if a school in which you work as a teacher's aide, a student teacher, or a teacher is 98% white and has recently experienced racial tension, you might decide to add such issues to a given case.

In addition to the types of diversity outlined in the tables, students in schools vary in other ways, including language, religious affiliation, and national creed. The reader is referred to other multicultural education sources for statistics on other groups and for additional data on the groups cited earlier.

Based on the percentages of various groups in the United States, as listed in Tables 1.1 and 1.2, the composition of a "typical" classroom of 30* students would be as shown in Table 1.3.

Table 1.3 Composition of a Classroom of 30 students*

Students	***Number***
White	20
African American	4
Asian	1
American Indian	1
Hispanic	3
Jewish	1
Muslim	1
Poor	6
With disabilities	2–3
Gay/lesbian/bisexual	3

*Based on estimated population of ethnic, socioeconomic class, poverty, exceptionality, and sexual orientation.

*Because a given student may well belong to more than one group, the total number of students listed exceeds 30.

Obviously, such a "typical" class rarely exists. It is constructed here for those who would want to set the cases provided in a classroom representing the diversity of persons in the general population. Because the student bodies in many schools consist of much greater proportions of ethnic diversity than does the general population, when analyzing a given case you should assume that the story takes place in such a school. Doing so will better prepare you for a career that might well include teaching in a school with a rich diversity of students.

Once you have predetermined the ethnic, socioeconomic, religious, exceptionality, and sexual orientation of the students in a case, establish other classroom, school, and community characteristics that will further provide the context for the case. For example, one could specify factors such as the following:

- Number of students served in the school
- Number of students in the particular classroom
- School budget
- Performance levels of students on statewide achievement tests

Furthermore, you could specify the following:

- Whether the school tracks students into several levels
- Whether the school has access to tutors and student teachers in a teacher education program in a local college
- The structure of the academic day (i.e., class schedule, etc.)
- Whether the school has stand-alone and online access to sophisticated computer and related technologies
- Whether the school has a well-developed parent-involvement program

Examples of contexts that might be designed as a basis for the analysis of a given case follow.

Example I. Longfellow School serves 1,000 low- and low-middle-income students living in the inner city. Typical classroom size is 25 students. The student body is 40% African American, 10% Hispanic American, 5% Asian American, 5% Native American, and 40% white. Approximately 20% of these students are Jewish. Student scores on standardized achievement tests are in the 70th percentile. The school divides students into three tracks. Thirty-nine percent of graduates go on to college. Reform efforts have moved the school to the fore in terms of offering a well-developed multicultural curriculum.

Example II. Lincoln School in a city of 40,000 serves 500 low-SES pupils. The student body is 70% white, 20% Native American, and 10% African American. Approximately 40% of the students come from farms. Fifty percent of pupils come from single-parent families, and half are from families that claim to be devoutly Catholic. Class size in Lincoln is 30 students per room. Each room has two computers with Internet interface, and two computer labs of 20 computers each are available to teachers. Except for the progressive approach to technology, the curriculum is relatively traditional. Parent involvement in school activities is low.

Each of these examples emphasizes different characteristics in terms of ethnicity, SES, religion, family structure, curriculum, and the like. Each could have been more or less elaborate, depending on the nature of the case to be analyzed, the needs and interests of the students analyzing the case, and the goals of the course or workshop within which the case is used.

Resource B

Banks's Approaches for the Integration of Multicultural Content

Approach	***Description***	***Examples***	***Strengths***	***Problems***
Contributions	Heroes, cultural components, holidays, and other discrete elements related to ethnic groups are added to the curriculum on special days, occasions, and celebrations.	Famous Mexican Americans are studied only during the week of Cinco de Mayo (May 5). African Americans are studied during African-American History Month in February but rarely during the rest of the year. Ethnic foods are studied in the first grade with little attention devoted to the cultures in which the foods are embedded.	Provides a quick and relatively easy way to put ethnic content into the curriculum. Gives ethnic heroes visibility in the curriculum alongside mainstream heroes. Is a popular approach among teachers and educators.	Results in a superficial understanding of ethnic cultures. Focuses on the lifestyles and artifacts of ethnic groups and reinforces stereotypes and misconceptions. Mainstream criteria are used to select heroes and cultural elements for inclusion in the curriculum.
Additive	This approach consists of the addition of content, concept, themes, and perspectives to the curriculum without changing its structures.	Adding the book *The Color Purple* to a literature unit without reconceptualizing the unity or giving the students the background knowledge to understand the book. Adding a unit on the Japanese-American internment to a U.S. history course without treating the Japanese in any other unit. Leaving the core curriculum intact but adding an ethnic studies course as an elective that focuses on a specific ethnic group.	Makes it possible to add ethnic content to the curriculum without changing its structure, which requires substantial curriculum changes and staff development. Can be implemented within the existing curriculum structure.	Reinforces the idea that ethnic history and culture are not integral parts of U.S. mainstream culture. Students view ethnic groups from Anglocentric and Eurocentric perspectives. Fails to help students understand how the dominant culture and ethnic cultures are interconnected and interrelated.

Note: Banks, J.A. (2005). *Multicultural education: Issues and perspectives* (5th ed.). New York: Wiley. Reprinted with permission of John Wiley & Sons, Inc.

Approach	*Description*	*Examples*	*Strengths*	*Problems*
Transformation	The basic goals, structure, and nature of the curriculum are changed to enable students to view concepts, events, issues, problems, and themes from the perspectives of diverse cultural, ethnic, and racial groups.	A unit on the American Revolution describes the meaning of the revolution to Anglo revolutionaries, Anglo loyalists, African Americans, Indians, and the British. A unit on 20th-century U.S. literature includes works by William Faulkner, Joyce Carol Oates, Langston Hughes, N. Scott Momaday, Saul Bellow, Maxine Hong Kingston, Rudolfo A. Anaya, and Piri Thomas.	Enables students to understand the complex ways in which diverse racial and cultural groups participated in the formation of U.S. society and culture. Helps reduce racial and ethnic encapsulation. Enables diverse ethnic, racial, and religious groups to see their cultures' ethos and perspectives in the school curriculum. Gives students a balanced view of the nature and development of U.S. culture and society. Helps to empower victimized racial, ethnic, and cultural groups.	The implementation of this approach requires substantial curriculum revision, in-service training, and the identification and development of materials written from the perspectives of various racial and cultural groups. Staff development for the institutionalization of this approach must be continual and ongoing.
Social Action	In this approach, students identify important social problems and issues, gather pertinent data, clarify their values on the issues, make decisions, and take reflective actions to help resolve the issue or problem.	A class studies prejudice and discrimination in its school and decides to take actions to improve race relations in the school. A class studies the treatment of ethnic groups in a local newspaper and writes a letter to the publisher suggesting ways that the treatment of ethnic groups in the newspaper should be improved.	Enables students to improve their thinking, value school and analysis, decision-making, and social-action skills. Enables students to improve their data gathering skills. Helps students develop a sense of political efficacy. Helps students improve their skills to work in groups.	Requires a considerable amount of curriculum planning and materials identification. May be longer in duration than more traditional teaching units. May focus on problems and issues considered controversial by some members of the school staff and citizens of the community. Students may be able to take few meaningful actions that contribute to the resolution of the social issue or problem.

Resource C

Design Your Own Case

Author Name(s): ______________________________

Title of Case: ______________ **Grade Level(s):** ______________

Subject Matter Area (e.g., science): ______________

Generic Teaching Topic (e.g., planning, assessment):

____

Contextual Information:

____

Community Factors:

____

School Factors:

____

Classroom Factors:

____

Teacher Characteristics:

____

Student Characteristics:

____

Characteristics of Curriculum:

____

Story:

____

____

____

____

Questions for Reflection:

1. ____

____

2. ____

____

3. ____

____

Activities for Extending Thinking:

1. ____

____

2. ____

____

Criteria for assessing responses to your Questions for Reflection:

List criteria (e.g., response is clear, consistent with research or best practice, generalized to an appropriate degree—not overgeneralized, valid—based on facts in the case, relevant to an issue in the case, other).

1. ____

____

2. ____

____

Responses to Questions for Reflection:

List what you would consider to be examples of acceptable and unacceptable responses.

	Acceptable	Unacceptable
1. a.	____________	____________
b.	____________	____________
2. a.	____________	____________
b.	____________	____________

Responses to Activities for Extending Thinking:

List examples of acceptable and unacceptable responses.

1.	____________	____________
2.	____________	____________

Resource D

Bibliography of Multicultural Children's Literature

Part I: Print Resources

African

Archibald, E. F. (1997). *A Sudanese family*. Minneapolis, MN: Lerner.

Berg, L. E. (1997). *An Eritrean family*. Minneapolis, MN: Lerner.

Bryan, N. (2004). *Somali Americans*. Edina, MN: Abdo Publishing.

Chicoine, S. (1997). *A Liberian family*. Minneapolis, MN: Lerner.

Dee, R. (1988). *Two ways to count to ten: A Liberian folk tale*. New York: Holt.

Hoffman, M. (2002). *The color of home*. New York: Phyllis Fogelman.

Kurtz, J. (1998). *The storyteller's beads*. Orlando, FL: Harcourt.

Pinkney, J. (2009). *The lion & the mouse*. New York: Little, Brown and Co. Books for Young Readers.

African American

Asim, J., & Pham, L. (2006). *Whose knees are these?* New York: LB Kids.

Asim, J., & Pham, L. (2006). *Whose toes are those?* New York: LB Kids.

Belton, S. (2008). *The tallest tree*. New York: Greenwillow Books.

Bradby, M. (1995). *More than anything else*. Illustrated by Chris K. Soentpiet. New York: Orchard.

Bridges, R. (1999). *Through my eyes*. New York: Scholastic.

Bryan, A. (1997). *Ashley Bryan's ABC of African American poetry*. New York: Atheneum Books for Young Readers.

Bryan, A. (2009). *Ashley Bryan: Words to my life's song*. New York: Antheneum.

Burg, S. (2008). *A thousand never evers. New York*: Delacorte Press.

Collier, B. (2000). *Uptown*. New York: Henry Holt.

Curtis, C. P. (2007). *Elijah of Buxton*. New York: Scholastic Press.

Duncan, A. F., & Keeter, S. (2005). *Honey baby sugar child*. New York: Simon & Schuster Children's Publishing.

Farris, C. K. (2008) *March on! The day my brother Martin changed the world*. New York: Scholastic.

Fitzgerald Howard, E. (2000). *Virgie goes to school with us boys*. Illustrated by E. B. Lewis. New York: Simon & Schuster Books for Young Readers.

Grimes, N. (2008). *Barack Obama: Son of promise, child of hope*. New York: Simon & Schuster.

Haber, L. (2007). *Black pioneers of science and invention.* Mooloolaba, QLD: Sandpiper.

Hoffman, M. (1991). *Amazing grace*. Illustrated by Caroline Binch. New York: Dial Books for Young Readers.

Hoose, P. (2009). *Claudette Colvin: Twice toward justice*. New York: Melanie Kroupa Books.

Hudson, W. (1993). *Pass it on: African-American poetry for children.* Illustrated by Floyd Cooper. New York: Scholastic.

Johnson, D. (2000). *Quinnie blue*. Illustrated by James Ransome. New York: Henry Holt.

Johnson, L. M., & McCann, S. (2008). *Sunny's adventures.* Newburyport, MA: Jabberwocky Books.

King Farris, C. (2003). *My brother Martin: A sister remembers growing up with the Rev. Dr. Martin Luther King Jr.* Illustrated by Chris Soentpiet. New York: Simon & Schuster Books for Young Readers.

King Mitchell, M. (1993). *Uncle Jed's barbershop.* Illustrated by James Ransome. New York: Simon & Schuster Books for Young Readers.

Kurtz, J. (2006). *JATS fairytale classics: Beauty and the beast.* New York: Hyperion Books.

Lee, S., Lee, T. L., & Nelson, K. (2005). *Please, puppy, please.* New York: Simon & Schuster Children's Publishing.

Lee, S., Lee, T. L., & Nelson, K. (2006). *Please, baby, please.* New York: Simon & Schuster Children's Publishing.

Littlesugar, A. (1999). *Tree of hope*. Illustrated by Floyd Cooper. New York: Philomel.

Littlesugar, A (2001). *Freedom school, yes!* Illustrated by Floyd Cooper. New York: Philomel.

Medearis, M., Medearis, A. S., & Johnson, L. (2008). *Daisy and the doll.* Atlanta, GA: August House.

Monk, I. (1999). *Hope*. Illustrated by Janice Lee Porter. Minneapolis, MN: Carolrhoda.

Munoz Ryan, P. (2002). *When Marion sang*. Illustrated by Brian Selznick. New York: Scholastic.

Nelson, K. (2005). *He's got the whole world in his hands.* New York: Dial.

Perdomo, W. (2002). *Visiting Langston*. Illustrated by Bryan Collier. New York: Holt.

Ringgold, F. (1991). *Tar beach*. New York: Crown.

Roos, M. (2006). *JATS Bible classics: God made the world.* New York: Hyperion Books

Steptoe, J. (1987). *Mufaro's beautiful daughters*. New York: Lothrop, Lee & Shepard.

Taulbert, C. L. (2001). *Little Cliff's first day of school*. Illustrated by E. B. Lewis. New York: Dial Books for Young Readers.

Taylor, M. D. (1987). *The friendship*. Illustrated by Max Ginsburg. New York: Dial Books for Readers.

Thomas, C. (2006). *I can too!* New York: Brittany's Books.

Walford, N. E. (2008). *The island hunters: Book 1—The backyard pirate adventures.* Charleston, SC: BookSurge Publishing.

Wesley, V. W., & Roos, M. (2005). *Willimena rules! Rule book #4: How to (almost) ruin your school play.* New York: Hyperion Book.

Wesley, V. W., & Roos, M. (2007). *Willimena rules! Rule book #6: How to face up to the class bully.* New York: Hyperion Book.

Williams, S. A. (1992). *Working cotton*. Illustrated by Carole Byard. New York: Harcourt Brace Jovanovich.

Woodson, J. (2001). *The other side*. Illustrated by E. B. Lewis. New York: Putnam.

Woodson, J. (2002). *Visiting day*. Illustrated by James E. Ransome. New York: Scholastic.

Woodson, J. (2007). *Feathers*. New York: The Penguin Group.

Woodson, J. (2008). *After Tupac & D. Foster*. New York: G. P. Putnam's Sons.

Woodson, J. (2009). *Peace, locomotion*. New York: Putnam.

Words with wings: A treasury of African-American poetry and art. (2000). New York: Harper.

Asian American

Hmong

A free people: Our stories, our voices, our dreams. (1994). Minneapolis, MN: The Project.

Brown, J. (2004). *Little cricket*. Albany, NY: Book House of Stuyvesant Plaza.

Cha, D. (2002). *Dia's story cloth.* St. Paul, MN: Minnesota Humanities Commission.

Murphy, N. (1997). *A Hmong family*. Minneapolis, MN: Lerner.

Snook, R., photographer.(2003). *Many ideas open the way: A collection of Hmong proverbs*. Fremont, CA. Shen Books.

Cambodian

Ho, M. (2003). *The Stone Goddess*. New York: Scholastic.

Lipp, F. (2001). *The caged birds of Phnom penh.* Illustrated by Ronald Himler. New York: Holiday House.

Chinese

Cheng, A. (2000). *Grandfather counts*. New York: Lee & Low.

Chin, O., & Alcorn, M. (2006). *The year of the dog: Tales from the Chinese zodiac.* San Francisco, CA: Immedium.

Chin, O., & Alcorn, M. (2007). *The year of the pig: Tales from the Chinese zodiac.* San Francisco, CA: Immedium.

Chin, O., & Alcorn, M. (2008). *The year of the rat: Tales from the Chinese zodiac.* San Francisco, CA: Immedium.

Chin, O., & Chua, C. (2008). *Julie black belt: The king fu chronicles.* San Francisco, CA: Immedium.

Chinn, K. (1995). *Sam and the lucky money*. New York: Lee & Low.

Demi. (1990). *The empty pot*. New York: Henry Holt.

Lee, M. (2001). *Earthquake*. Illustrated by Yangsook Choi. New York: Frances Foster.

Lewis, R. (2000). *I love you like crazy cakes*. Illustrated by Jane Dyer. New York: Little, Brown.

Lin, G. (2009). *Where the mountain meets the moon.* New York: Little, Brown and Company Books for Young Readers.

Roth, S. L. (2001). *Happy birthday Mr. Kang*. Washington, DC: National Geographic Society.

Wong, J. S. (1994). *Good luck gold and other poems*. New York: Margaret K. McElderry.

Wong, J. S. (1996). *A suitcase of seaweed and other poems*. New York: Margaret K. McElderry.

Wong, J. S. (2000). *The trip back home*. Illustrated by Bo Jia. New York: Harcourt.

Wong, J. S. (2000). *This next New Year*. Illustrated by Yangsook Choi. New York: Frances Foster.

Wong, J. S. (2002). *Apple pie 4th of July*. Illustrated by Margaret Chodes-Irvine. New York: Harcourt.

Japanese

Bunting, E. (1998). *So far from the sea*. Illustrated by Chris K. Soentpiet. New York: Scholastic.

Mochizuki, K. (1993). *Baseball saved us*. Illustrated by Dom Lee. New York: Lee & Low.

Say, A. (1993). *Grandfather's journey*. Boston: Houghton Mifflin.

Uchida, Y. (1993). *The bracelet*. Illustrated by Joanna Yardley. New York: Philomel.

Wong McSween, M. (2009). *Gordon and Li Li: Words for everyday (Mandarin for Kids)*. New York: McWong Ink.

Korean

Balgassi, H. (1996). *Peacebound trains*. Boston: Clarion.

Balgassi, H. (1997). *Tae's sonata*. Boston: Clarion.

Choi, Y. (2001). *The name jar*. New York: Knopf.

Pak, S. (1999). *Dear Juno*. Illustrated by Susan Kathleen Hartung. New York: Viking.

Pak, S. (2002). *A place to grow*. Illustrated by Marcelino Truong. New York: Arthur A. Levine.

Park, F., & Park, G. (1998). *My freedom trip: A child's escape from North Korea*. Illustrated by Debra Reid Jenkins. Washington, DC: National Geographic.

Park, F., & Park, G. (2002). *Good-bye, 382 Shin Dang Dong*. Washington, DC: National Geographic.

Recorvits, H. (2003). *My name is Yoon*. Illustrated by Gabi Swiatkowska. New York: Frances Foster.

Laotian

Raines Day, N. (2001). *Piecing earth and sky together: A creation story from the Mien Tribe of Laos*, illustrated by G. Panzarella. Fremont, CA: Shen Books.

Philippino

de la Paz, M. J. (2001). *Abadeha, The Philippine Cinderella*, illustrated by Youshan Tang. Auburn, CA: Shen's Books.

Gilles, A. A. (2001). *Willie wins*. New York: Lee & Low.

Olesky, W. (2002). *The Philippines*. New York, Children's Press.

Thai

Ho, M. (1996). *Hush: A Thai lullaby*. Illustrated by Holly Meade. New York: Orchard.

Krudop, W. L. (2000). *The man who caught fish*. New York: Farrar Straus Giroux.

Tibetan

Dolphin, L. (1997). *Our journey from Tibet*. New York: Dutton Children's Books.

Perry, A. (1999). *The Tibetans*. New York: Viking Studio.

Vietnamese

Bartlett, T. (2001). *When You Were Born in Vietnam: A Memory for Children Adopted from Vietnam*. Photographs by W. Bartlett. St. Paul: Yeong & Yeong.

Breckler, R. (1996). Sweet dried apples: A Vietnamese wartime childhood. Boston: Houghton Mifflin.

Garland, S. (1993). *The Lotus seed*. Illustrated by Tatsuro Kiuchi. New York: Harcourt Brace.

McKay, L., Jr. (1998). *Journey home*. New York: Lee & Low.

McLeod, M. W., & Nguyen Thi Dieu. (2001). *Culture and customs of Vietnam*. Westport, CN: Greenwood.

O'Connor, K. (1992). *Dan Thuy's new life in America*. Minneapolis, MN: Lerner.

Shea, P. D. (2003). *Ten mice for Tet*. San Francisco: Chronicle Books.

Shea, P. D. (1995). *The whispering cloth*. Illustrated by Anita Riggio. Stitched by You Yang. Boyds Mills, Pennsylvania: Boyds Mills Press.

Truong, T. (2003). *Going home, coming home/Vê Nhà, Tham Quê Huong*. Illustrated by Ann Phong. San Francisco: Children's Book Press.

American Indian

Compton, M. (2008). *American Indian fairy tales*. Charleston, SC: Forgotten Books.

Granum, H. (2006). *The great eagle spirit*. Frederick, MD: PublishAmerica.

Robins, A., Robins, F. J., & Bouthyette, V. (2007). *The beautiful princess without a face*. Bloomington, IN: AuthorHouse.

Afghani

Kazem, H. (2003). *Afghanistan*. Strongsville, OH: Gareth Stevens.

Khan, R. (1998). *King of the skies*. Toronto: Stoddart Kids.

Khan, R. (1998). *The roses in my carpets*. Toronto: Stoddart Kids.

Khan, R. (2003). *Ruler of the courtyard*. East Rutherford, NJ: Viking Children's Books.

Bosnian

Landew Silverman, R. (1997). *A Bosnian family*. Minneapolis, MN: Lerner.

Indian

Krishnaswami, U. (2003). *Monsoon*. New York: Farrar, Straus, Giroux.

Islam/Muslim

Chalfonte, J. (1996). *I am Muslim.* New York: PowerKids Press.
Demi, (2003). *Muhammad.* New York: Simon & Schuster.
Khan, R. (1998). *Muslim child.* Toronto: Napoleon.
Macaulay, D. (2003). *Mosque.* Boston: Houghton Mifflin.
Nye, N. S. (2002). *The flag of childhood: Poems from the Middle East.* New York: Aladdin Paperbacks.
Stanley, D. (2002). *Saladin: Noble prince of Islam.* New York: HarperCollins.

Jewish American

Adelman, P. (1998). *The Bible from alef to tav.* Los Angeles: Tora Aura.
Batternamn, L. C. (1997). *Two cents and a milk bottle.* Los Angeles: Tora Aura.
Bierman, C. (1998). *Journey to Ellis Island.* New York: Hyperion.
Blos, J. (1994). *Brooklyn doesn't rhyme.* New York: Atheneum.
Hurwitz, J. (1992). *Once I was a plum tree.* Sag Harbor, NY: Beech Tree.
Kimmel, E. A. (2008). *The mysterious guests: A Sukkot story.* New York: Holiday House.
Kimmelman, L. (2000). *Dance, sing, remember: A celebration of Jewish holidays.* New York: HarperCollins.
Lasky, K. (1998). *Dreams in the golden country: The diary of Zipporah Felman, a Jewish immigrant girl.* New York: Scholastic.

Palestinian

Clinton, C. (2002). *A stone in my hand.* Cambridge, MA: Candlewick.
Nye, N. (1997). *Sitti's secret.* New York: Four Winds.

Latino

Ada, A. F. (1997). *Gathering the sun: An alphabet in Spanish and English.* Illustrated by Simon Silva. New York: HarperCollins.
Ada, A. F. (2002). *I love Saturdays y domingos.* Illustrated by Elivia Savadier. New York: Atheneum Books for Young Readers.
Ada, A. F., & Suarez, M. (2006). *Mama goose: A Latino nursery treasure.* Hyperion Book, New York.
Altman, L. J. (1993). *Amelia's road.* Illustrated by Enrique O. Sanchez. New York: Lee & Low.
Anaya, R. A., & Cordova, A. (2009). *Juan and the jackalope: A children's book in verse.* Albuquerque: University of New Mexico Press.
Ancona, G., Ada, A. F., & Campoy, F. I. (2005). *Mis Amigos.* San Francisco: Children's Press.
Ancona, G., Ada, A. F., & Campoy, F. I. (2005). *Mi Barrio.* San Francisco: Children's Press.
Ancona, G., Ada, A. F., & Campoy, F. I. (2005). *Mi Escuela.* San Francisco: Children's Press.
Ancona, G., Ada, A. F., & Campoy, F. I. (2006). *Mis Abuelos.* San Francisco: Children's Press.
Ancona, G., Ada, A. F., & Campoy, F. I. (2006). *Mis Bailes.* San Francisco: Children's Press.
Ancona, G., Ada, A. F., & Campoy, F. I. (2006). *Mis Comidas.* San Francisco: Children's Press.

Ancona, G., Ada, A. F., & Campoy, F. I. (2006). *Mis Fiestas.* San Francisco: Children's Press.

Ancona, G., Ada, A. F., & Campoy, F. I. (2006). *Mi Fimilia.* San Francisco: Children's Press.

Ancona, G., Ada, A. F., & Campoy, F. I. (2006). *Mis Juegos.* San Francisco: Children's Press.

Ancona, G., Ada, A. F., & Campoy, F. I. (2006). *Mis Musica.* San Francisco: Children's Press.

Ancona, G., Ada, A. F., & Campoy, F. I. (2006). *Mis Quehaceres.* San Francisco: Children's Press.

Anzaldua, G. (1993). *Friends from the other side: Amigos delotro lado.* Illustrated by Consuelo Mendez. San Francisco: Children's Press.

Cool salsa: Bilingual poems on growing up Latino in the United States. (1994). New York: Fawcett Juniper.

Delacre, L. (1993). *Vejigante masquerader.* New York: Scholastic.

Dorros, A. (1991). *Abuela.* Illustrated by Elisa Kleven. New York: Puffin.

Dorros, A. (1995). *Isla.* Illustrated by Elisa Kleven. New York: Dutton Children's Books.

Engle, M., (2008). *The surrender tree: Poems of Cuba's struggle for freedom.* New York: Henry Holt.

Fine, B. H. (1999). *Under the lemon moon.* Illustrated by Rene King Moreno. New York: Lee & Low.

Garza, C. L. (1996). *In my family: En mi familia.* San Francisco: Children's Press.

Gnojewski, C. (2005). *Day of the dead: A Latino celebration of family and life.* Berkeley Heights, NJ: Enslow Publishers.

Gonzalez, L. (2008). *The storyteller's candle.* San Fransisco: Children's Book Press.

Grolle, S., & Arsdalen, K. V. (2007). *Cranky Frankie: A springtime Latino tradition.* Bloomington, IN: Trafford Publishing.

Grossman, P. (1994). *Saturday market.* Illustrated by Enrique O. Sanchez. New York: Lothrop, Lee & Shepard.

Herrera, J. F. (2005). *Downtown boy.* New York: Scholastic Press.

Isabel, D., Vasallo, E. A., & Burris, P. G. (2007). *La cancion de Gabriela: Como me adapto a un lugar nuevo?* New York: Rayo.

Jimenez, F. (1998). *La mariposa.* Illustrated by Simon Silva. Boston: Houghton Mifflin.

Jimenez, F. (2008). *Reaching out.* Boston: Houghton Mifflin Company.

Johnston, T. (2001). *Uncle rain cloud.* Illustrated by Fabricio VandenBroeck. Watertown, MA: Charlesbridge.

Katz, K. (1999). *The colors of us.* New York: Holt.

Krull, K. (2003). *Harvesting hope: The story of Cesar Chavez.* Illustrated by Yuyi Morales. New York: Harcourt.

Mora, P., & Lopez, R. (2009). *Book fiesta! Celebrate children's day.* Rayo, New York.

Mora, P. (1996). *Confetti: Poems for children.* Illustrated by Enrique O. Sanchez. New York: Lee & Low.

Mora, P. (1997). *Tomas and the library lady.* Illustrated by Raul Colón. New York: Knopf.

Mora, P. (1999). *The rainbow tulip.* Illustrated by Elizabeth Sayles. New York: Viking.

Mora, P. (2001). *Love to mama: A tribute to mothers.* Illustrated by Paula S. Barragan. New York: Lee & Low.

Morales, Y. (2008). *Just in case.* New York: Roaring Brook Press.

Nimmo, J. (2007). *Charlie Bone and the beast.* London: Orchard Books.

Nimmo, J. (2008). *Charlie Bone and the shadow.* London: Orchard Books.

Perez, A. I. (2009). *My diary from here to there/ Mi diario de aqui hasta alla.* San Francisco: Children's Book Press.

Perez, L. K. (2002). *First day in grapes.* Illustrated by Robert Casilla. New York: Lee & Low.

Picayo, M., & Griswold, E. (2007). *Caribbean journey from A to Y.* New York: Campanita Books.

Pinkney, M., & Pinkney, S. (2007). *I am Latino: The beauty in me.* New York: Little, Brown Young Readers.

Ramos, L. (2008). *The invincible Anita: Book 1.* Bloomington, IN: IUniverse.

Robleda, M., & Ramirez, D. (2005). *Maria: Una Nina Latina en Estados Unidos/A Latino Girl in the United States.* Doral, FL: Santillana USA Publishing Company.

Rosa-Casanova, S. (1997). *Mama provi and the pot of rice.* Illustrated by Robert Roth. New York: Aladdin Paperbacks.

Soto, G. (1993). *Too many tamales.* Illustrated by Ed Martinez. New York: Putnam.

Soto, G. (2002). *If the shoe fits.* Illustrated by Terry Widener. New York: Putnam.

Winter, J. (2004). *Calavera Abecedario: A Day of the Dead alphabet book.* New York: Harcourt Brace.

Wolf, B. (1994). *Beneath the stone: A Mexican Zapotec tale.* New York: Orchard.

Native American

Bruchac, J., & London, J. (1992). *Thirteen moons on turtle's back.* Illustrated by Thomas Locker. New York: Philomel.

Bruchac, J. (1993). *The first strawberries: A Cherokee story.* Illustrated by Anna Vojtech. New York: Dial Books for Young Readers.

Bruchac, J. (1994). *A boy called slow.* Illustrated by Rocco Baviera. New York: Philomel.

Bruchac, J. (1996). *The circle of thanks: Native American poems and songs of thanksgiving.* Illustrated by Murv Jacob. Mahwah, NJ: Bridgewater.

Bruchac, J. (1997). *Many nations: An alphabet of Native America.* Illustrated by Robert F. Goetzl. Mahwah, NJ: Bridgewater.

Bruchac, J. & Bruchac, J. (2008). *The girl who helped thunder and other Native American folktales.* New York: Sterling.

Goble, P. (1999). *Paul Goble gallery: Three Native American stories.* New York: Simon & Schuster Books for Young Readers.

Grossman, V. (1991). *Ten little rabbits.* Illustrated by Sylvia Long. San Francisco: Chronicle.

Highway, T. (2001). *Caribou song.* Illustrated by Brian Deines. Toronto: HarperCollins.

Hobbs, W. (1997). *Beardream.* Illustrated by Jill Kastner. New York: Aladdin Paperbacks.

Leitich Smith, C. (2000). *Jingle dancer.* Illustrated by Cornelius Van Wright and Ying-Hwa Hu. New York: Morrow Junior Books.

Littlechild, G. (1993). *This land is my land.* San Francisco: Children's Press.

Martin, R. (1992). *The rough-face girl.* Illustrated by David Shannon. New York: Putnam.

Mass, W., (2008). *Every soul a star.* New York: Little, Brown.

Mitchell, B. (1996). *Red bird.* Illustrated by Todd L. W. Doney. New York: Lothrop, Lee & Shepard.

McLerran, A. (1995). *The ghost dance.* Paintings by Paul Morin. New York: Clarion.
Ortiz, S. J. (2001). *The people shall continue.* San Francisco: Children's Press.
Osofsky, A. (1992). *Dreamcatcher.* Illustrated by Ed Young. New York: Orchard.
Oughton, J. (1992). *How the stars fell into the sky: A Navajo legend.* Boston: Houghton Mifflin.
Pearsall, S. (2006). *All of the above*. New York: Little, Brown.
Swann, G. (1998). *Touching the distance: Native American riddle-poems.* Illustrated by Maria Rendon. New York: Browndeer.
Waboose, J. B. (2000). *Sky sisters.* Illustrated by Brian Deines. Toronto: Kids Can.

Multiracial

Igus, T. (1997). *Two Mrs. Gibsons*. Berkeley, CA: Children's Book Press.
Wing, N. (1996). *Jalapeno bagels*. New York: Antheneum.
Davis, B. M. (2009). *The biracial and multiracial student experience*. Thousand Oaks, CA: Corwin Press.

Race Relations

McKee, D. (1979). *Tusk tusk.* La Jolla, CA: Kane/Miller.
Scholes, K. (1989). *Peace begins with you.* New York: Little, Brown Children's.
Vaugelade, A. (2001). *The war*. Minneapolis, MN: Carolrhoda.
Wood, D. (1991). *Old turtle*. Duluth, MN: Pfeifer-Hamilton.

Chapter Books

Ada, A. F. (1993). *My name is Maria Isabel.* New York: Aladdin Paperbacks.
American eyes: New Asian-American short stories for young adults. (1994). New York: Holt.
Atkin, S. B. (1993). *Voices from the fields: Children of migrant farm workers tell their stories.* New York: Little, Brown.
Bruchac, J. (1997). *Eagle song*. New York: Puffin
Clinton, C. (2002). *A stone in my hand*. Cambridge, MA: Candlewick.
Curtis, C. P. (1995). *The Watsons go to Birmingham—1963*. New York: Bantam Doubleday Bell Books for Young Readers.
Curtis, C. P. (1999). *Bud, not buddy*. New York: Delacorte.
Danticat, E. (2002). *Behind the mountains*. New York: Orchard.
Dorris, M. (1992). *Morning girl*. New York: Scholastic.
Dorris, M. (1994). *Guests*. New York: Scholastic.
Erdrich, L. (1999). *The birchbark house*. New York: Hyperion Books for Children.
Flake, S. G. (1998). *The skin I'm in*. New York: Hyperion Books for Children.
Forester, S. (1999). *Dust from old bones*. New York: Morrow/Harper.
Hamilton, V. (1993). *Many thousand gone: African Americans from slavery to freedom.* Illustrated by Leo and Diane Dillon. New York: Knopf.
Hesse, K. (1992). *Letters from Rifka*. New York: Holt.
Ho, M. (1991). *The clay marble*. New York: Farrar Straus Giroux.
Jimenez, F. (2001). *Breaking through*. Boston: Houghton Mifflin.

Leitich Smith, C. (2001). *Rain is not my Indian name*. New York: HarperCollins.
Lowry, L. (1989). *Number the stars*. New York: Bantam Doubleday Bell Books for Young Readers.
Mohr, N. (1979). *Felita*. New York: Puffin.
Mohr, N. (1986). *Going home*. New York: Puffin.
Munoz Ryan, P. (2000). *Esperanza rising*. New York: Scholastic.
Na, A. (2001). *A step from heaven*. New York: Front Street.
Naidoo, B. (1986). *Journey to Jo'burg: A South African story*. New York: Harper Row.
Naidoo, B. (2000). *The other side of truth*. New York: Amistad.
Naidoo, B. (2003). *Out of bounds: Seven stories of conflict and hope*. New York: HarperCollins.
Namioka, L. (1992). *Yang the youngest and his terrible ear*. New York: Bantam Doubleday Bell Books for Young Readers.
Nye, N. (1997). *Habibi*. New York: Simon & Schuster.
Reilly Giff, P. (1997). *Lily's crossing*. New York: Dell Yearling.
Soto, G. (1990). *Baseball in April and other stories*. New York: Harcourt Brace.
Soto, G. (1992). *The skirt*. New York: Dell Publishing.
Taylor, M. D. (1976). *Roll of thunder, hear my cry*. New York: Puffin.
Taylor, M. D. (1981). *Let the circle be unbroken*. New York: Puffin.
Taylor, M. D. (1989). *The friendship and the gold Cadillac*. New York: Bantam Skylark.
Taylor, M. D. (1990). *Mississippi bridge*. New York: Skylark.
Taylor, M. D. (1990). *The road to Memphis*. New York: Puffin.
Taylor, M. D. (1995). *The well*. New York: Scholastic.
Taylor, M. D. (2001). *The land*. New York: Phyllis Fogelman.
Uchida, Y. (1978). *Journey home*. New York: Aladdin Paperbacks.
Uchida, Y. (1981). *A jar of dreams*. New York: Aladdin Paperbacks.
Veciana-Suarez, A. (2002). *Flight to freedom*. New York: Orchard.
Yep, L. (1989). *The cook's family*. New York: Penguin Putnam.
Yep, L. (1991). *The star fisher*. New York: Puffin.
Yep, L. (2000). *Cockroach cooties*. New York: Hyperion Paperbacks for Children.

Reviews, Guides, Curricular References on Multicultural Children's Literature

Birdseye, D. T. (1997). *Under our skin: Kids talk about race*. New York: Holiday House.
Blakemore, C. (2002). *Faraway places: Your source for picture books that fly children to 82 countries*. Albany, WI: Adams-Pomeroy.
Galda, L., & Cullinan, B. E. (2002). *Literature and the child* (5th ed.). Belmont, CA: Wadsworth/Thomson Learning.
Gangi, J. M. (2004). *Encountering children's literature: An arts approach*. New York: Pearson.
Harris, V. J. (1997). *Using multiethnic literature in the K–8 classroom*. Massachusetts: Christopher-Gordon.

Helbig, A. (2001). *Many peoples, one land: A guide to new multicultural literature for children and young adults.* Westport, CT: Greenwood.

Kruse, G. M., & Horning, K. T. (1991–1996). *Multicultural literature for children and young adults* (Vol. 2). Madison: Cooperative Children's Book Center of the University of Wisconsin–Madison.

Mitchell, D. (2003). *Children's literature: An invitation to the world.* Boston: Allyn and Bacon.

New press guide to multicultural resources for young readers. (1997). New York: Norton.

Nodelman, P., & Reimer, M. (2003). *The pleasures of children's literature.* New York: Allyn & Bacon.

Norton, D. E. (2009). *Multicultural children's literature: Through the eyes of many children* (3rd ed.). New York: Allyn & Bacon.

Open the books and see all the people. (2000). Jamaica, NY: Queens Borough Public Library.

Opitz, M. F. (1998). *Literacy instruction for culturally and linguistically diverse students.* Newark, DE: International Reading Association.

Risko, V. J., & Bromley, K. (2001). *Collaboration for diverse learners: Viewpoints and practices.* Newark, DE: International Reading Association.

Schon, I. (2000). *Recommended books in Spanish for children and young adults 1996–1999.* Lanham, MD: Scarecrow.

Smith, D. J. (2002). *If the world were a village: A book about the world's people.* New York: Philomel.

Part II: Internet Resources

Children's Literature—General

Carol Hurst's Children's Literature Site
http://www.carolhurst.com/

Children's Book Council
http://www.cbcbooks.org/

Children's Literature Research
http://www.tarleton.edu/library/subguides/childlit_sg.html

Children's Literature Web Guide
http://www.acs.ucalgary.ca/~dkbrown/index.html

Early Childhood Research and Practice (Multicultural Education and Children's Picture Books: Selected citations from the ERIC database)
http://ecrp.uiuc.edu/v3n2/search.html

Kathy Schrock's Guide for Educators: Literature and Language Arts
http://school.discoveryeducation.com/schrockguide/arts/artlit.html

Kay E. Vandergrift's Special Interest Page
http://comminfo.rutgers.edu/professional-development/childlit/

Book Links
http://www.ala.org/ala/aboutala/offices/publishing/booklinks/index.cfm

Horn Book
http://www.hbook.com/

Caldecott Medal Home Page
http://www.ala.org/ala/mgrps/divs/alsc/awardsgrants/bookmedia/caldecottmedal/caldecottmedal.cfm

John Newberry Medal Home Page
http://www.ala.org/alsc/newberry.cfm

Coretta Scott King Award
http://www.ala.org/ala/mgrps/rts/cskbookawards/recipients.cfm

The Americas Award
http://www.uwm.edu/Dept/CLACS/outreachamericas.html

The Pura Belpré Award
http://www.ala.org/alsc/belpre.cfm

Michael L. Printz Award
http://www.ala.org/yalsa/printz

University of Iowa (Bibliographies of fiction, nonfiction, and picture books)
http://www.education.uiowa.edu/crl/bibliographies/index.html

Advocacy and Educational Equity

Children's Defense Fund
http://www.childrensdefense.org/

Diversity University, Inc.
http://www.du.org/

Equity Assistance Centers
http://www.edgateway.net/pub/docs/262

South Central Equity Assistance Center
http://www.idra.org/scce/

Women and Minorities in Science and Engineering
http://www.mills.edu/

African American

Black History Activities
http://www.kn.pacbell.com/wired/BHM/AfroAm.html

Black History Treasure Hunt and Quiz
http://www.kn.pacbell.com/wired/BHM/bh_hunt_quiz.html

Juneteenth
http://www.juneteenth.com/

African Art—Aesthetics and Meaning
http://www.lib.virginia.edu/clemons/RMC/exhib/93.ray.aa/African.html

Asian American

AskAsia Homepage
http://www.askasia.org/

China the Beautiful, Chinese Art and Literature
http://www.chinapage.com/china.html

Japanese American National Museum
http://www.janm.org/

Joseph Wu's Origami Page
http://www.origami.vancouver.bc.ca

Lo Latino

Artes e Historia de Mexico
http://www.arts-history.mx

Azteca Web Page
http://www.azteca.net/aztec

Centro Virtual Cervantes
http://www.cvc.cervantes.es/portada.htm

Cinco de Mayo
http://latino.sscnet.ucla.edu/demo/cinco.html

Hispanic Contributions to History
http://www.neta.com/~1stbooks/content.htm

Hispanic Magazine
http://www.hisp.com/

Hispanic Reading Room, Library of Congress
http://lcweb.loc.gov/rr/hispanic

Indigenous Mexican Images
http://www.azteca.net/aztec/prehisp/index.shtml

Latin American Network Information Center
http://lanic.utexas.edu

Mexico para Ninos
http://www.elbalero.gob.mx

Mundo Latino
http://www.mundolatino.org/cultura

Mundo Maya
http://www.mayadiscovery.com/

National Council of La Raza
http://www.nclr.org/

National Latino Communications Center
http://clnet.ucla.edu/community/nlcc

Nuestro México
http://www.mexico.udg.mx/

Oaxacan Pottery
http://www.manos-de-oaxaca.com/

Society for the Advancement of Chicanos and Native Americans in Science
http://www.sacnas.org/

Multicultural Education

Amigos
http://edweb.sdsu.edu/people/cguanipa/amigos

Institute for Global Communications
http://www.igc.org/igc

Multicultural Book Review
http://www.isomedia.com/homes/jmele/homepage.html

Virtual Library on Migration & Ethnic Relations
http://www.ercomer.eu/wwwvl/

Native Americans

American Indian Heritage Foundation
http://www.indians.org/About_Us/about_us.html

Bureau of Indians Affairs
http://www.bia.gov/

National Museum of the American Indian
http://www.nmai.si.edu/

Native American Indian Resources
http://www.kstrom.net/isk/mainmenu.html

Native American Stories: Books and E-texts
http://www.kstrom.net/isk/stories/ebooks.html

NativeWeb—an Internet Community
http://www.nativeweb.org/

Society for the Advancement of Chicanos and Native Americans in Science
http://www.sacnas.org/

WWW Virtual Library: American Indians
http://www.hanksville.org/NAresources/

Women and Girls

Bilingual Women of NASA
http://quest.arc.nasa.gov/women/espanol/intro.html

Computer Research Association: Women
http://www.cra-w.org/projects

Exploring Your Future in Math and Science
http://www.cs.wisc.edu/~karavan/afl/home.html

Girl Games Inc
http://www.girlgamesinc.com/

Girl Tech
http://www.girltech.com/index.aspx

GrayMill—Gender Equity
http://www.graymill.com/

National Women's History Project
http://www.nwhp.org/

New Moon Publishing
http://www.newmoon.org/

Tapping Interest Resources for Women in Computer Science
http://tap.mills.edu/ada/

University of Wisconsin Women and Science Programs
http://www.uwosh.edu/wis

Women of NASA
http://quest.arc.nasa.gov/women/intro.html

Resource E

Sample Rubrics for Assessing Student Responses to Cases

The following two rubrics for assessing student responses to cases have proven to be useful. The first, entitled "Rubric for Assessment of Case Analysis Process," provides a format for student self-assessment, peer assessment, and instructor assessment of the process aspects of case analysis (i.e., the level of participation of each student). When working in small groups, students seem to appreciate the opportunity to assess peer contributions, that is, to be able to reward active participation and hold accountable those who might be less participatory. This form may be used regularly after each small-group case analysis or periodically; its impending use may be announced at the beginning of the term and/or on each day it is to be used.

The second rubric, entitled "Rubric for Instructor Rating of Case Analysis Products," has been helpful in delineating criteria for assessing the products submitted by individuals or groups of students. As with any rubric, criteria may be altered for any given case analysis. For example, if the "Questions for Reflection" ask students to relate a given case to lesson planning, then the criterion (bottom left-hand side of the rubric), which asks students to relate the issues in the case to up to six factors, might be adjusted by the instructor to focus on that same criteria. As with the first form described, this rubric may be used regularly or periodically, and announced at the will of the instructor.

Rubric for Assessment of Case Analysis Process

PARTICIPATION, FACILITATION, AND ATTITUDINAL ASPECTS — **Name:** ______

Use the following rating scale for your assessments: (high) 5, 4, 3.5, 3 (low) — **Case #:** ______

	Self	***Peer***	***Instructor***	***Total***
1. Demonstrated *participation skills,* e.g., helped others, shared ideas, listened to others, refrained from distraction/annoying other, used appropriate humor, sought clarity, was prepared prior to group meeting	Rating: ______ Evidence: ______	Name 1: ______ Rating: ______ Evidence: ______ Name 2: ______ Rating: ______ Evidence: ______ Name 3: ______ Rating: ______ Evidence: ______	Rating: ______ Evidence: ______	______
2. Employed *facilitation skills* when appropriate, e.g., suggested direction, provided encouragement, monitored time and group progress, helped facilitate decision making, generated new ways of viewing a simulation	Rating: ______ Evidence: ______	Name 1: ______ Rating: ______ Evidence: ______ Name 2: ______ Rating: ______ Evidence: ______ Name 3: ______ Rating: ______ Evidence: ______	Rating: ______ Evidence: ______	______
3. Demonstrated *positive attitudes,* such as sensitivity to thoughts and feelings of others, thoughtfulness, commitment to task, honesty, integrity, and open-mindedness	Rating: ______ Evidence: ______	Name 1: ______ Rating: ______ Evidence: ______ Name 2: ______ Rating: ______ Evidence: ______ Name 3: ______ Rating: ______ Evidence: ______	Rating: ______ Evidence: ______	______

Rubric for Instructor Rating of Case Analysis Products

Criteria	*5*	*4*	*3.5*	*3*	*Rating*	*Evidence*
Identifies and addresses the important diversity issues embedded within the case	Diversity issues are identified and specifically addressed (e.g., race, class, gender, affectional orientation, age).	Diversity issues are identified but not specifically addressed.	Diversity issues are not identified or addressed.	Component not submitted.		
Acknowledges that there might be more than one view or perspective (i.e., multiple interpretations)	Multiple perspectives are acknowledged, and these perspectives are thoroughly expressed within the case response.	Multiple perspectives are acknowledged, but the expressions of these perspectives are limited with the case response.	A single perspective is acknowledged and expressed.	Component not submitted.		
Reconciles differences in suggested conclusions, and derives preferred approach to the issue based on evidence cited	Identifies preferred approach and provides thorough evidence to support key assertions.	Provides limited evidence to support assertions.	Provides no evidence to support assertions	Component not submitted.		
Presents responses (problems, evidence, conclusions, etc.) in a clear way	Case response is clearly articulated and is free of grammatical, usage, and mechanical errors.	Case response is articulated, and a few grammatical, usage, or mechanical errors exist.	Case response is not clearly articulated, and grammatical, usage and mechanical errors impede comprehension.	Component not submitted.		
Relates key issues in the case to diversity-based: (1) lesson and unit planning, (2) instructional strategies, (3) student needs, (4) cultural backgrounds of students, (5) field experiences, and/or (6) professional standards in education	Key issues of the case are thoroughly related with best diversity-based instructional practices. The issues/practices alignment is clearly stated. Four out of the six practices are incorporated in the response.	Key issues of the case are somewhat related to best diversity-based, instructional practices. The issues/practices alignment is stated. Three out of the six practices are incorporated in the response.	Key issues of the case need to be identified and are not related to best diversity-based instructions/practices. The issues/practices alignment is not stated. Only one or two of the practices are incorporated in the response.	Component not submitted.		

Bibliography

General Education

Berger, E. H. (2008). *Parents as partners in education: Families and schools working together* (7th ed.). Upper Saddle River, NJ: Prentice Hall.

Boykin, A. W. (1994). Afrocultural expression and its implications for schooling. In Hollins, E., King, J., and Hayman, W. (Eds.), *Teaching diverse populations: Formulating a knowledge base* (pp. 243–256). Albany: SUNY Press.

Collins, P. H. (2009). *Another kind of public education: Race, schools, the media, and democratic possibilities*. Boston: Beacon.

Covington, M. (1984). The self-worth theory of motivation. *Elementary School Journal, 85*(1), 5–20.

Cuban, L. (2008). *Frogs to princes: Writings on school reform*. New York: Teachers College Press.

Danielson, C. (1996). *Enhancing professional practice: A framework for teaching*. Alexandria, VA: Association for Supervision and Curriculum Development.

Darling-Hammond, L., (2009). *The flat world of education: How America's commitment to equity will determine our future*. New York: Teachers College Press.

Davis, L. (1996, April). Equality in education: An agenda for urban schools. *Equity & Excellence in Education*, 61–67.

Friend, M., & Cook, L. (2007). *Interactions: Collaboration skills for school professionals* (5th ed.). Boston: Allyn & Bacon.

Frey, D., & Carlock, C. J. (1989). *Enhancing self-esteem*. Muncie, IN: Accelerated Development.

Gage, N. L. (1978). *The scientific basis of the art of teaching*. New York: Perennial Library.

Glasser, W. (1985). *Control theory in the classroom*. New York: Teachers College Press.

Kellough, R. D., & Carjuzaa, J. (2006). *Teaching in the middle and secondary schools* (8th ed.). Upper Saddle River, NJ: Pearson Prentice Hall.

Kolata, G., Laumann, E., Michael, R., & Gagnon, J. (1994). *Sex in America*. Chicago: National Opinion Research Center, University of Chicago.

Marzano, R. J. (1992). *A different kind of classroom: Teaching with dimensions of learning*. Alexandria, VA: Association for Supervision and Curriculum Development.

McCollough, C. (2008). *The art of parables*. Kelowna, British Columbis: Copperhouse.

McNergney, R., Herbert, J., & Ford, R. (1994). Cooperation and competition in cases-based education. *Journal of Teacher Education, 45*(5), 339–345.

Monroe, C. R. (2009). *Teachers closing the discipline gap in an urban middle school*. Urban Education, *44*, 322–347.

National Center for Education Statistics. (2007). *The condition of education*, 2007. Washington, DC: Author.

Olson, K., (2009). *Wounded by school: Recapturing the joy in learning and standing up to old school culture*. New York: Teachers College Press.

Redman, G. L. (1992). *Building self-esteem in students: A skill and strategy workbook for teachers*. Arden Hills, MN: Author.

Reed, S., & Sautter, R. (1990). Children of poverty—The status of 12 million young Americans. *Phi Delta Kappan, 71*(10), K1–K12.

Riley, S. S. (1984). *How to generate values in young children: Integrity, honesty, individuality, self-confidence, and wisdom.* Washington, DC: National Association for the Education of Young Children.

U.S. Department of Education. (1988). *Tenth annual report to Congress on the implementation of the handicapped act.* Washington, DC: Author.

Sources Containing Case Studies

Campoy, R., (2005). *Case study analysis in the classroom: Becoming a reflective teacher.* Thousand Oaks, CA: Sage Publications.

Gorski, P. (2005). *Multicultural education and the Internet.* New York: Pearson Education.

Greenword, G. E., & Fillmer, H. T. (1997). *Professional core cases for teacher decision-making.* Upper Saddle River, NJ: Merrill/Prentice Hall.

Hinely, R., & Ford, K. (1995). *Education in Edge City: Cases for reflection and action.* Hillsdale, NJ: Erlbaum.

Kaufman, J. M., Mostert, M. P., Nuttycombe, D. G., Trent, S. C., & Hallahan, D. P. (1993). *Managing classroom behavior: A reflective case-based approach.* Boston: Allyn & Bacon.

Kowalski, T. J., Weaver, R. A., & Henson, K. T. (1990). *Case studies on teaching.* New York: Longman.

Shulman, J. H., & Mesa-Bains, A. (Eds.). (1990). *Diversity in the classroom: A casebook for teachers and teacher education.* San Francisco: Research for Better Schools.

Silverman, R., Welty, W. M., & Lyons, S. (1994a). *Classroom assessment cases for teacher problem solving.* New York: McGraw-Hill.

Silverman, R., Welty, W. M., & Lyons, S. (1994b). *Classroom management cases for teacher problem solving.* New York: McGraw-Hill.

Silverman, R., Welty, W. M., & Lyons, S. (1994c). *Educational psychology cases for teacher problem solving.* New York: McGraw-Hill.

Silverman, R., Welty, W. M., & Lyons, S. (1994d). *Multicultural education cases for teacher problem solving.* New York: McGraw-Hill.

Silverman, R., Welty, W. M., & Lyons, S. (1994e). *Primis Education Series: Case studies for teacher problem solving.* New York: McGraw-Hill.

Silverman, R., Welty, W. M., & Lyons, S. (1996). *Case studies for teacher problem solving.* New York: McGraw-Hill.

Stipek, D. J. (1988). *Motivation to learn.* Upper Saddle River, NJ: Prentice Hall.

Taylor, L. S., & Whittaker, C.A. (2009) *Bridging multiple worlds: Case studies of diverse educational communities.* New York: Pearson.

Wasserman, S. (1993). *Getting down to cases: Learning to teach with case studies.* New York: Teachers College Press.

Watson, C. R. (1997). *Middle school case studies.* Upper Saddle River, NJ: Merrill/Prentice Hall.

Yin, R. K. (ed.). (2005). *Introducing the world of education: A case study reader.* Thousand Oaks, CA: Sage Publications.

Reviews: Case Methods

Anderson, L. M., Blumenfeld, P., Pintrich, P. R., Clark, C. M., Marx, R. W., & Peterson, P. (1995). Educational psychology for teachers: Reforming our courses, rethinking our roles. *Educational Psychologist, 30*(3), 143–158.

Harrington, H., & Garrison, M. (1992). Cases as shared inquiry: A dialogical model of teacher preparation. *American Educational Research Journal, 29,* 715–735.

Merseth, K. (1996). Cases and case methods in teacher education. In J. Sikula (Ed.), *Handbook of research on teacher education* (pp. 722–746). New York: Macmillan/Simon & Schuster.

Empirical Studies: Case Methods

Levin, B. B. (1994). Using the case method in teacher education: The role of discussion and experience in teachers' thinking about cases. *Teacher and Teacher Education, 10*(2), 1–17.

Levin, B. B. (1996, April). *Learning from discussion: A comparison of computer-based versus face-to-face case discussions.* Paper presented at the American Educational Research Association Conference, New York.

Lundeberg, M. A. (1993). Case discussions in educational psychology. In V. Wolf (Ed.), *Improving the climate of the college classroom* (pp. 159–164). Madison: University of Wisconsin System Office of Equal Opportunity Programs and Policy Studies.

Lundeberg, M. A., Coballes-Vega, C., Daly, K., Bowman, G., Uhren, P., & Greenberg, D. (1995). Wandering around the world: Building multicultural perspectives through K–12 telecommunications projects. *Journal of Technology and Teacher Education, 3*(4), 301–321.

Lundeberg, M. A., & Fawver, J. E. (1994). Thinking like a teacher: Encouraging cognitive growth in case analysis. *Journal of Teacher Education, 45*(4), 289–297.

Lundeberg, M. A., Matthew, D., & Scheurman, G. (1996, April). *Looking twice means seeing more: How knowledge affects case analysis.* Paper presented at the American Educational Research Association Conference, New York.

Case Methodology

Clandinin, D. J. (1992). Narrative and story in teacher education. In T. Russell & H. Munby (Eds.), *Teachers and teaching: From classroom to reflection.* Washington, DC: Falmer Press.

Cordeiro, P. (1998). Problem-based learning in educational administration: Enhancing learning transfer. *Journal of School Leadership, 8*(3), 280–302.

Dolmans, D., & Snellen-Balendong, H. (1997). Seven principles of effective case design for a problem-based curriculum. *Medical Teacher, 19*(3), 185–90.

Greenwood, G., & Parkay, F. W. (1989). *Case studies for teacher decision making.* New York: Random House.

Grossman, P. L. (1992). Teaching and learning with cases: Unanswered questions. In J. H. Shulman (Ed.), *Case methods in teacher education.* New York: Teachers College Press.

Hansen, A. (1997). Writing cases for teaching: Observations of a practitioner. *Phi Delta Kappan, 78*(5), 398–404.

Honan, J. P., & Rule, C. S. (2002). *Using cases in higher education: A guide for faculty and administrators*. San Francisco: Jossey-Bass.

Hutchings, P. (1993). *Using cases to improve college teaching: A guide to more reflective practice.* Washington, DC: American Association for Higher Education.

Kagan, D. M., & Tippins, D. J. (1993). Classroom cases as gauges of professional growth. In M. O'Hair & S. Odell (Eds.), *Teacher education yearbook 1: Diversity and teaching* (pp. 98–110). New York: Harcourt Brace Jovanovich and the Association of Teacher Educators.

Merriam, S. B. (1998). *Qualitative research and case study applications in education.* San Francisco: Jossey-Bass.

Merseth, K. (1991). *The case for cases in teacher education.* Washington, DC: American Association for Higher Education.

Schon, D. A. (1983). *The reflective practitioner: How professions think in action.* New York: Basic Books.

Schon, D. A. (1991). *The reflective turn: Case studies in and on educational practice.* New York: Teachers College Press.

Shulman, J. H. (Ed.). (1992). *Case methods in teacher education.* New York: Teachers College Press.

Shulman, J. H., & Mesa-Bains, A. (Eds.). (1993). *Diversity in the classroom: A casebook for teachers and teacher educators.* Hillsdale, NJ: Research for Better Schools and Erlbaum.

Shulman, L. (1996). Tender feelings, hidden thoughts: Confronting bias, innocence and racism through case discussion. In A. Colbert, P. Desberg, & K. Trimble (Eds.), *The case for education: Contemporary approaches for using case methods* (pp. 137–158). Boston: Allyn & Bacon.

Sykes, G., & Bird, T. (1992). Teacher education and the case idea. In G. E. Grant (Ed.), *Review of research in education, Vol. 18.* Washington, DC: American Educational Research Association.

Tillman, B. (1995). Reflections on case method teaching. *Action in Teacher Education, XVII*(1), 1–8.

Tripathy, M. R., (2008). Case methodology for adult learning: A critical review of theory and practice. *Asian Journal of Management Cases, 5*(1), 5–19.

Yin, R. K. (2009). *Case study research: Design and methods* (4th ed.). Los Angeles, CA: Sage.

Journal Articles and Papers on Case Methods

Albanese, M., & Mitchell, S. (1993). Problem-based learning: A review of literature on its outcomes and implementation issues. *Academic Medicine, 68,* 52–81.

Capon, N., & Kuhn, D. (2004). What's so good about problem-based learning. *Cognition & Instruction, 22*(1), 61–79.

Carter, K. (1993). The place of story in research on teaching and teacher education. *Educational Researcher, 22*(1), 5–12.

Carter, K., & Gonzalez, L. (1993). Beginning teachers' knowledge of classroom events. *Journal of Teacher Education, 44,* 223–232.

Fourtner, A. W., Fourtner, C. R., & Herreid, C. F. (1994). Bad blood: A study of the Tuskegee syphilis project. *Journal of College Science Teaching, 23,* 277–285.

Harrington, H. L. (1994). Perspectives on cases. *International Journal of Qualitative Studies in Education, 7*(2), 117–133.

Harrington, H. L., & Garrison, J. (1992). Cases as shared inquiry: A dialogical model of teacher preparation. *American Educational Research Journal, 29*(4), 715–735.

Herreid, C. F. (1994). Case studies in science: A novel method of science education. *Journal of College Science Teaching, 23,* 221–229.

Kagan, D. M. (1993, Winter). Contexts for the use of classroom cases. *American Educational Research Journal, 30*(4), 703–723.

Kaste, J. (2004). Scaffolding through cases: diverse constructivist teaching in the literacy methods course. *Teaching and Teacher Education, 20*(1), 31–45.

Kleinfeld, J. (1990a). Creating cases on your own. Fairbanks, AK: Department of Education, Rural College, University of Alaska.

Kleinfeld, J. (1990b). The special virtues of the case method in preparing teachers for minority schools. *Teacher Education Quarterly, 17*(1), 43–51.

Kunselman, J., & Johnson, P. (2004). Using the case method to facilitate learning. *College Teaching, 52*(3), 87–92.

Merseth, K. K., & Lacey, C. A. (1993). Weaving stronger fabric: The pedagogical promise of hypermedia and case methods in teacher education. *Teaching and Teacher Education, 9*(3), 283–299.

Sykes, G., & Bird, T. (1992). Teacher education and the case idea. *Review of Research in Education, 18,* 457–521.

Multiculturalism

Adams, M., Bell, L. A., & Griffin, P. (1997). *Teaching for diversity and social justice*. New York: Routledge.

Aday, R., Rice, C., and Evans, E., Intergenerational partners project: A model Linking elementary students with senior center volunteers. *The Gerontologist, 31*(2), 263–266.

Alexander, L. B., & Morton, M. L. (2007). Multicultural Cinderella: Results of a collaborative project in an elementary school. *School Libraries Worldwide, 13*(2), 32–45.

Alexander, L. B., & Sanez, M. (2006). Using children's folktales to explore multiculturalism. *School Library Media Activities Monthly, 23*(3), 22–24.

Allen, R. (2005). Promoting diverse leadership: Shared cultural backgrounds can strengthen bridges. *Education Update, 47*(3), 1–3, 8.

Andrzejewski, J., & Alessio, J. (1999). *Education for global citizenship and social responsibility.* (Monograph). Burlington, VT: John Dewey Project on Progressive Education.

Averill, R., Anderson, D., Easton, H., Te Maro, P., Smith, D., & Hynds, A. (2009). Culturally responsive teaching of mathematics: Three models from linked studies. *Journal for Research in Mathematics Education, 40*(2), 157–186.

Ayers, W. (2008). *City kids, city schools.* New York: The New Press.

Banks, C. A. M. (2005). *Improving multicultural education: Lessons from the intergroup education movement.* New York: Teachers College Press.

Banks, C. A. M., & Banks, J. A. (1995). Equity pedagogy: An essential component of multicultural education. *Theory into practice, 34*(3), 152–158.

Banks, J. A. (1991). A curriculum for empowerment, action, and change. In C. E. Sleeter (Ed.), *Empowerment through multicultural education* (pp. 125–142). Albany: State University of New York Press.

Banks, J. A. (1994a). *An introduction to multicultural education.* Boston: Allyn & Bacon.

Banks, J. A. (1994b). *Multiethnic education.* Boston: Allyn & Bacon.

Banks, J. A. (2005). *Multicultural education: Issues and perspectives* (5th ed.). New York: Wiley.

Banks, J. A. (2006). *Cultural diversity and education: Foundations, curriculum, and teaching.* Boston: Allyn & Bacon.

Banks, J. A. (2007). *Diversity and citizenship education: Global perspectives.* San Francisco: Jossey-Bass.

Banks, J. A. (2009). *Teaching strategies for ethnic studies* (9th ed.). Boston: Allyn & Bacon.

Banks, J. A., & Banks, C. A. M. (Eds.). (1997). *Multicultural education: Issues and perspectives.* Boston: Allyn & Bacon.

Banks, J. A., & Banks, C. A. M. (Eds.). (2004). *Handbook of research on multicultural education* (2nd ed.). San Francisco: Jossey-Bass.

Banks, J. A., & Banks, C. A. M. (Eds.). (2007). *Multicultural education: Issues and perspectives* (6th ed.). New York: Wiley.

Banks, J. A., Banks, C. A. M., Cortes, C. E., Hahn, C., Merryfield, M., Moodley, K. A., et al. (2005). *Democracy and diversity: Principles and concepts for educating citizens in a global age.* Seattle, WA: Center for Multicultural Education, University of Washington.

Barndt, J. (2009). *Understanding and dismantling racism: The twenty-first century challenge to white America.* Minneapolis, MN: Fortress Press.

Bell, D. (1992). *Faces at the bottom of the wall: The permanence of racism.* New York: Basic Books.

Calderon, M. E. (2009). *Teaching reading to English language learners, grades 6–12.*Thousand Oaks, CA: Corwin Press.

Carey, K. (2004). The real value of teachers: Using new information about teacher effectiveness to close the achievement gap. *Thinking K–16: A Publication of the Education Trust, 8*(1), 3–42.

Chisholm, I. M. (1994). Culture and technology: Implications for multicultural teacher education. *Journal of Information Technology and Teacher Education, 3*(2), 213–228.

Christensen, L. (1994). Unlearning the myths that bind us. In B. Bigelow, L. Christensen, & J. Karp (Eds.), *Rethinking our classrooms: Teaching for equity and justice* (pp. 8–13). Milwaukee, WI: Rethinking Our Schools.

Christensen, R., & Karp, S. (Eds.). (2003). *Rethinking school reform: Views from the classroom.* Milwaukee, WI: Rethinking Our Schools.

Cochran-Smith, M. (1999). Learning to teach for social justice. In G. S. Griffin (Ed.), *The education of teachers: Ninety-eighth yearbook of the national society for the study of education* (pp. 114–144). Chicago: University of Chicago Press.

Coggins, D., Kalvin, Drew, C., Grace, D., & Carroll, M. D. (2007). *English language learners in the mathematics classroom.* Thousand Oaks, CA: Corwin Press.

Cornbleth, C. (2008). *Diversity and the new teacher: Learning from experience in urban schools.* New York: Teachers College Press.

Cox, S. S.-K. (2003). International adoption of mixed race children. In M. P. P. Root & M. Kelle (Eds.), *Multiracial child resource book: Living complex identities* (pp. 116–123). Seattle, WA: Mavin Foundation.

Cushner, K., & Brennan, S. (2007) *Intercultural student teaching: A bridge to global competence.* Lanham, MD: Rowman and Littlefield/Association of Teacher Educators.

Darder, A. (1991). *Culture and power in the classroom.* New York: Bergin and Garvey.

Darling-Hammond, L., & Bransford, J. (2005). *Preparing teachers for a changing world: What teachers should learn and be able to do.* San Francisco: Jossey-Bass.

Derman-Sparks, L., Phillips, C. B., & Hilliard, A. G., III. (1997). *Teaching/learning anti-racism: A developmental approach.* New York: Teachers College Press.

Davis, B. (2007) *How to coach teachers who don't think like you: Using literacy strategies to coach across content areas.* Thousand Oaks, CA: Corwin Press.

Davis, E. J., Smith, T. J., & Leflore, D. (2008). *Chaos in the classroom: A new theory of teaching and learning.* Durham, NC: Carolina Academic.

Delgado, R., & Stefanic, J. (2001). *Critical race theory: An introduction.* New York: NYU Press.

Delpit, L. (2008). *Skin that we speak.* New York: The New Press.

Dilg, M. (2003). *Thriving in the multicultural classroom: Principles and practices for effective teaching.* New York: Teachers College Press.

Doddington, C. (2007). *Child-centered education: Reviving the creative tradition.* Los Angeles, CA: Sage Publications.

Entin, R. C., & Vogt, L. (Eds.). (2008). *Controversies in the classroom: A radical teacher reader.* New York: Teachers College Press.

Fishman, S. M. (2007). *John Dewey and the philosophy and practice of hope.* Urbana: University of Illinois Press.

Fuller, C. (2009). *Sociology, gender and educational aspirations: Girls and their ambitions.* New York: Continuum.

Gaff, J. G. (1992). Beyond politics: The educational issues inherent in multicultural education. *Change, 24*(1), 31–35.

Gallavan, N. P. (2010). *Annual editions: Multicultural education* (15th ed.). New York: McGraw-Hill.

Garcia, E. (2004). Educating Mexican American students: Past treatment and recent developments in theory, research, policy, and practice. In J. A. Banks & C. A. M. Banks (Eds.), *Handbook of research on multicultural education* (2nd ed., pp. 491–514). San Francisco: Jossey-Bass.

Garcia, E., & Jensen, B. (2009). Early educational opportunities for children of Hispanic origins. *Social Policy Report, 23*(2), 1–20.

Gaunt, K. D. (2006). *The games black girls play: Learning the ropes from double dutch to hip-hop.* New York: NYU Press.

Gay, G. (1994). *At the essence of learning: Multicultural education.* West Lafayette, IN: Kappa Delta Pi.

Gay, G. (2000). *Culturally responsive teaching: Theory, research, and practice.* New York: Teachers College Press.

Gay, G. (2005a). Educational equality for students of color. In J. A. Banks & C. A. M. Banks (Eds.), *Multicultural education: Issues and perspectives* (5th ed., pp. 211–241). Hoboken, NJ: Wiley.

Gay, G. (2005b). Politics of multicultural teacher education. *Journal of Teacher Education, 56*(10), 221–228.

Gay, G. (January/February–March/April, 2010). Acting on beliefs in teacher education for cultural diversity. *Journal of Teacher Education.* Thousand Oaks, CA: Sage Publications.

Gillborn, D., & Ladson-Billings, G. (Eds.). (2004). *The Routledge Falmer multicultural education reader.* New York: Routledge Falmer.

Glass, G. V. (2008). *Fertilizers, pills, and magnetic strips: The fate of public education in America.* Charlotte, NC: Information Age.

Gollnick, D. M., & Chinn, P. C. (2009). *Multicultural education in a pluralistic society* (8th ed.). Upper Saddle River: Pearson Allyn & Bacon.

Gonzalez-Mena, J. (2010). *50 strategies for communicating and working with diverse families* (2nd ed). Upper Saddle River: Pearson.

Gonzales, L., & Leonard, J. (2007). *New hope for urban high schools: cultural reform, moral leadership and community partnership*. New York: Praeger.

Goodlad, J. I. (2008). Narratives of the education surround. In B. Z. Presseisen (Ed.), *Teaching for intelligence* (2nd ed., pp. 17–31). Thousand Oaks, CA: Corwin.

Goodwin, A. L. (1994). Making the transitions from self to other: What do preservice teachers Really think about multicultural education? *Journal of Teacher Education, 45,* 119–131.

Goodwin, A. L. (2002). The case of one child: making the shift from personal knowledge to professionally informed practice. *Teaching Education, 13*(2), 137–154.

Gorski, P. C. (2005). *Multicultural education and the Internet: Intersections and integrations* (2nd ed.). New York: McGraw-Hill.

Gorski, P. C. (2009). Insisting of digital equity: Reframing the dominant discourse on multicultural education and technology. *Urban Education, 44*(3), 348–364.

Grant, C. A., & Gomez, M. L. (Eds.). (1996). *Making schooling multicultural: Campus and classroom.* Upper Saddle River, NJ: Merrill/Prentice Hall.

Grant, C. A., & Sleeter, C. E. (1998). *Turning on learning.* Upper Saddle River, NJ: Merrill/Prentice Hall.

Green, R. L. (2005). *Expectations: How teacher expectations can increase student achievement and assist in closing the achievement gap.* Columbus, OH: SRA/McGraw-Hill.

Guthrie. J. W. (Ed.). (2003). *No Child Left Behind Act of 2001. Encyclopedia of education* (2nd ed., Vol. 8, pp. 3087–3090). New York: Macmillan Reference U.S.A.

Harris, I. M., & Morrison, M. L. (2003). *Peace education* (2nd ed.). Jefferson, NC: McFarland.

He, M. F., Sapp, J., Bryant, E. C., Botelho, M. J., Eng, B. C., Dejean, W. F., & Aguilar, J. (2009). A guide to new resources. *Multicultural Perspectives, 11*(2), 116–122.

Helms, J. (Ed.). (1990). *Black and white racial identity: Theory, research, and practice.* Westport, CT: Praeger.

Higgins, J. J. (2003). *Multicultural children's literature: Creating and applying an evaluation tool in response to the needs of urban educators.* New Horizons for Learning. Retrieved from http://www.newhorizons.org/startegies/multicultural/higgis.htm

Hittleman, D. (1978). *Developmental reading: A psycholinguistic perspective.* Chicago: Rand-McNally.

Hoover, J. J., Klingner, J. K., & Patton, J. M. (2008). *Methods for teaching culturally and linguistically diverse exceptional learners.* Upper Saddle River, N J: Pearson Merrill.

Howard, A. (2008). *Learning privilege: Lessons of power and identity in affluent schooling.* New York: Routledge.

Howard, G. (2006) *We can't teach what we don't know: White teachers, multicultural schools* (2nd ed.) New York: Teachers College Press.

Irvine, J. I. (2003). *Educating teachers for diversity: Seeing with a cultural eye.* New York: Teachers College Press.

Irizarry, J. G. (2009). Representin': Drawing from hip hop and urban youth culture to inform teacher education. *Education and Urban Society, 41*, 489–515.

Jennings, T. (1994). Self in connection as a component of human-rights advocacy. *The Journal of Moral Education, 23*(3), 285–295.

Jimenez, T. E., & Graf, V. L. (2008). *Education for all: Critical issues in the education of children and youth with disabilities.* San Francisco: Jossey-Bass.

Kincheloe, J. L., & Hayes, K. (2007). *Teaching city kids: Understanding and appreciating them.* New York: Peter Lang.

King, J. L. (2004). Culture-centered knowledge: Black studies, curriculum transformation, and social action. In J. A. Banks & C. A. M. Banks (Eds.), *Handbook of research on multicultural education* (2nd ed., pp. 349–378). San Francisco: Jossey-Bass.

Kopetz, P. B., Lease, A., & Warren-Kring, B. (2006). *Comprehensive urban education.* Upper Saddle River, NJ: Pearson Allyn & Bacon.

Kosmin, B. A. (1991). *Highlights of the CJF 1990 national Jewish population survey.* New York: Council of the Jewish Federation, pp. 3–6, 10, 20–22, 25–26. Reprinted in Feagin, J., & Feagin, C. (1993). *Racial and ethnic relations* (4th ed.). Upper Saddle River, NJ: Prentice Hall.

Kubota, R. (2009). *Race, culture, and identities in second language education: Exploring critically engaged practice.* New York: Routledge.

Kunjufu, J. (2008). *100+ educational strategies to teach children of color.* Sauk Village, IL: African American Images.

Ladson-Billings, G. (2005a). *Culturally relevant teaching.* Mahwah, NJErlbaum.

Ladson-Billings, G. (2005b). Is the team all right? Diversity and teacher education. *Journal of Teacher Education, 56*(10), 229–234.

Ladson-Billings, G. (2007). *Crossing over to Canaan: The journey of new teachers in diverse classrooms.* San Francisco: Jossey-Bass.

Ladson-Billing, G. (2009). *The dreamkeepers: Successful teachers of African American children* (2nd ed.). San Fransisco: Jossey-Bass.

Leonard, J. (2009). *Culturally specific pedagogy in the mathematics classroom: Strategies for teachers and students.* New York: Routledge.

Leanardo, Z. (2009). *Race, Whiteness, and education.* New York: Routledge.

Leonhardt, D. (2004, August 27). More Americans were uninsured and poor in 2003, census finds. *New York Times,* p. A18.

Levine, A., & Cureton, J. (1992). The quiet revolution: Eleven facts about multiculturalism and the curriculum. *Change, 24*(1), 25–29.

Levine, D. (2008). *Rethinking schools.* San Francisco: Jossey-Bass.

Li, G. (2008). *Culturally contested literacies: America's "rainbow underclass" and urban schools.* Routledge.

Litchner, J. H., & Johnson, D. (1973). Changes in attitudes toward Negroes by White elementary students after the use of multiethnic readers. *Journal of Educational Psychology, 65*, 295–299.

Suarez-Orozco, M. M., & Paez, M. M. (Eds.). (2002). *Latinos remaking America*. Berkeley, CA: University of California Press.

Takaki, Ronald (1998). *Strangers from a different shore: A history of Asian Americans.* Boston: Back Bay Books.

Tatum, B. D. (1992). Talking about race, learning about racism: The application of racial identity development theory in the classroom. *Harvard Education Review, 62*(1), 1–24.

Teaching tolerance. Available from Teaching Tolerance, Order Department, 400 Washington Avenue, Montgomery, AL 36104.

Tiedt, P., & Tiedt, I. (2006). *Multicultural teaching: A handbook of activities, information, and resources* (7th ed.). Boston: Allyn and Bacon.

Tomlinson, C. A., Brimijoin, K., & Narvaez, L. (2008). *Differentiated school: Making revolutionary changes in teaching and learning.* Alexandria, VA: ASCD.

Tomlinson, C. A., & Eidson, C. C. (2003). *Differentiation in practice: A resource guide for differentiation curriculum grades 5–9.* Alexandria, VA: ASCD.

Tomlinson, C. A., & McTighe, J. (2006). *Integrating differentiated Instruction & understanding by design (connecting content and kids).* Alexandria, VA: ASCD.

Tomlinson, C. A., & Strickland, C. A. (2005). *Differentiation in practice: A resource guide for differentiating curriculum grades 9–12.* Alexandria, VA: ASCD.

Torres-Guzman, M. E., & Gomez, J. (2009). *Global perspectives on multilingualism: Unity in diversity.* New York: Teachers College Press.

Trudgill, P. (1984). *Sociolinguistics: An introduction to language and society.* New York: Penguin.

Turner-Vorbeck, T., & Marsh, M. M. (2008). *Other kinds of families: Embracing diversity in schools.* New York: Teachers College Press.

Tutwiler, S. J. W. (2005). *Teachers as collaborative partners: Working with diverse families and communities.* Mahwah, NJ: Erlbaum.

Understanding Islam and the Muslims. (1989). Washington, DC: The Embassy of Saudi Arabia. Reprinted in Bennett, C. (1995). *Comprehensive multicultural education theory and practice.* Needham Heights, MA: Allyn & Bacon.

UNESCO. (2004). *Shared values, cultural diversity and education: What to learn and how.* Case study for the International conference on Education. Retrieved on March 8, 2004, from www.ibe.unesco.org/International/ICE/pdf/pdfbg3e.pdf

United for a Fair Economy. (2004). *Distribution of U.S. wealth ownership in 2001.* Retrieved March 16, 2005, from http://www.faireconomy.org/research/wealth_charts:html

U.S. Census Bureau. (2001). *Statistical abstract of the United States: 2000* (120th ed.). Washington, DC: U.S. Government Printing Office.

U.S. Census Bureau. (2003). *Statistical abstract of the United States: 2003* (123rd ed.). Washington, DC: U.S. Government Printing Office.

Villegas, A. M., & Lucas, T. (2002). Preparing culturally responsive teachers. *Journal of Teacher Education, 53*(1), 20–32.

Vinson, K., Gibson, R., & Ross, E. W. (2001). *High-stakes testing and standardization: The threat to authenticity.* Monograph in *Progressive Perspectives.* Burlington: University of Vermont, John Dewey Project on Progressive Education.

Internet Resources

General Educational Resources

Edweb	http://www.edwebproject.org/
ERIC	http://ericir.syr.edu/ (lesson plans, databases, and so on)

Internet Public Library	http://www.ipl.org/
Kathy Schrock's Guide	http://school.discoveryeducation.com/schrockguide/
TeacherLingo URL:	http://www.teacherlingo.com/
Teachers (Library of Congress)	http://www.loc.gov/teachers/
U.S. Department of Education	http://www.ed.gov/

Teaching with Technology

T.H.E. Online	http://www.thejournal.com/ (Journal of Technology in Higher Education)

Studying Teaching Using Technology

http://www.goingpublicwithteaching.org/yhutchinson/

Yvonne Hutchinson's Web site in which she builds on the oral traditions of her students' cultures and seeks to support the development of their literary skills. Uses video clips and commentary to analyze an instructional period ("A Class Anatomy").

http://quest.carnegiefoundation.org/insideteaching/

K–12 teachers and teacher educators document their practice and reflect on their teaching. The site contains multimedia records of teaching practice, videos of teaching, examples of lesson plans, practitioner reflections, images of student work, and other documents of teaching and learning. Individual Web sites are categorized by grade level, subject area, and name.

http://www.tc.edu/ncrest/teachers/venson/

Emily Venson's Web site documenting the use of literature circles in a ninth-grade humanities class in a public high school in Manhattan in 2007, the primary focus of which was to help students develop a critical perspective and to recognize their own biases as well as those of others.

http://www.gallery.carnegiefoundation.org/

This site provides digital representations of knowledge on teaching and learning. Included are links to subject areas, Carnegie Collections, case studies, and more.

Classroom Resources for Equity and Social Justice

Rethinking Schools	http://www.rethinkingschools.org/

Listservs and Newsgroups

Multicultural Education	E-mail:MULTCED@umddumd.edu http://www.wmht.org/

Glossary

Chapter 2

critical thinking

Higher-level thinking (analytical, carefully judging, synthesis) such as carefully judging the merit or truth of text material.

discrimination

The denial of fair treatment and justice by both individuals and institutions in areas such as education, housing, employment, banking, and political rights; actions that often follow prejudicial thought.

gender

Culturally determined characteristics of femininity and masculinity.

gender identity

An individual's feeling of being female, male, androgynous, or undifferentiated.

gender equity (gender fair)

Fair, just, impartial treatment of males and females within a society and its institutions.

prejudice

A preconceived attitude or opinion formed without sufficient knowledge; frequently based on stereotypes; usually unfavorable but can be favorable in intent (although even "favorable" prejudices have the unfavorable effect of categorizing individuals or groups).

reinforcement (of learning and/or behavior)

Encouraging or rewarding; strengthening.

relevant curriculum

Curriculum that has meaning because it connects with the prior knowledge and experience of the learner.

sexism

Economic, political, and social structures that give one sex group an advantage over the other. Stereotypes and misinformation about the biological characteristics of each sex group reinforce discrimination. Historically, in most societies, women have been victimized; however, males are also victimized by sexist beliefs and practices.

sexual orientation

The object(s) of an individual's sexual interest (i.e., heterosexual, homosexual, bisexual, or asexual).

social-emotional classroom climate

Feeling tones experienced by students within a classroom (e.g., warmth, acceptance, affection, distance, intimidation, confusion, frustration).

teacher flexibility and responsiveness

The degree to which a teacher is flexible in terms of curriculum and instruction and is responsive to student needs and interests.

teacher–student interaction patterns

The quantity and quality of verbal and nonverbal communication that goes on between teacher and students. Such patterns can either build or denigrate student self-esteem and can either warm or cool the social–emotional classroom climate.

traditional social and role concepts

Social status and roles historically assigned to males and females (e.g., for males—masculine/athletic, independent, breadwinner; for females—feminine, nurturant, dependent).

wait time

The amount of time a teacher waits after posing a question before rephrasing, answering it, giving a cue, or making another comment. (Recommended wait time is at least three to five seconds for most simple questions; longer for those that require more complex thinking, e.g., analysis, synthesis, evaluation.)

Chapter 3

cultural competence

Culturally relevant teaching often associated with positive perspectives of parents and families, communication of high expectations, learning within the context of culture, student-centered instruction, reshaping the curriculum, and teachers as facilitator (Gay, 2000).

cultural norms

Widespread practices or customs characteristic of a particular culture.

culture

The sum total of ways of living, including values, beliefs, aesthetic standards, linguistic expression, patterns of thinking, behavioral norms, and styles of communication that a group of people has developed to ensure its survival in a particular physical and human environment (Pusch, 1979).

democracy in the classroom

The degree to which students are empowered to participate in decision making (e.g., regarding classroom rules or procedures).

ethnic group

A social construct that divides people into social groups based on characteristics such as shared sense of group membership, history, ancestral geographic base, language, political and economic interests, behavioral patterns and values. Examples of ethnic groups are: Haitian and African American (Black); Cherokee and Navajo (Native American); Polish, Irish, & French (White); Chinese, Korean, and Vietnamese (Asian); Cuban, Mexican, and Puerto Rican (Latino) (Adams, Bell, and Griffin, 1997).

ethnocentrism

Pride in and focus on one's own ethnicity. If overextended, can lead to feeling of superiority and to discrimination against people of different ethnicities.

interdisciplinary teaching

Teaching based on demonstrating connections between and among two or more disciplines (subject matter areas).

learning styles (cultural)

Learning preferences linked to the cultural ethos of a group of people, for example, stylistic behaviors of many African Americans such as: a preference for oral modalities of communication, an emphasis on affect/emotions, a spiritual rather than a mechanistic view of life, movement expressiveness emphasizing movement, rhythm, music, and dance, among others (Boykin, 1994).

multiculturalism

A philosophical view, a movement/approach that includes and honors the history, heritage, culture, and contributions of gender, racial, ethnic, linguistic, religious, economic, special needs, sexual orientation, and other groups in curriculum, instruction, and the total school environment.

rule consequence

The result of following or violating a classroom rule or procedure (e.g., restitution, time-out, dismissal from class).

social justice curriculum

Curriculum that in content and process provides equal access to and equal outcomes for all students; that seeks excellence and equity; that actively seeks to eliminate preexisting social, political, and economic inequities.

stereotype

An overgeneralized, often negative view of an entire population or group of people without regard for their individual differences. Although some stereotypes may be meant to be complimentary, even they are hurtful in that they categorize people without regard for individuality.

Chapter 4

access

A barrier-free opportunity to learn and use materials, resources, and events in natural settings (Moll, 2005).

agent group

A group that often targets another group or groups for discrimination. In U.S. society, white males are normally considered positioned to be this agent group.

classism

Prejudice and/or discrimination against people because of their real or perceived economic status.

equity pedagogy

Teaching that facilitates the academic achievement of students from diverse racial, cultural, gender, and social-class groups (Banks & Banks, 1995).

experiential knowledge

Knowledge or practical wisdom gained from what one has observed, encountered, or undergone.

Hip-hop culture

A microculture, originating on the streets by African-American youth, but which now has appeal throughout the world as reflected in styles of clothing and music.

institutional racism

The network of institutional structures, policies, and practices that create advantages and benefits for whites and discrimination, oppression, and disadvantages for people from targeted groups. The advantages created for whites are often invisible to them or are considered "rights" available to everyone as opposed to "privileges" awarded only to some (Adams, Bell, & Griffin, 1997).

knowledge base

Research-derived knowledge on which a discipline (e.g., sociology, teacher education, or psychology) is built.

oppression

A state of deprivation of human rights or privilege; persecution of a group of people by another with the power to make and enforce laws on a broad scale.

power

The ability to make and enforce laws that affect a large group of people (e.g., a nation) over a period of time.

race as a socially constructed concept

Categories based on perceived physical differences between and among human groups; a social construct that arbitrarily divides people on characteristics such as skin color, facial form, or eye shape, ancestral history, heritage, and culture, and the social, political, and economic needs of a society at a particular period of time.

racial identity theories

Theories that suggest that persons pass through stages of development as they form their racial identity.

racism

Prejudice or discrimination toward persons because of their race.

social action activities

Activities that encourage students to think about and take action with the purpose of creating a more fair or just condition (e.g., eliminating some form of injustice or oppression in a classroom, school, or community).

student self-esteem

A student's feeling of being lovable and capable; a student's assessment of his or her own value or worth.

target group

A group of people who are targeted for bias or discrimination (e.g., persons of color, GLBT orientation).

tracking

The placement of students in classroom based on ability (i.e., homogeneous grouping). Generally thought to have detrimental effects on the psychological and academic growth of all students, especially of those in tracks other than the "highest" track.

white privilege

The concrete benefits of access to resources and social rewards and the power to shape the norms and values of society that whites receive, unconsciously or consciously, by virtue of their skin color in a racist society (Adams, Bell, & Griffin, 1997).

Chapter 5

assessment criteria

Standards used to assess the degree to which a goal has been attained.

behavior modification

The direct altering of unwanted behaviors by means of reinforcement, ignoring, and/or punishment (conditioning), or biofeedback.

effects of child-rearing practices

Emotional/psychological/physical effects of a given approach to parenting in general, or behavior management more specifically.

emotional literacy

Awareness of knowledge and dispositions related to self and how one relates to others; level of self-awareness and understanding of own thoughts and feelings.

establishing incentives

The process of setting up positive consequences of specified behavior, for example, a reward; a desired (motivating) outcome of completing a task.

free and reduced-price lunch programs

School programs designed to serve meals in schools with high proportions of students of poverty.

hegemony

The established view of how things are in a society that serves the interests of those in privileged or dominant positions. When a school presents a comfortable view of the mainstream and its establishment ideology, and the inherent truth of school knowledge, that is hegemonic.

high-poverty school

A school with a high proportion of students of poverty.

meritocracy

A system based on the notion that accomplishments are based on an individual's hard work and personal traits and hence that those who accomplish the most deserve the greatest social and financial rewards.

poverty

As measured by the government on the basis of income, a family of three with an income of less than $13,314 per year (Rose, 2000).

SES

The socioeconomic status of a person or group.

Chapter 6

agnostic

One who doubts the existence of God (i.e., claims that it is unknown if a God exists).

anti-Semitism

Prejudice and/or discrimination against Jews; can be based on hatred of Jews because of their ethnicity, religious beliefs, or the erroneous belief that Jews are a race.

atheist

One who denies the existence of God.

Buddhism

Key tenets: reincarnation and emphasis on discernment, insight, good conduct, morality, virtue meditation, wisdom, and enlightenment. Founded in 535 BC by

Siddhartha Gautama, considered a prince of India. Currently the fourth-largest religion in the world.

Hinduism

Key tenets: the goodness of an individual's life will dictate how he or she will be reincarnated, more than one god and numerous religious texts. Currently the largest religion in India and the third largest in the world.

Islam

The term Islam means peace. The Islam religion creed consists of a two-part statement: "There is no god but God; and Prophet Muhammad is the messenger of God." Anyone who makes this declaration—known as the shahadah, meaning bearing witness—freely and sincerely is a Muslim. Muhammad is a model of love, gentleness, fairness, equality and brotherhood (Sardar & Davies, 2004).

Judaism

A monotheistic religion, based on the Holy Scripture and the Talmud, provides the historical basis of both Protestantism and Catholicism.

provisions of the First Amendment to the Constitution

Practices allowed and not allowed by the First Amendment to the U.S. Constitution.

religious symbols

Emblem, sign, or representation of a religion.

separation of school and state

The requirement that religion (or absence of) not be promoted or demoted by the public schools.

Sikhism

Key tenets: a universal single God, reincarnation, karma. Founder, Guru Nanak, accepted ideas from Islam and Hinduism, but rejected the Hindu belief in the caste system. Founded in 15th-century BCE in India.

spirituality

Belief in a life-giving force; for some, presence of God; related to sacred or religious matters.

values

Deeply held beliefs that have been chosen freely from alternatives and are cherished and acted on over time. A belief or attitude that is highly treasured and that guides behavior.

Chapter 7

ableism

Prejudicial attitudes and discriminatory behaviors directed against people with disabilities.

accommodation

A modification of curriculum or instruction to more effectively meet the needs of students, especially special-needs students.

culturally and linguistically diverse (CLD)

Students with a cultural background and a language that is different from that of dominant society.

disability

A physical, mental, or sensory condition that interferes with a person's ability to do something (e.g., learn, walk, see, hear). Preferred usage is as a descriptive noun and adjective, as in "person with disabilities."

FERPA

Family Educational & Privacy Act—a federal law that protects the privacy of student education records. It applies to all schools that receive funds under an applicable program of the U.S. Department of Education. Parents and eligible students have the right to inspect the records maintained by the school.

free appropriate public education (FAPE)

The Section 504 regulation requires a school district to provide a "free appropriate public education" to each qualified person with a disability who is in the school district's jurisdiction, regardless of the nature or severity of the person's disability.

grouping strategies

Various ways of organizing students into groups for the purpose of learning.

Individualized Education Program (IEP)

A program designed specifically to meet the needs of a particular student, especially a student with a special need (e.g., a visual or hearing impaired student).

Individuals with Disabilities Education Act (IDEA)

Provides for a free appropriate public education for all students with disabilities, in the least-restrictive environment.

Individuals with Disabilities Education Improvement Act (2004) (IDEIA)

Aligns with the No Child Left Behind Act and focuses outcomes for students with disabilities rather than on the special-education process; also emphasizes the need to reduce paperwork and expand possibilities for reducing disagreements between schools and parents. It became effective July 1, 2005.

language immersion

An approach to foreign language instruction in which the usual curricular activities are conducted in a foreign language. Students follow the same curricula, and in some cases, use the same materials (translated into the target language) as those used in the non-immersion schools in their district.

learning disabled

Any condition characterized in school-age children by difficulty in accomplishing specific tasks, especially reading and writing, and associated with impaired development of a part of the central nervous system.

mainstreaming

The process of placing students with exceptionalities in regular classrooms for part of all of the day.

Chapter 8

bisexual

A male or female who is attracted sexually and emotionally to both males and females.

family

"Two or more persons who share resources, responsibilities for decisions, values, and goals, and have commitments to one another over a period of time. The family is that climate that one comes home to; and it is that network of sharing and commitments that most accurately describes the family unit, regardless of blood, or adoption, or marriage" (American Home Economics Association).

gay

A generic term that applies to both men and women who are attracted to another of the same sex. Some people object to the use of gay when applied to lesbians as well as gay men and use the word only to mean a homosexual male. The word has its origins in the 13th century meaning "merry," associated with troubadours who sang of courtly, and sometimes same-sex, love.

gender dysphoria

A psychological term used to describe the feelings of pain and anguish that arise from a transgender person's conflict between his or her gender identity (internal experience) and his or her biological sex (external experience).

GLBT

This acronym for gay/lesbian/bisexual/transgender is an umbrella term that covers both sexual orientation and gender identification. Other variations include LGBT, LGBTA (allies), GLBTI (intersex) and LGBTQ (questioning/queer).

heterosexism

The institutionalized assumption that everyone is heterosexual and that heterosexuality or bisexuality is the exception. This institution is maintained by pervasive images of heterosexuals in the media and also by the assumption that everyone is heterosexual. These images and assumptions allow straight people the privilege to not have to "come out."

heterosexual

Someone who forms sexual and affectionate relationships with members of the other gender. Also referred to as "straight."

heterosexual privilege

The basic civil rights and social privileges that a heterosexual individual automatically receives, and which are systematically denied to gay, lesbian, or bisexual persons on the sole basis of their sexual orientation (e.g., marriage, hospital visitation rights, holding hands without fear of repercussion).

homophobia

The irrational fear of, hatred of, aversion to, or discrimination against homosexuals or homosexual behaviors. Homophobia consists of three separate components: sexism, xenophobia (fear of difference), and erotophobia (fear of sexual desire). "Biphobia" and "transphobia" are more specific terms when discussing prejudice toward bisexual and transgender persons, respectively.

homosexual

A man or woman who is attracted sexually/erotically and emotionally to persons of the same sex. Most gay, lesbian, and bisexual people today do not like to use this term to define themselves because of the word's history of use to anthologize and medicalize same-sex behavior.

inclusive language

The use of gender-nonspecific language (e.g., "partner" instead of "husband") to avoid heterosexist assumptions.

internalized homophobia

The experience of shame, aversion, or self-hatred in reaction to one's own feelings of attraction for a person of the same sex.

intersexed individuals

People born with a combination of male and female characteristics of the reproductive and sexual systems. These characteristics may be noticeable immediately at birth or sometimes not until the onset of puberty. Intersexed individuals were formally known as hermaphrodites, although this term is now considered offensive. It was formerly believed that intersexed individuals needed to be placed firmly into one sex via surgery and/or hormones at the onset of visible intersexed characteristic. Many times these treatments were administered without regard to the individual's desires. This treatment is now considered malpractice, and organizations, such as the Intersex Society of North America, exist to provide public education and support for intersexed individuals.

lesbian

Used as an adjective or noun in reference to a female who has a same-sex orientation (i.e., attraction to another of the same gender).

LGBT

Abbreviations for lesbian, gay, bisexual, transgender persons; many prefer it to the older GLBT, which placed men in the traditional first place.

out

To be open about one's sexual orientation or gender identity.

partner or significant other

Primary domestic partner or spousal relationship(s). May refer to "girlfriend/boyfriend," "lover," "roommate," "life partner," "wife/husband," or other terms.

pink triangle

A popular symbol for the GLBT rights movement. The symbol was originally used in Nazi Germany death camps, when homosexual prisoners were forced to wear pink inverted triangles.

queer

Used by some within the GLBT community to refer to a person who is gay, lesbian, bisexual, or transgender, or someone who is supportive of GLBT issues. This term is often as much a political statement as a label. Those who use the term feel it is more inclusive, allowing for the variety in race, class, ability, age, and gender that is present in GLBT communities. Others are offended by this word and view it as a pejorative.

questioning

A term or label used to identify those who are exploring personal issues of sexual orientation and/or gender identity.

sexual orientation

The inclination or capacity to develop intimate emotional and sexual relationships with people of the same gender, the other gender, or either gender. One's sexual orientation, therefore, may be heterosexual, homosexual, bisexual, or asexual.

transgender

A broad umbrella term used to describe the continuum of individuals whose gender identity and expression does not correspond with their genetic sex, for example, transsexuals and transvestites (male or female impersonators). Some transgender persons wish to change their self-perception; others have no such desire. There is no correlation between sexual orientation and gender identity; transgender persons can be heterosexual, gay, lesbian, or bisexual. Some people abbreviate the term "trans" or even "T."

transsexual

An individual who presents him-/herself and lives as the genetic "opposite" to his/her genetic gender at birth. Most transsexuals alter, or would like to alter, their bodies through hormonal therapy, sex reassignment surgery (SRS), or other means. Transsexualism is sometimes divided into two stages: primary transsexualism (emerging in childhood) and secondary transsexualism (emerging during or after puberty).